I0868295

# EX AUDITU

An International Journal of Theological Interpretation of Scripture

Volume 9 1993

*Ex Auditu* is published annually by Pickwick Publications, 4137 Timberlane Drive, Allison Park, Pennsylvania 15101-2932, U.S.A.

---

Subscriptions
  Individuals:
    U.S.A. - $15.00
    Canada - $12.00 (in U.S. Funds)
    All other countries - $15.00 (in U.S. Funds)
    Students - $10.00

  Institutions:
    U.S.A. - $25.00
    Canada - $20.00
    All other countries - $25.00 (in U.S. Funds)

---

Indexed in *Religion Index One: Periodicals*, published by the American Theological Library Association, Chicago, Illinois, available online in the ATLA Religion Database through BRS Information Technologies (Latham, New York); DIALOGUE Information Services (Palo Alto, California); *Interlationale Zeitschriftenshau für Bibelwissenschaft und Grenzgebeite; Religion and Theological Abstracts;* and *Old Testament Abstracts.*

Please address all subscription correspondence and change of address information to Pickwick Publications.


ISSN 08883-0053

# EX AUDITU

*An International Journal of Theological Interpretation of Scripture*



THE EDITORIAL BOARD MEMBERS AND CONSULTANTS represent various disciplines and denominations. Theological Interpretation of Scripture is a task to be taken seriously by scholars who are committed to the Christian faith and tradition. However, as one editorial consultant stated: "let people gradually get used to the idea that a sane hermeneutics is both oriented in advance toward agreement/consent and is simultaneously exigent, discriminating, critical."

EDITORIAL CONSULTANTS

# EX AUDITU

Volume 9 1993

CONTENTS

Introduction
*Klyne R. Snodgrass* v

Salvation By Resurrection
*Clark H. Pinnock* 1

Resurrection as Humanly Intelligible Destiny
*Ben F. Meyer* 13

If Mortals Die, Will They Live Again?
Ben C. Ollenburger 29

The Resurrection of Jesus and the Resurrection of the Dead
*Peter Stuhlmacher* 45

Resurrection: What Kind of Body?
*Ted Peters* 57

Resurrection and Ethics in Chrysostom
*Stanley Samuel Harakas* 77

The Women at the Tomb: What are They Doing There?
*Carolyn Osiek* 97

Facing Toward the Millennial Year 2000 Under Biblical Guidance With a Focus on the Resurrection
*John P. Newport* 109

Resurrection, Cosmic Liberation, and Christian Earth Keeping
*Roger E. Olson* 123

Response to Roger Olson's Paper
*Steven Bouma-Prediger* 133

Sermon: The Famine of the Word
*Elizabeth Achtemeier* 137

Bibliography 143

# INTRODUCTION

To believe in Jesus is to believe that God raised him from the dead. To believe in Jesus is to believe that he will raise you on the last day. To believe in Jesus is to be involved in his death and resurrection so that you live new life now. Texts such as the ones from which these statements were drawn (Rom 10:9; John 6:40; Rom 6:4 respectively) underscore the absolutely central role the resurrection plays in Christian theology. As has often been pointed out, Christianity brings no new ethic or doctrine other than belief that the end-time resurrection has already occurred for Jesus. Christianity has no other reason for being except belief in his resurrection, and, no doubt, apart from belief in his resurrection, we probably would never have heard of Jesus of Nazareth.

Surely however, one of the anomalies of life is the failure of the Church to focus on the resurrection. Despite the fundamental, all-encompassing role of the resurrection in the belief system reflected in the New Testament, modern Christians give relatively little attention in their belief systems to either Jesus' resurrection or the hope of future resurrection for humans. An appropriate nod on Easter or at funerals is usually all these twin beliefs receive.

Why are we so impoverished in our thinking about and celebration of the resurrection? Much more attention has been given to the death of Christ than to his resurrection. We are quite capable of focusing on the death of Christ in moving ways, such as a Good Friday Tenebrae service at the conclusion of which we leave quietly from a darkened sanctuary. The problem is that we are still mute on Easter morning. We do not need less focus on the death of Jesus, but we do need more focus on what Paul Minear called the "twin event" (*To Die and To Live: Christ's Resurrection and Christian Vocation,* New York: Seabury Press, 1977), for without the resurrection, the death of Christ is meaningless.

This year's North Park Symposium on the Theological Interpretation of Scripture addressed the subject of the resurrection to draw attention to its theological importance. No conference can do adequate justice to such a topic, and this one is no exception. Some aspects of the discussion are not treated. Most regretable is the fact that Romans 6 received so little attention. At the same time, the papers presented at the symposium are strong statements on the resurrection and will contribute significantly to discussion of and reflection on the central role of Jesus' resurrection. As is to be expected, the contributors differ among themselves on several issues, and of course, the opinions expressed are those of the writers and not those of the editorial board. Given such qualifiers, however, these papers make telling points about issues of the greatest importance, issues concerning salvation and morality, future hope and present living. For example, Clark Pinnock's confessions of not doing justice to the soteriological impact of the resurrection and his attempt to rectify the problem deserve a broad audience. Ben Meyer combines philosophical and exegetical expertise in a way few can to focus on the resurrection as the destiny of humanity. If he is correct, his argument is comforting; if not, humanity really is in trouble.

One of the more difficult areas of the discussion is the treatment of resurrection in the Old Testament, which is addressed in Ben Ollenburger's paper. Granted that other Semitic peoples believed in the afterlife, why does the Old Testament have so few passages treating the future life and resurrection? Some of the passages mentioning resurrection, such as Isaiah 26:19 or Ezekiel 37, are often set aside as metaphorical. That is, they deal with the reviving of the nation, not the resurrection of the dead. One must ask, of course, from where do such metaphors originate? Where do the writers get the language of resurrection to use it metaphorically? In addition, what is the significance of such images as the "tree of life" in Genesis 3 or the "translations" of Enoch and Elijah? And as Ben points out—even if one does not choose to follow M. Dahood in his Anchor Bible commentary on the psalms when he finds numerous references to the afterlife—the psalms express the conviction that death will not separate God from his people. Otherwise, statements like "Precious in the sight of the Lord is the death of his faithful ones" (Ps 116:15) make no sense. Even though the paucity of references to resurrection in the Old Testament is surprising, the subject is more complex than it appears.

The sermon presented at the worship service concluding the symposium is included. A bibliography on the resurrection has been provided to assist further research.

The next symposium will take place October 14-16, 1994, and will focus on the Church. For information, please write to Ms. Jackson Blanchard, North Park Theological Seminary, 3225 W. Foster, Chicago, IL 60625.

Klyne R. Snodgrass
Editor

To live in the light of the resurrection—that is the meaning of Easter.

I should like to speak of God not on the borders of life but at its center, not in weakness but in strength, not, therefore, in man's suffering and death but in his life and prosperity. On the borders it seems to me better to hold our peace and leave the problem unsolved. Belief in the Resurrection is not the solution of the problem of death. The "beyond" of God is not the beyond of our perception faculties. . . . God is the "beyond" in the midst of our life. The Church stands not where human powers give out, on the borders, but in the center of the village.

Dietrich Bonhoeffer
*Letters and Papers from the Prison,*
pp. 154, 165-6

# SALVATION BY RESURRECTION

CLARK H. PINNOCK

Why are modern Christians unable to speak readily of the saving function of the resurrection of Jesus? How might they be enabled to do so more readily? Facing such questions in the context of this symposium allowed me to search the inadequacy of my own theology and to correct it.

The apostle Paul evidently had no difficulty speaking of the resurrection, but testified eloquently to the saving function of resurrection in several places:

> If while we were enemies we were reconciled to God by the death of his Son, much more now that we are reconciled shall we be saved by his life (Rom 5:10)
>
> If Christ has not been raised, your faith is futile and you are still in your sins (1 Cor 15:17)
>
> If you confess with your lips that Jesus is Lord and believe in your heart that God raised him from the dead, you will be saved (Rom 10:9)
>
> It will be reckoned to us who believe in him that raised from the dead Jesus our Lord, who was put to death for our trespasses and raised for our justification (Rom 4:24-25).

In such texts Paul declares that we are saved by the resurrection, not only by the cross, and that the two are jointly the cause of our salvation. Yet this is not what one normally hears today, at least in my circles. There is a discrepancy between what Christians say and what the apostle taught. We seldom speak of the saving significance of the resurrection, but are one-sidedly oriented to the cross when it comes to soteriology. The resurrection seems to have lost its redemptive significance among us. We have allowed the emphasis to shift elsewhere and the resurrection to diminish to a largely apologetic and subjective significance. Who today among evangelicals would say that humanity is saved *more* by Christ's life than by his death, as Paul does? Who today would make the resurrection the point of departure for theology? Has not the cross (or more properly, a theory of the atonement) usurped center stage in theology? Many more books and sermons ask "Why the cross?" than ask "Why the resurrection?" We seem to look for soteriological signficance only in the cross.[1]

Further evidence of this are the systematic theologies which are dominated by long sections on atonement, but totally lose eloquence when it comes to treating the resurrection. Millard Erickson, for example, devotes one page to the resurrection in his long work of 1500 pages and even that solitary page is taken up with apologetic, not with soteriological issues. This is just as true of Hodge, Shedd, Warfield, Berkhof, Murray, Demarest/Lewis, and the others (all Reformed). My impression is that we have more hymns on the cross than on the resurrection also. Is it not an irony that evangelicals, who think of themselves and are thought of by others as Paulinists, should have ignored the apostle's theology of the soteriological function of resurrection?[2]

Evangelicals stress the cross more than the resurrection. They see resurrection as a symbol of life, but not as central to the paradigm of salvation. The soteriological significance of Jesus' resurrection lies largely unappropriated by them. The otherwise favorable influence on me by the Inter-Varsity Fellowship reinforced that fact, because the movement started in Cambridge and focused on the issue of the blood of Christ as absolutely central.[3]

This discrepency between the New Testament and our own outlook merits attention. Why do we seldom discuss the redemptive significance of the resurrection? How can we correct the mistake and recover its significance as constitutive to the work of Christ? Given the prominence of resurrection in the New Testament, it is a fair test of any theology whether it can handle Jesus' resurrection as integral to the work of Christ or not.[4]

## THE LAW COURT

What seems to have happened is that Western theology has allowed itself to be dominated by a legalistic view of sin and a forensic model of atonement which leaves little room for resurrection.

When the atonement is thought of chiefly in terms of merit and the law, the cross becomes central, but the resurrection drops into the category of subjective redemption. A Latin idea of atonement does not have much room for resurrection which can go almost unmentioned because it is not required.[5]

If the human problem is one of dishonoring and if honor to God has been restored by the satisfaction of the cross, what problem is there left for the resurrection to address? Or, if the human problem is one of guilt and its penalty has been paid in full in a penal manner, what problem remains for the resurrection to address? If the redemptive work of Christ was finished on the cross, there are surely negative implications for the resurrection. The legal framework has no need for the resurrection to play a soteriological role. The human problem, if it is one requiring the propitiation of God, is taken care of by the cross, and the resurrection is not needed to complete the work as understood in this way. In this paradigm, the cross must become central and the resurrection becomes an afterthought. Christ's death is the real means of salvation and the resurrection is only confirmation. Do not Christians speak of the "finished work" of Christ on the cross, oblivious to the obviously unfinished character of salvation in relation to death?

There are other problems too. Salvation in a juridical context is also understood primarily as justification and not the redemption of the whole person, for which the resurrection would be relevant. The juridical view also tends to a theory of limited atonement and a denial of the universal scope of redemption, at least among the Calvinists, because penal substitution implies the lifting of guilt from all for whom the punishment was inflicted. The penalty cannot be directed to any other persons than those who are actually to be saved. If it were so directed, the non-elect would also necessarily be saved. To avoid that Reformed theologians cannot think of the event as a racial substitution. At numerous points Western theology has gone amiss in its thinking about atonement because of its juridical framework.[6]

This interpretation of atonement in forensic terms was an apologetic move by theologians seeking rationality in a medieval culture. It was their attempt to provide a rationale for the incarnation—*cur deus homo*? Unfortunately they did not pay sufficient attention to biblical theology on the subject of sin and the work of Christ, but rather distorted it. It was a case of the apologetic tail wagging the theological dog.[7] Because they saw sin chiefly as infraction rather than a broken relationship, they saw atonement chiefly as satisfaction rather than healing.

Resurrection must be central to any understanding of the work of Christ which claims to be based on the New Testament. A theory that renders the resurrection unimportant is automatically suspect. I do not oppose a theology seeking rationality, but I object to a theology accepting a rationality which is not biblically recognizable. The passion to put God into a conceptual box of our own making is always strong and must always be resisted. Christian theology is meant to be done on the basis of the biblical canon.

## THE NEED TO REFORM

When theology takes a wrong turn and needs reforming, it is best to return to the New Testament and to the theology of the first millennium. My biblical source here is chiefly Paul, though I recognize the importance of integrating other scriptural strands, and my early church source is Irenaeus, though I sense that his themes are common to Greek theology generally.

How did the early witnesses make room for the resurrection? What model did they use for soteriology inclusive of the resurrection?[8] In the texts cited from Paul it is plain that cross and resurrection together save humanity. Paul says that we have been reconciled by the cross and saved by the resurrection (Rom 5:10); that apart from resurrection, we would be still in our sins (1 Cor 15:17); that faith in the resurrection saves us, without the cross even being mentioned (Rom10:9); that Jesus was put to death for our trespasses and raised for our justification (Rom 4:25).

Somehow by his life, death and resurrection then, the divine Son rescued us from wrath and delivered us from this present evil age. By partaking in our humanity, Jesus made possible our adoption as sons and daughters of God. The key thing is to see that his work took place in the incarnation as a whole, not only in the event of the cross. He saved us by taking on our human nature and functioning as our representative in solidarity with us across the whole of his human experience. His entire life was the vicarious work of God for our salvation as a total event. His humanity as the last Adam was inclusive of cross and resurrection, not just of the cross. Paul saw Christ as last Adam and true Israel coming into the world to do battle with the powers of evil, from the beginning to the end of his life. Humanity which is subject to the powers of darkness needs deliverance from sin, death, and Satan, and Christ has set us free from them by his triumph in life, death and resurrection. Having disarmed the hostile powers and won a victory over them, the Christus Victor has freed us from our sins and made us alive unto God. The divine warrior has bared his holy arm and triumphed over the powers of evil such that there is a new creation and new relationship created between God and the world.

The Greek fathers saw Christ's work in this way as a triumph over sin and death.

The incarnation was the work of God himself overcoming the powers hostile to his will through the total Christ event. When asked, "For what purpose did Christ come down from heaven?" Irenaeus replied, "He came to destroy sin, overcome death, and give life to man" (*Against Heresies* 3, 18, 7). Christ as the last Adam has rescued humanity from sin and death and from both the guilt and power of sin. By his life, death, and resurrection, Jesus broke the power of evil and sin over us. Aulén comments, "The divine victory accomplished in Christ stands at the center of Irenaeus' thought and forms the central element in the *recapitulatio,* in the restoring and perfecting of the creation, which is his most comprehensive theological idea."[9]

We can learn from these early Greek theologians to view the incarnation as a holistic saving event and not concentrate so much on the cross in isolation. Certainly we ought not to focus so radically on it in a forensic way. This would make it possible for the resurrection to become central for us again. This approach of the early Greek theologians does not lack the theme of sacrifice. Rather, sacrifice is one of the aspects rather than the whole of the work of Christ, and sacrifice is not thought of as the propitiation of God by a third party. The sacrifice is God's gift and provision, not the work of another person placating God. Christ does not have to intervene to persuade God to be merciful; on the contrary, God gives himself to us in the giving of the Son. God expends his own life, suffering for the people and immersing himself in the depth of their trouble. The cross does not point to God's vindictive punishing of Christ, but to God's fidelity to his own promise of salvation of which the cross is the concrete symbol.

The entire earthly life of Jesus was a continual process of conflict with the powers of evil, and his death was the decisive final battle. Christ came down from heaven because no power less than God's own would be able to bring about reconciliation. The work of Christ not only saves us from guilt but also from the power of sin and evil. In the cross, God absorbs all that sinners can do without striking back at them. If the cross delivers us from the power of sin, the resurrection delivers us from the power of death. Through them both God delivers us from sin and triumphs over evil.

The idea of atonement in the early church, including the New Testament witness, is that Jesus as our representative brought the age of fallen humanity to an end. He conquered death and rose to new life making it possible for us to escape the power of sin and enter into the new age with him. The resurrection is God's deed by which the crucified was exalted to messianic glory. It marks the conquest of death and the vanquishing of sin. We are risen with Christ and we will share in God's victory. In the resurrection a new day has dawned for all nations.

## THEOLOGY OF RESURRECTION

How as hearers of the word of God should we express our faith in salvation through resurrection? My thoughts here are drawn from Paul and Irenaeus, but similar ideas are also present in the soteriology of Karl Barth and in the focus of both James and Thomas Torrance on the theme of the vicarious humanity of Christ.[10]

*First,* the fundamental category for understanding the soteriological role of the resurrection is Christ's solidarity with humanity as the last Adam. Salvation was accomplished in Christ's human nature which he had assumed for our sakes. The Word took our humanity and became flesh. He became a universal person. He came into solidarity with us in his baptism. He lived his life as man, took our place and died for our sins, was raised to life, and now ever lives unto God. Salvation was completed in his representative human nature before it could be completed in ours. Forensic thinking does not think biblically enough about cross or resurrection because it removes the Christ event from the context of solidarity and creates a framework of its own, alien to the New Testament.

Paul thinks of cross and resurrection in terms of Christ's solidarity with us. We tend to lose sight of this fact. Paul wrote, "If one died for all, all died" (2 Cor 5:14) and "If Christ arose, we will be raised" (1 Cor 15:21). His resurrection saves us because in his resurrection we all rise. Because resurrection was part of the redemption of Christ, it is part of our redemption. The resurrection was Christ's deliverance from the power of death which was in force until the Father lifted it. Christ's resurrection is the resurrection of the last Adam. Christ saved humanity by taking it through death into resurrection. In rising Christ was adopted as the last Adam (Rom 1:4), justified (1 Tim 3:16), sanctified (Rom 6:11), and glorified (l Cor 15:49). He experienced redemption for our sake in solidarity with us. In all of this the Adamic factor is obviously pivotal. We cannot understand Paul if we forget this. As we have participated in the sin and death of the old Adam, so shall we participate in the life and salvation of the new Adam. God has chosen and saved us in Jesus Christ.[11]

Solidarity is at the heart of Pauline christology and key to the meaning of Christ's resurrection. Paul viewed Jesus as true Israel, true humanity, and our redeeming representative. As the last Adam, Jesus, who represents us all in our intended role as God's creatures, was obedient to God in death and through being raised up has entered a new mode of existence which we one day will share with him. Since Israel failed God, since all humanity has failed, God decided to mediate salvation through Jesus as the last Adam. God therefore involved us in his dying and rising, as we had been involved in Adam's living and dying. Christ is the representative of humanity and having been raised has entered a new mode of existence. He has become both the pattern and the life-giving source of our resurrection.

The christology which underlies this notion is Jesus as the last Adam. According to this category, Christ assumed the corporate identity of the race and reversed the disobedience of sinners by his own obedience to God's will. His life, death and resurrection are not solitary but race-involving events. In his death and resurrection, we die and rise with him through his representation and our solidarity with him. As humanity's representative, Jesus turned what Adam did right around and restored the image of God. Jesus followed Adam's path to death and became the new Adam in the resurrection wherein he is crowned with glory and honor on behalf of us all. Christ lifted humanity up to glory and called us to follow in his footsteps, that we might go through death and resurrection and enter into God's purpose.[12]

Paul portrayed Christ as a corporate being, as more than just an individual person. His Adamic significance for the world is the central fact. Jesus glorified God by fulfilling the role God intended for humanity. In the resurrection God set Jesus on high as priest and king. The stone which was rejected has become head of the corner. He has become Lord and Christ and to him every knee will bow (Phil 2:10f). The resurrection ushered in a new phase of the divine sonship. Now he is Son of God with power (Rom 1:4). The one who humbled himself unto death is the exalted son of man who participates in the lordship of God and is head over all humanity. He is the royal man and second Adam in whom the justification and sanctification of all humanity has in principle (*de jure*) taken place.

There is a solidarity between Christ and humanity in death and resurrection. In him we die, in him we rise. He was raised up in his role as last Adam to become the first fruits of those who slept and the first born among a large family of sisters and brothers. Between Jesus' resurrection and our own there is an organic connection. We see them as two episodes of a single resurrection. Because he rose, we will be raised: first in conversion (Eph 2:5); later in glory (Phil 3:21). Because Christ is raised, we will be raised by virtue of union with him. The solidarity is worked out in two stages: now and not yet. Now we experience death and resurrection with Christ in conversion. Like sleepers we awaken and rise from the dead (Eph 5:14) and are summoned to walk in newness of life (Rom 6:4). But we also wait for the redemption of the body when we will come alive in Christ at the final resurrection.

The Greek fathers spoke of salvation by recapitulation in the work of the last Adam. *Precapitulation* might be a better term in view of the fact that Christ did not merely restore what Adam lost but also established what we will all become. But the idea is correct. The dominion of the age of death is broken by resurrection and a new age of life beyond death has emerged. This is because we are "in him" who is the last Adam and who has fulfilled the role God had given to humanity.

Jesus through vicarious humanity became part of the human tragedy in order to redeem it. By identifying with humanity, he changed the situation for us from the inside. Both his death and his resurrection were vicarious because of his universal representation. Here at last is a man who answers to God's purposes and embodies what God has wanted. Therefore he can bring God and humanity together where Israel had failed. The process of racial renewal can now commence with the goal of bringing humans into conformity to Christ. God has summed up humanity in Jesus as a way of drawing history together and overcoming divisions.

In resurrection Jesus anticipated the general resurrection, and in death, he anticipated the end-time suffering of the world, vicariously experiencing them both. God accepts the godless in his death and raises the dead by his resurrection. Christ experienced God's end-time judgment for sinners and signals acquittal and not condemnation for sinners in his resurrection. Jesus' resurrection points to the resurrection of humanity and the renewal of creation through the power of the Spirit.

Does this make sense today? Rationality is important so long as it does not twist revelation. What might be the rationality of solidarity? Certainly the idea of God's dealing with humanity through a representative man is a powerful symbol if we can make sense of it. It might help us to remember that God made us persons, which modern humanity celebrates, but also persons-in-relationship which modernity forgets. God made us social and corporate beings, as well as individuals, so that our choices affect other people. We are like a flock of birds in flight; there is a racial solidarity in sin and redemption. Our turning away from God characterizes us at the racial as well as at the individual level. There is a universal penchant toward sin. Only a small step is required to realize that redemption operates at the corporate level also. Humanity as a whole needs to be impacted by redemption. The dispositional solidarity of the race needs to be changed from rebellion to faith. The Enlightenment with its distorted emphasis on the individual as an island has made it difficult for us to think in corporate terms, but this is now changing. In the postmodern situation, it is more accepted that we are co-human.

God's wisdom reckoned that the best way to save humanity would be for God to be for-us-in-human form. The best thing would be to self-insert into humanity as deeply as possible in order to draw humanity back to sharing the divine life. In this way God can be seen as having accepted humanity unequivocally and to be working graciously at the deepest level for human salvation. C. S. Lewis in his brilliantly intuitive way caught this truth when he spoke of God becoming man and affecting the whole human mass, as a drop of dye colours the whole glass of water.[13]

If we are not sure about this idea, it is still true that Jesus' resurrection did validate and confirm his mission, including the dimension of representation. It vindicated his pre-Easter claims and endorsed the idea of representation of humanity implicit in them. The resurrection gave God's verdict about Jesus being the one through whom he deals with humanity. The resurrection showed Jesus to be God's son and true covenant partner.

*Second,* Jesus' resurrection must be seen in the context of the apocalyptic horizon as an event that relates to the salvation of the whole person and the creation. (Apocalyptic speaks of theodicy and of the judgment of God upon the wicked, e.g., Daniel 12, but Paul does not make this connection.)

In solidarity with us, Christ not only identified with our sinful past, but also with our redeemed future. Today we tend to misunderstand the resurrection, as though it were an isolated and strange event that happened only to Jesus long ago. But resurrection in the context of the first century would stimulate people to think about the resurrection of humanity on the last day, when God brings in the kingdom. In those minds Jesus' resurrection would signal the birth of a new world order. It would have been seen as anticipating the general rssurrection and would have spelled hope for the race. As Paul put it, Jesus through his resurrection brought life and immortality to light through the gospel (2 Tim 1:10). Jesus' resurrection on our behalf must be seen as an eschatological event, the first-fruits of the resurrection of the dead. Jesus was not resuscitated like Lazarus who had to die again, but represents a new glorifed humanity coming forth from death. The resurrection means that there is a new creation, and thus it opens up a future for the world. Resurrection speaks of the fulfillment of humanity in its wholeness and prefigures the redemption of the whole cosmos. Because Christ was raised, the end of the world has begun.[14]

For Paul the resurrection of Jesus was an eschatological event which speaks of eternal life as in the classical model of Irenaeus. Jesus brought immortality to light; his resurrection is the prolepsis of a new creation, not an isolated event. It is the demonstration that God is serious about making all things new, and it saves us because it inaugurates the resurrection in which we too will participate. It is the anticipation and foretaste of that last resurrection. It is the beginning of a new creation and world transformation and looks forward to a new humanity.

Paul wrote that Christ is the first fruits of all who sleep (1 Cor 15:20). He assures us that the God who raised the Lord will also raise us by his power (1 Cor 6:14). He said that even now God has endowed our mortal bodies with resurrection life (Rom 8:11). The resurrection is a preview of the future in Christ. The end has begun and the future has become present. The goal of history has become manifest as it previews what is to come. The resurrection guarantees eternal life because it is the representative beginning of the final resurrection and the pledge of future transformation.

Paul referred to two creations. In a compressed statement, he spoke first about a physical and then a spiritual creation (1 Cor 15:46). He seemed to be saying that God always had in mind a different body than the one Adam first received and that the original creation was always destined to be taken to a higher plane. He wrote of a new world order that is coming, one characterized as spiritual, meaning one controlled by the life-giving Spirit of God, an order into which Christ has now entered by his resurrection. Christ was transformed and became a life giving Spirit (1 Cor 15:45). His resurrection is the beginning of the new world order, the dawning of the new creation. The groaning creation now subject to frustration will be set free (Rom 8:18-24). The hope is that "God will transform the body of our humiliation that it may be conformed to the body of his glory by the power that enables him to make all things subject to himself" (Phil 3:21).

Resurrection shows us that God is serious about the creation. Salvation does not cast the material order aside, but exalts it to glory. Resurrection is the fulfillment of creation.[15]

Can we make sense of this today? Early Christians could look at reality in this way, but can we? I think we can, if we make the connection between Jesus' resurrection and the hope for history symbolized by the resurrection. We are beings destined for death and not being immortal will need resurrection, if salvation is to be complete. God must supply a fulfillment beyond the limits of this earthly life, if we are to live in fellowship with him and if death is not to have the final word. Resurrection is meaningful then because humans hope for salvation of the whole person beyond death, and resurrection is the event which promises this. Resurrection will be relevant as long as people hope for fulfillment—which will be always.

Salvation is not a purely spiritual affair according to scriptures. It is more than justification, more than a judicial pardon, though it includes that. Salvation reaches all the way from regeneration to glorification. It involves the redemption of the whole person—body, mind, and spirit. We need to be transformed in material as well as immaterial ways. This is why there must be resurrection.[16]

Resurrection spells fulfillment for creation. Here we glimpse the goal for which we and it were made. The hope of resurrection gives earthly life deep significance. Not to have such a perspective renders human life deeply problematic. To hope for resurrection is to hope for final meaning. By his resurrection, Christ became the avant garde, the embodiment in advance of the new order to come. His victory over death was part of something much bigger, the triumph of God over all his enemies. It was the advance installment of the new order.

In the words of Clement of Rome: "Let us consider, beloved, how the Lord continually proves to us that there will be a future resurrection, of which he has rendered the Lord Jesus Christ the first fruits by raising him from the dead" (1 Clem 42). We have hope because we trust in the God who "gives life to the dead and calls into existence things that do not exist" (Rom 4:17).

*Third,* addressing the issue of credibility, the effective cause of Jesus' resurrection is the Holy Spirit, the Lord and giver of life. We have to recover the muscular quality of the Spirit's effects as agent in creation and recreation in order to grasp this.

The resurrection of Jesus could happen because God is powerful enough to give life to the dead. Paul refers to the immeasurable greatness of his power and the working of his great might in Christ when he raised him from the dead (Eph 1:19f). Only God's power could take on the forces of death and destruction and nullify them as it did.

World transformation can be accomplished by the power of the Spirit. In the past we have seen a place for the Spirit's activity in the sphere of redemption, but have neglected his cosmic operations. We have tended to forget that the Spirit is the Spirit of life itself (Ps 104:29f). We have cut the Spirit off from bodily life and from nature. Plato has won a victory over the Bible in our theology in this and in other matters. We must recapture the cosmic work of the Spirit which is the energy of creation. The Spirit is a more muscular power than we have tended to imagine. To bring this out Pannenberg daringly calls the Spirit "a field of force." The Spirit carries the omnipotent power of God, and we should connect this thought with the resurrection by the power of God. At work in creation, the Spirit is also at work in new creation. The Spirit of Jesus is also the Spirit of all life. The power that brought creation forth also breathed life into Jesus and raised him up. Let us not overlook the cosmic and eschatological work of the Spirit. The indwelling Spirit who makes us long for consummation is the Spirit who will transform the world. According to the prophets he is active in these last times bringing about newness. He is the power by which Jesus was raised and which will raise us up immortal and imperishable. "If the Spirit of him who raised Jesus from the dead dwells in you, he who raised Christ Jesus from the dead will give life to your mortal bodies also through his Spirit" (Rom 8:11). The Spirit is the ontology of new creation and makes it a possibility.

The Spirit thus makes us long for the consummation by keeping hope alive and bearing witness in our hearts and by being the earnest, pledge, and seal (2 Cor 1:22: Eph 1:13f). The Spirit points us to a transformed future. The Spirit is also restless and presses on to fulfillment. The resurrection of Jesus was an eschatological act of the Spirit whereby God's promise of hope was fulfilled and confirmed for the rest of creation. He transformed Jesus and will transform us. Dying in dishonor, like him we will be raised in glory. The Spirit is the power of the transformed future, the power by which this present age will be changed into the kingdom of God. He is the means God will use to effect transformation.[17]

Does this make sense? It does if we give thought to the power of God in creation. Can we not detect the power of God at work in evolutionary history? How could the world possibly have come into existence by chance? Is the world not a finely tuned, law governed, life producing order? There are so many special conditions which had to be fulfilled in the structure of the universe for human life just to have existed. It is apparent that the power of the Spirit is active in the universe in which we live. It does not require much faith to infer that a divine power is at work who values persons and rules over the immensities of time and space. And, if we can see the Spirit at work in the old creation, it is natural to expect him to be at work in the new. If the Spirit gave life to the old creation, he can give life to the new also. The master artist who brought the world to fruition in its order, beauty, value, and form can carry on with this to the consummation. The teleological pull evident in the old creation can bring the world to completion and perfection. The pull toward the realization of God's purposes for creation operates for the new creation too. It is the Spirit who orchestrates, lures, persuades, steers, directs, and prods the order of creation. Moving beyond natural theology, it is the Spirit who raised Jesus from the dead. This solidly founded historical event shows that the power of the new creation is already operating in history. It requires no great leap of faith to believe it.

*Fourth*, there is also existential power in the resurrection proclamation. Bultmann was wrong about Jesus' resurrection in some respects, but not in all. He was mistaken to view the resurrection as something that happened only to the disciples, as the rise of Easter faith in them, when the New Testament plainly regards it as something that affected Jesus himself and his body.

But Bultmann was right to see a strong existential dimension in the resurrection and to recognize that faith is called for. There may be good evidence for the resurrection as an event, but historical evidence cannot demonstrate it. It can create a climate for faith; it cannot create faith.

Although the event of the resurrection is prior to its proclamation, not until it is proclaimed and a witness is borne to it does it engage the human heart. If the order of being has resurrection before proclamation, the order of knowing has it the other way around. People learn about resurrection from preaching and witness. One cannot make the resurrection a historical construct and expect people to be transformed by it. It does not happen that way. The word of the resurrection is not believed because it is proclaimed in lofty speech or because it can be proven to have happened. It is believed when it engages the hearer, when the Spirit of resurrection breathes hope into the human heart, a hope for new creation.

To be grasped by the resurrection we have to enter the world of the gospel narrative. We have to stand beside the empty tomb and see things from a new perspective. This announcement offers us hope. It issues an invitation to new life. God sets life and death before us. The proclamation calls us to faith in the risen One. Easter is a symbol of hope, a symbol of God's victory over death, when Christ is proclaimed as crucified and risen. Faith is called for. Will we accept or reject it? Like the disciples, we are invited to believe the good news. The proclamation has the potential of arousing faith in us through the Spirit. Hearing the good news, we can surrender to God, believe in the crucified, follow him, and live in newness of life by faith, or we can turn away.

Pascal saw that it involved a wager. How many Christians can prove that it happened? How many can prove it as more than a probability? No one can. We believe the proclamation when it comes in the power of the Spirit. We believe because we see the possibility of hope in it, not because we can prove its historicity. The word sets before us life and death and challenges us to choose life. Thomas was given the evidence he asked for, but Jesus also added: "Blessed are those who have not seen yet believe" (John 20:24-29).

Bultmann was right to recognize that most people respond to the resurrection through the proclamation. They have no way of knowing how to confirm its event character, not being historians. Apologetics cannot convince people that resurrection has the meaning that preaching assigns to it. Christ meets us in the word of preaching. No one can eliminate the risk which believing involves. Faith comes by hearing, and hearing by the word of Christ (Rom 10:17).

Does this make sense? It does if one recognises the good news as God's address to us. As a society of persons, the triune God is an elusive presence even in revelation. More than learning facts about God, we see the Lord with the eyes of our heart. We grasp who God is through love and relationship. The historian who can defend the historicity of the resurrection is at no particular advantage when it comes to knowing the risen One. Like the majority who cannot evaluate the historical claims, the historian too has to believe. Formal proof will not bring one to salvation. After all the proofs are given, it will still be necessary to believe, to see beyond the proofs to God. It is important that God should remain hidden that faith be possible. Knowledge does not transform us, and information may only feed our curiosity, while Jesus wants a change of heart. In the last analysis there has to be a human reaching out to God. There are reasons enough to believe, but not so many that one can avoid the call to love and trust God.[18]

## CONCLUSION

The resurrection is a pivotal category for the doctrine of salvation. We have salvation because of Christ's death and resurrection by which we have access in one Spirit to the Father.

From the redemptive historical angle, resurrection was the climax of the life of Christ. By this event, the new age is inaugurated and Jesus has become the firstborn among many brothers and sisters. As our representative the last Adam came to life, and in his resurrection we glimpse our own future. This is not a solitary figure, nor an isolated event. In the Spirit we see the power credible enough to raise the dead, and by the same Spirit our hearts radiate with hope as we await the redemption of the body and the universe.

## NOTES

1. Theodore R. Clark points this out in *Saved by his Life: A Study of the New Testament Doctrine of Reconciliation and Salvation* (New York: Macmillan, 1959).

2. Richard Gaffin admits this for the Reformed tradition and tries to correct it. See his *Resurrection and Redemption: A Study in Paul's Soteriology* (Grand Rapids: Baker, 1978), 11-12.

3. John Stott refers to these events in *The Cross of Christ* (Downers Grove: InterVarsity Press, 1986), 7-9.

4. James Orr presses the point of testing theology on this issue in *The Resurrection of Jesus* (New York: Eaton and Mains, n.d.), 274-88.

5. H. J. Holtzmann followed by A. Schweitzer found the problem in Paul himself, claiming the apostle combined two irreconcilable ideas in his thought: the juridical and the mystical. David M. Stanley reviews such recent positions on the resurrection in Pauline soteriology in *Christ's Resurrection in Pauline Soteriology* (Rome: Pontificio Instituto Biblico, 1961), 4-22.

6. Though J. I. Packer is aware of the dangers of allowing philosophy to overcome the biblical witness, it does so in his own work when he is forced to deny the universality of atonement because of the penal substitutionary logic even in the face of strong biblical evidence like 1 Jn 2:2 and Jn 1:29. See Packer, "What did the cross achieve? The logic of penal substitution" *Tyn Bul* 25 (1974), 36-39.

7. Evangelicals are beginning to see the need of reform: John V. Dahms, "Dying with Christ" *JETS* 36 (1993), 15-23. He interprets the sacrifice of Christ not in juridical terms but as the full surrender to God which we could not actualize.

8. I found Gustaf Aulén helpful because he takes us back behind Anselm to the theology of the New Testament and the early church to an understanding which he terms the classic model. See his *Christus Victor: An Historical Study of the Three Main Types of the Idea of the Atonement* (London: SPCK, 1953).

9. Aulén, *Christus Victor*, 37.

10. On this theme see Christian D. Kettler, *The Vicarious Humanity of Christ and the Reality of Salvation* (Lanham, MD: University Press of America, 1991) and Karl Barth, *Church Dogmatics*: Vol. 4, *The Doctine of Reconciliation* (Edinburgh: T. & T. Clark, 1974).

11. See Harry R. Boer, *An Ember Still Glowing: Humankind as the Image of God* (Grand Rapids: Eerdmans, 1990), 10.

12. On the last Adam christology, see James D. G. Dunn, *Christology in the Making: A New Testament Inquiry into the Origins of the Doctrine of the Incarnation* (Philadelphia: Westminster, 1980), Chap. 4, and N. T. Wright, *The Climax of the Covenant: Christ and the Law in Pauline Theology* (Minneapolis: Fortress Press, 1992), Chap. 2.

13. Lewis, *Mere Christianity* (London: Fontana, 1952), 141. Further on the rationality of substitution, see Wolfhart Pannenberg, *Jesus—God and Man* (Philadelphia: Westminster, 1968), 264-69.

14. Lutherans seem to grasp these matters better than Calvinists do: See Ted Peters, *God—the World's Future* ( Minneapolis: Fortress Press, 1992), 312-16.

15. See Walter Künneth, *The Theology of the Resurrection* (St Louis: Concordia, 1965), 161-79.

16. Murray J. Harris, *Raised Immortal: Resurrection and Immortality in the New Testament* (Grand Rapids: Eerdmans, 1983), 165-71.

17. N. Q. Hamilton, *The Holy Spirit and Eschatology in Paul* (Edinburgh: Oliver and Boyd, 1957).

18. Pascal was sensitive to such dynamics of faith and knowledge. Thomas V. Morris, *Making Sense of It All: Pascal and the Meaning of Life* (Grand Rapids: Eerdmans, 1992).

INDIVIDUALS ATTENDING
1993
NORTH PARK SYMPOSIUM ON
THEOLOGICAL INTERPRETATION OF SCRIPTURE

Elizabeth Achtemeier*
Lawrence Adams
Frances M. Anderson
Linda Belleville
jackson Blanchard
Steve Boum-Prediger*
John Bray
Marjorie Carlson
Richard Carlson
Helen Cepero
David Dahlberg
Robert Dvorak
Linda Forbes
Herb Freedholm
Robert Geelhoed
David Gill
Larry Griffin
Linda Gutfeldt
Michael Gutfeldt
Dikran Hadidian
Stephen Hall
Stanley Harakas*
David Horner
Timothy Horner
Cal Katter
Karl Klockars
Paul Koptak
Paul Larsen
Sang Book Lee
Jennifer J. Leese
Mohn Martz*
Bruce Metzger*
Walter Michel*
Donald Miller
Dean Nelson
John Newport*
David Nystrom
Ben Ollenburger*
Roger Olson*
Grant Osborne*
Carolyn Osiek*
Thomas Parker*
Ted Peters*
Jamie Phelps*
Clark Pinnock*
David M. Scholer
Klyne Snodgrass
Cathy Stanley
Tim Stohlberg
Irmgard Stuhlmacher
Peter Stuhlmacher*
John Sundquist
Norma S. Sutton
Glen Wagner
Wayne Weld
Everett L. Wilson

* Program Participant

# RESURRECTION AS HUMANLY INTELLIGIBLE DESTINY

BEN F. MEYER

Two now elderly Christian philosophers, Jean Guitton and Josef Pieper, have pondered the theme of human destiny in the perspective of Christianity, posed philosophic questions, and ventured philosophic answers on this theme. Human destiny as Christianity has defined it—namely, resurrection and eternal life—has seemed, from Paul's encounter with confidently dogmatic Epicureans and Stoics in Athens (Acts 17) to our own time, to be burdened with a kind of a priori implausibility. Whether ancient or modern skepticism is the more impenetrable is moot, but the plausibility-block to which we allude cannot in any case be ascribed exclusively to skepticism. Guitton speaks of "the enigma of resurrection"[1] and Pieper points out that, left to itself, human reason "quickly runs out of ideas here"; that, moreover, the truths of faith, though revealed, still "remain hidden"; but, finally, that all our lives up to the very moment of death we are hopers, intent on a "hoped-for" that cannot but burst the bounds of this world.[2]

## EARLY CHRISTIANITY AND HUMAN DESTINY: PRELIMINARY CONSIDERATIONS

Human destiny in Christian perspective transcends the sphere proper to human resources and operations. Any such transcendence generates tension between itself and humanism of whatever kind. But human destiny in the Christian field of meaning transcends not only human nature, but any and all created natures, so that the tension between Christianity and humanism is radical and maximal.

Guitton has been well aware of the gap between contemporary Western culture and the article in the Apostles' creed, "(I believe in) the resurrection of the body." "All life's experience," he observes, "protests against this belief; one wonders whether it is truly believed in the Christianity of today."[3] His own efforts looked to the diminishing of this credibility gap by drawing on resources of reason.[4] Pieper, in three or four short works, drew on prophetic knowledge—as Plato and Aristotle had drawn *ex ακοες* (Phaedo, 61 d 9) on the intuitions immanent in pre-philosophic religious tradition—to illuminate the darkness of the future.[5]

Like Guitton, we shall conclude this study with an effort to show a certain positive force in the Christian view of destiny. This will not be so much an effort to diminish the unbelievability of "the resurrection of the body," but it will point up some differences between the Christian view, which has an undeniable richness, and competing views from the nineteenth century to the postmodernism of today, which, on themes like human destiny, cannot conceal their poverty. Like Pieper, we shall return to Aquinas for one critical starting point and shall focus on hope precisely with reference to the resurrection of the body.

The New Testament offers ample evidence of a human destiny (knowing and loving God as he really is) that cannot be other than absolutely supernatural (not, to be sure, in the modern sense of "spooky" or "unexplained," but in the sense "independent of human destiny and of human or any created nature and powers." The word "destiny" has the sense here of the final "lot" that falls to man, without further specification.

"Destiny" is not a biblical theme. To biblical writers words like "destiny," "fate," "fortune," and the like referred to alien views. No New Testament writer draws on this vocabulary of destiny to express Christian views, e.g., *moira* and *aisa* (final lot, share, portion); *potmos* (fate), *tuchē* (fortune, chance), *heimarmenē* and *anagkē* (fate, necessity). "Destiny" in the sense in which we use it is akin to "goal" in the line of Pindar: "We do not know the goal that fate *(potmos)* has marked for our running" (*Nem.* 6:6-7). In this limited sense (final state, lot, goal), the New Testament offers many texts pertinent to human "destiny." In dealing with these texts, however, we must observe the rule of attending not only to what the writer says but to the larger fields of meaning—the hermeneutic and historic contexts—that qualify his saying it. By surveying this evidence we may hope to find a way of making the Christian view of human destiny intelligible to ourselves—the condition of our making it intelligible in any way at all to others.

Was Christianity unified enough that we can speak of "destiny in early Christian perspective"? Gregory Dix defined the major historical question engaging New Testament scholars during the hundred-year-period between Ferdinand Christian Baur (d. 1860) and Dix's own time (d. 1952) as whether from the Jerusalem community to the post-Pauline Church, Christianity exhibited an enduring ecclesial identity.[6] Seven years ago I offered an incurious public a monograph (*The Early Christians: Their World Mission and Self-Discovery)*[7] designed to lay the groundwork for an affirmative answer to Dix's question. An affirmative answer must, to be sure, take account of the changes that the first Christians underwent. Most significant of these is the sequence of changes in the horizons/fields of vision of the participants: from Jesus' disciples, who were probably all *hebraioi* (Aramaic-speaking Jews), to the Jerusalem Christian *hebraioi* and *hellēnistai,* to the dialectic of Jerusalem and Antioch in the early days of the world mission, to the missionary communities founded in the Mediterranean basin in the fifties and sixties, to Christianity, post-Petrine and post-Pauline, toward the end of the Apostolic Age. The purpose of my monograph was to highlight evidence of a Christian universe of meaning in this period, defined by "the gospel," and wide and capacious enough to accommodate many diverse conceptualities and culturally conditioned self-definitions. It seemed to me that what had been conspicuously absent from the views of Walter Bauer[8] and Ernst Käsemann,[9] of scholars writing on "unity and diversity,"[10] and of recent introductions (e.g., that of Helmut Koester)[11] was solid evidence supporting *not diversity, but division.* (Who doubts that diversities, rich and enriching as well as problematic and distracting, were everywhere present in early Christianity from the Levant to the western Mediterranean and from the first community to the end of the Apostolic Age?) Division is incompatible with unity; diversity is not. True contraries are unity and division, uniformity and diversity. Diversity can hardly be the key issue, for it is compatible equally with unity and division. Every New Testament writer asserts or betrays a certain recoil from division, but *unity without diversity would have been impossible* and all early Christian writers seem to know this.

*Dialectical oppositions* (those in which each of the opponents considers repudiation of the views of the other side as the one and only intelligent, reasonable and responsible stand) among the early Christians were rare. This question, under considerration as we have said for over a hundred years, remains to plague every issue, including the present one. Although space does not permit substantiation, relatively few dialectical oppositions arose in early Christianity, and none of them were left unsettled. In the present instance, the question of resurrection, our position is happily identical with the claim of Paul in 1 Cor 15:1-11, which concludes, "So, be it I or they [other missionaries], it is in these terms that we proclaim the gospel and it was in these terms that you accepted it in faith" (v. 11).

A common confession and conviction in faith respecting human destiny was a datum of early Christianity. This "datum" does not include *a priori* the notion that their conceptualities, or interrelated modes of understanding, were simply identical. It does signify, however, that these conceptions were not in ultimate contradiction on the reality of human destiny.

Moreover, the major themes of the New Testament have proven to be reciprocally pervasive. By affinity, not by entailment, they imply one another. Just as nearly every narrative pericope in the gospel tradition was a kind of summary of the gospel (as the form critics and their successors pointed out), so with numerous main New Testament themes. They made up, not a system, but a circle of revelation and reflection. Poor judgment can, of course, defeat any hermeneutic. We should have sense enough not even to think of taking our bearings on human destiny from ideologues. We are not a subdivision of the avant-garde, and we need a more discerning estimate of our own situation than any such ideological faction can offer. Academics, unaware of (or greatly underestimating the decisiveness of) self-reversal on the part of ideologies, have often betrayed a weakness for celebrated nihilists. On this we have a trenchant recent comment from a most unlikely source, Ernst Junger, a figure from the past but an active, now nearly 100-year-old sage, who sees nihilism as appealing today chiefly to the bored and empty-headed rich.[12]

Our situation is time conditioned, but we have no basis for supposing from the start a flat contradiction between "human" and "time-transcendent." Our historic situation might be variously depicted (as the post-Cold-War quest of a viable world order; as an ongoing competition to give final definition to modernity; as the challenge posed by a civilization in decline, digging its grave with a relentless consistency). But the New Testament writers' ways of dealing with the issue of human destiny, while they touch the diverse historic situations of human beings, focus rather on an ultimate situation, a state of life beyond death. Early Christianity proclaims a new destiny that has reached into time and that also reaches *beyond time*. This was once an idealist theme. The break with idealism led many, such as Martin Heidegger, to posit time as intrinsic to human existence. Whoever adopts this view, remarked Josef Pieper, "will find hidden from him not only the life *'beyond time'* but also the very meaning of life *in* time."[13]

## HUMAN DESTINY AS TRANSCENDENT: BIBLE, EUCHARIST, BAPTISM

The instruction of the elementary class *(rudes)* of North African converts to Christianity ca. 400 A.D., according to St. Augustine, had the form of a Lenten initiation to the Bible from Genesis to the Apocalypse and the effect of inducting the converts into a great drama. The scriptures presented this drama partly as history, partly as prophecy. Its beginning was the creation of the world and of man, its middle the advent of Christ and what has followed, including the prospective converts' own present faith and struggle, and the promised ending included the resurrection of the dead, the coming of Christ, the judgment of the world, and the reign of God.

These converts of the late Roman Empire thereby moved out from under the sense of fate *(fatum)* that weighed on pagan antiquity and became burdensome in the course of the Roman ascendancy. The story to which the converts were responding—more, into which they were entering—had been conceived in terms other than fate, yet the response of joyous liberation from fate was wholly appropriate. It was liberation-by-baptism. The flipside and real cause of this joy was an eternal destiny of life in Christ with God.

Respecting human destiny, our situation is hardly different from that of North African converts in Augustine's time. Escape for us is not from fate, but from meaninglessness and ideologies that rationalize it. For our time too the human drama is revealed in the scriptures. We too have a history-transcending destiny of resurrection, judgment, and eternal life. This is far from the strange mix of hard empiricism and pragmatism with the feckless superstition and sentimentally humanitarian morality that dominates contemporary secular culture. The theme of Christ's impact on human destiny is among the themes most generative of an accurate and realistic grasp of New Testament texts.

Heuristic reflection on the human problem, that is, reflection born of the utter incompatibility of God, his goodness, wisdom, and power with the cumulative surd of evil evident in the world and all through its history, leads the inquirer to posit a divine solution to the human problem of evil, to analyze the problem so as to discern what traits a genuine solution must have, and to inquire historically whether any candidate for the anticipated divine "solution" has broken surface in history.[14]

Transactions with the New Testament render inevitable the identity of this solution with salvation in Christ. The prophets of Israel had envisaged a change of direction, a "restoration of fortunes" *(šûb šĕbût)*; but the fulfillment of this hope outsoared its original form, for the event of salvation in Christ effected a radical reorganization of human destiny. The ultimate destiny of man was to be *entry into the mystery of God.* This shifted the center of gravity of hope, adding to historic existence and natural immortality a focus on posthistoric existence and resurrection on the model of Christ. Given Christ's actual mission, Israel's hope of prevailing in the contests of earthly life yielded by necessity to a transformation and became "fundamental hope," bent not on having, but on selfhood or being (Josef Pieper); it became "real hope," transcending the objects that had enkindled it (Gabriel Marcel).[15]

The supernatural destiny in question is one of knowing and loving God, not as in a glass darkly, but face to face (1 Cor 13:12). In the dimensions it has actually assumed, God's solution to the human problem—the "problem" of impotent immersion in evil—entails a searing reorganization, one that, devaluing any mere humanism, calls for a heightening and transcending (*Erhebung* and *Aufhebung*) of natural humanity and solicits from the human heart the heroic love of a Maximilian Kolbe at Auschwitz. This solution is also the promise of a future in the risen body and a material universe, a future of which the scriptures offer barely a glimmer.

We shall begin our account of New Testament data on the transcendent destiny of the human race with Jesus' own scenario of the eschatological future. This scenario, drawing on age-old biblical lore, evoked the messianic banquet on the world mountain. In the symbolic idiom of Jesus, Abraham, Isaac, and Jacob recline to banquet with the saved of Israel and the nations. Here the central images are the bread of life and wine of salvation. Jesus grasped his own role in the life of Israel as definitive. To borrow from the words of John the Baptist in the question he sent Jesus from prison, it is the role of one after whom we are to await no other (Matt 11:2-6/Luke 7:18-23). Consequently, this role or mission is *bound up with the total fulfillment of all the scriptures.*

Jesus accordingly took it that his personal mission somehow included the dispensing of the bread of life. Without the need of allusion to Moses, this belonged to the blessings that it was his mission to announce and effect (Luke 6:21/Matt 5:6). The bread of life was first for Israel, then for the world (Matt 8:11/Luke 13:29; cf. Matt 15:26-27). It was "the bread of tomorrow" which he taught his disciples to pray to receive even today (Matt 6:11/Luke 11: 3).

Leaving aside historicity questions on the miracle of the loaves, we should recall how symbol-charged the presentation of the event is both in the Synoptic versions and in John. It recalls Israel in the wilderness nourished by bread from heaven and tacitly evokes the eucharistic practice of the listeners/readers. In the gospel of John it replaces, and in the Synoptists it anticipates, the eucharistic words of Jesus at the Last Supper. This rich, polyphonic story promises bread galore for the life of the world.

At the Last Supper, probably a Passover meal, Jesus highlighted the bread and wine symbols, associated them with the sacrificial idiom of "flesh" (John 6:51-56; *Ign. Smyrn.* 7:1; *Rom.* 7:3; *Phld.* 4:1; *Trall.* 8:1; Justin, *Apol.* I 66:2) and blood, and founded the rite that would replace the cult of the temple of Jerusalem, doomed to destruction in the looming ordeal. German scholars for many years have urged a more exact terminology than "interpretative words" *(Deuteworte)* and gestures, for the eucharistic words and acts went beyond interpreting. They were words and acts of giving, a supreme self-giving. Hence the use of phrases such as "words" and "gestures of bestowal" *(Gabeworte, Gabegeste).*[16]

Which words were original continues to be disputed. In 1988 Peter Stuhlmacher offered a helpful principle: in looking for the most probably original set of eucharistic words, "that version is to be preferred which most easily makes historically understandable how the other versions arose."[17] On this basis a solid case can be made for the originality of the Markan word on the cup: "This is my blood, covenant-blood, (to be) poured out for many" (Mark 14:24; Aram: *Dên (hû)ʾadam q̆eyamî demištĕpêkʿal saggîʾîn).*

The eucharistic words and acts indicate the final terms in which Jesus cast his mission. It was a mission that fulfilled the type of the Servant (Isa 53:10-12) and offered the root solution to the human problem of immersion in sin. The Markan word on the cup shows a convergence of two categories: that of fulfillment (of the type of the Servant in Isa 53:11-12 and of the prophecy and promise in Jer 31 and Ezek 36 of a new covenant=new heart/new spirit) and, second, the category of solution (to the problem of sin to be forgiven, cf. Isa 53:10-12, and of chronic liability to sin: "the heart of stone," Ezek 36:26).

On the understanding that Jesus' words and acts were effective, evidenced in the expression "in the sight of God," the eucharistic words and acts are the divine revelation of a definitively settled human destiny (which, to be sure, may or may not be achieved). This reaches thematic, explicit status in the climax of the speech on the bread of heaven in the gospel of John:

> I am the living bread that has come down from heaven; if anyone eats this bread he will live for ever; and the bread which I shall give is my own flesh, for the life of the world . . . Truly, truly I say to you, unless you eat the flesh

> of the Son of man and drink his blood, you can have no life in you; whoever eats my flesh and drinks my blood has eternal life, and I will raise him up at the last day. For my flesh is real food and my blood is real drink. Whoever eats my flesh and drinks my blood dwells in me and I in him (6:51, 53-56).

John presents a midrash on scriptural texts ("he gave them bread [from heaven] to eat," Exod 16:16; cf. v. 4) and represents a Jewish repudiation of Jesus/the eucharist. Paul, on the other hand, shows how hard it was for gentile converts to take in the full force of the words of Jesus, of the rite of loaf and cup which he founded, of its continuously renewed creation of the Church, of its realization of present salvation, of its promise for the realization of human destiny. This gentile incapacity held despite the fact that all these things were thematic in Paul's teaching: the words of Jesus (1 Cor 11:23-25); the founder of the rite (1 Cor 11:23, 24e, 25 b, e); its ever-renewed creation of the Church (1 Cor 10:17); its realization of present salvation (1 Cor 10:16-17; 11:26-27, 29); its promise of the realization of human destiny (1 Cor 11:26b, c). But the real sense and force and value of these truths could not be taken in by pagan converts swiftly, firmly, and accurately. By force of cultural instinct (on automatic pilot, as it would seem to us, and without full attention), they correlated the Lord's Supper with a culturally familiar, standard Hellenistic memorial practice.

That the Lord's Supper was utterly different from and far more than that is shown by 1 Cor 10 and 11. The fault that Paul found with the manner of the Corinthian community's celebration of the Lord's Supper had to do with the division between rich and poor at the common meal (1 Cor 11:17-22), a division particularly odious in view of the presiding presence in the community of "the Lord," who had made himself poor for their sake (2 Cor 8;9; cf. Phil 2:6-7b) and by his totally selfless eucharistic self-giving, sealed by death and resurrection, had made them one (1 Cor 10:16-17)!

Why did Paul cite the aetiological text of the rite (1 Cor 11: 23-25)? And what was his point in the words with which he followed his citation of the aetiology (1 Cor 11:26-32)? Otfried Hofius, in an article offering a brilliantly independent reconstruction of eucharistic celebration in Corinth,[18] has argued that it was in order to recall the *pro vobis/huper hûmôn/* "for you" motif (1 Cor 11:24) that showed a spirit flatly contrary to that of the rich in the face of the have-nots among them. There can be little doubt that this has its moment of truth; but can it bear the full weight of the explanation we need? The same question should be asked of Hans-Josef Klauck's remarkable study of the eucharist and *koinōnia*-ecclesiology in Paul.[19] Klauck appeals both to the "for you" motif and the motif of "covenant" cited in the eucharistic words.

Still, it should be noticed that immediately following his citation of the eucharistic words, Paul does nothing to highlight either the "for you" motif or the covenant motif, neither of which moreover would require a full citation of the eucharistic words. Another account seems called for. Earlier in 1 Cor 8 and 10 Paul had taken up two questions. The first dealt with eating meat that had been used in idolatrous cult, on which he offered a precise distinction: offering food to idols is an empty act, but better no meat at all than that, glorying in my own freedom, I occasion the sin of "the weak," a brother for whom Christ died. The other question was on participation in idolatrous cult (1 Cor 10), which he apodictically repudiated. Cult is entry into communion. Idolatrous cult is entry into communion with demons (Deut 32:17; cf. Ps 106:37-38). You cannot be in simultaneous communion with Christ and with demons. The text that makes the point on communion (*koinōnia*) with Christ is Paul's exploitation of what was probably a fragment of eucharistic catechesis in Antioch or in some Mediterranean mission community. For the sake of the rhetorically forceful conclusion of v. 17, he has changed the order of "cup" and "loaf." 1 Cor 10:16-17 reads:

> The cup of blessing that we bless, is it not a sharing in the blood of Christ? The loaf we break, is it not a sharing in the body of Christ? Because there is one loaf, we, though many, are one body, for we all partake of the one loaf.

*Koinōnia,* a nonbiblical word widely used in hellenistic religion, means a sacral bond, both a "sharing in" and a "communion with." Here Paul evokes the ineffable bond that binds the Christian to Christ and creates communion with Christ, a sharing in the reality of and redemptive fruits of Christ's self-offering to the Father. Tacitly supposed are: 1) the eucharistic rite understood as communion with and sharing in the body and blood of Christ; 2) hence, the distribution of eucharistic elements, and their being eaten and drunk; 3) a realist understanding of the whole; that is, the body and blood are the body and blood of the crucified and exalted Lord. On this basis Paul interprets the reality of "the-Church-as-body-of-Christ" as deriving from participation in the one loaf, Christ.

Thus armed with some preliminary understanding of Paul's eucharistic theology, we return to the question of why he cited the entire aetiological text of eucharistic acts and words of Jesus (1 Cor 11:23-25). He had charged that what the Corinthians did was a great error. Allowing factions of rich and poor to arise in the very assembly gathered for transformation of "many" into "one" body-of-Christ was not, and could not well be called, the Lord's Supper: "It is not the Lord's Supper that you eat" (1 Cor 11:20). What was the defect to be corrected? Some isolated particular? Some specific oversight? No, the correction as it actually stands (1 Cor 11:23-32) is a rehearsal from the top, a basic, rudimentary instruction starting with the most fundamental eucharistic text (1 Cor 11:23-25). This is followed by Paul's defining exactly what "you," the commmunity, are doing when you are celebrating the Lord's Supper. As often as you eat this bread and drink this cup, *you are proclaiming the death of the Lord.* Since this proclaiming is never lacking ( "as often as"), it must refer primarily at least to the community's fulfillment of the Lord's "Do this!" The fulfillment of this mandate comprises the eucharistic words and acts announcing the death of the Lord, just as at the Last Supper.

The referent of "you are proclaiming" (*kataggellete,* a rare word in the LXX, and rendering no Hebrew text) may include the kind of homily we find in John 6. (Hofius argues rather for the psalms as our main guide to the "proclaiming" of 1 Cor 11:26.[20] Should this be correct, then the object of the proclaiming ought indeed to be widened, as Hofius proposes, to take in the resurrection.) If, however, we take the text as it stands, with "the death of the Lord" as the object of the proclaiming, the proclaiming must be in the first instance the sacral, solemn affirmation in word (the words just cited by Paul) and act (in accord with the aetiological function of the words) of the sacrificial and saving death of Christ. The reference is to his death, for this is what the motifs "body" and "blood" evoke. (The original words, in all probability, were the specifically sacrificial terms, "flesh" and "blood.") The proclaiming is not directed to some other party, as in missionary proclamation, but is primarily confessional. It is the entire community's solemn, thankful, cultic expression of faith before God. This emerges not only from the cultic situation itself, but from the complementary "until he come(s)" (1 Cor 11:26d). For this clause as Jeremias and Hofius have shown[21] is temporal. The eucharist will be celebrated till the day of the Lord. But it is not only temporal; it is also final (a purpose or result clause). It implies the community's call for the Lord's coming, for the death of the

Lord is no isolated event of the past, but the inauguration of final salvation. The celebrative remembering of the death of the Lord is itself intercessory. It is a petitioning for the parousia. In the "proclaiming" of the Lord's death we hear, accordingly, the *maran ʾatāʾ* (Maranatha), Lord, come! (1 Cor 16:22).

What follows in vv. 27-32 is a conclusion (it begins with "Therefore") that excludes the kind of spurious Lord's Supper described in vv. 17-22. The heart of the matter is expressed in vv. 27-29. The normative reality of the Lord's Supper is the presence of the risen Lord as both host of the community and self-offering to the Father. Observance of the Supper is the making-present of Christ's death for the world. Therefore, anyone who (like the self-centered, mindlessly feasting rich in the community of Corinth) shares in the eating and drinking without discerning "the body"—that is, without discerning in bread and cup the risen Christ himself present as both Lord and sacrificial offering—eats and drinks judgment (i.e. condemnation) on himself! Paul's correction does not say: "Think about love and the poor." It says: "Think about *what you are doing* when you eat this bread and drink this cup."

Baptism and the eucharist are alike in that both are symbols of eschatological fulfillment (*eschatologische Erfüllungszeichen*).[22] "Eschatological" should not be soft-pedaled. Paul's debate with Judaism turned on the subjects of the human destiny epitomized in "new creation" and "new covenant," themes familiar to and in use among Jews of the time. Who were these subjects? Jews alone, in accord with the historic election of Israel? Or Israel first, and gentiles in dependence on Israel, in accord with the scheme of the eschaton? The answer hinged on whether history already had undergone a qualitatively new development, whether the mission of Jesus (clearly, unambiguously eschatological, as the gospel traditions familiar to Paul show) had been authentic, and whether the eschaton had broken out. This issue in a variety of sets of terms dominated Paul's debate or dialogue with the Jews, which hovers in the background of Galatians and Romans. Both letters, from start to finish, are thoroughly eschatological. The affirmations of Paul in the cultic sphere (e.g., Rom 3:25-26; 1 Cor 6:11) hinge on the reality of the inbreaking eschaton.

How otherwise could the human subject by the cultic acts of baptism and eucharist enter into the saving mystery, the risen Christ in whom his self-offering and death continue? The "putting on" of Christ (Gal 3:27) in baptism and the entry into his death (Rom 6:3) constituted "new creation" in which the righteous Servant (Isa 53:11) made many righteous, so inaugurating a new and final destiny for the human race. We meet here the Christian conception of the human dilemma. The dilemma has to do with sin and death, with an immersion in sin that was the guarantee of death. The making "righteous," then, was a liberation from this state, without which there could be no destiny of "life" with the living God. Baptism and the eucharist were tied into the break with sin, the new state of righteousness, and the eschatological future. Sacramantal acts bore an eschatological destiny, i.e., entry into the reign of God. The unrighteous will not inherit the reign of God . . . but

> you have had yourselves washed *(apelousasthe)*,
> you have been consecrated *(hēgiasthēte)*,
> you have been made righteous *(edikaiothēte)*.

in the name of our Lord Jesus Christ and in the Spirit of our God (1 Cor 6:9-11).

Here again we have a traditional text, lapidary and hieratic, which Paul probably adopted from the Antiochene baptismal liturgy. In addition to motifs such as washing, consecration, righteousness, reference to Christ and the Spirit, the Antiochene baptismal liturgy is the probable source of the motif of "conformity to the image of God's Son" (Rom 8:29-30). This supposed the loss (it was Adam's loss in paradise) of the "glory" of God (Rom 3:23; *Apoc. Moses* 20), i.e., the unblemished image and likeness of God. Its recovery belongs to eschatological participation in Christ that begins in baptism (1 Cor 12:13) and consists in being "transformed from glory to glory into his likeness" (2 Cor 3:18). The Spirit effects "new creation" (2 Cor 5:17) by faith (Gal 3:2-5, 14)/baptism (1 Cor 12:13). This gives the subject a new mode of being and new principles of life, which the living out of the Christ-life makes wholly operative. Thus faith/baptism inaugurates by the power of the Spirit a sequence of "with-Christ" happenings: to co-suffer with Christ (Rom 8:17) in a process of "growing conformity" with his death (Phil 3:10); to be co-crucified with him (Gal 2:19; Rom 6:6); made co-natural with him, in a death like his (Rom 6:5); carrying his death in one's own body (2 Cor 4:10; cf. Gal 6:17); to be co-buried with him (Rom 6:4); to be his co-heir to glory (Rom 8:17); to be co-glorified with him soon (Rom 8:17). *This is what it means to be co(n)formed to the image of God's Son.* It is a richly, extravagantly transformed recovery of the lost likeness of God, an again-becoming-son to God by being made one with God's Son. The new principle of existence is simultaneously a new destiny, not in the sense of an isolated abstract goal, but in that of *co-destiny to glory with the Son.* It is a baptismal and eucharistic entry into the pattern of Christ, his sufferings (Phil 3:10; 2 Cor 1:5-7; Gal 6:17), his death (2 Cor 4:10; Gal 2:19; Rom 6:5-6), his resurrection (1 Cor 15:21, 49; Rom 6:5, 8), his very being as image and glory and Son of God (1 Cor 11:7; 2 Cor 3:18; 5:21 [cf. 1 Cor 1:30]; Rom 8:29).

Pre-faith/baptism man is an "old" self; the new self is "dead to sin" and "alive to God" (Rom 6:5-11; cf. Gal 2:17-20). To be in Christ is not to be alone with a lonely destiny, but to be with others who are in him, with them to constitute a new mode of human existencel. On the level of historic society this new mode of existence is a *gens tertia* with Jews and Gentiles of the old order, but in the reality grasped by faith and a transcendent new man, freed of the old divisions, conflicts, and bondages:

> There is neither "Jew" nor "Greek," there is neither slave nor free, there is no "male and female" [Gen 1:27], for you are all one in Christ Jesus. (Gal 3:28).

In Gal 6 "new creation" transposed easily into an election-historical title "the Israel of God" (Gal 6:16). In the eschatological reality of Christ--that is, by sacramental *koinōnia*/communion with the Son of God—the age old promise of the election of Israel and the eschatological refashioning of humanity was realized at once. Humanity was refashioned for a destiny of risen life, life in the "spiritual body" (1 Cor 15:44), and eternal life on the pattern of Christ (1 Cor 15:45-46), knowing and loving God as he is.

## ENTAILMENTS OF THE NEW TESTAMENT THEME OF HUMAN DESTINY

World literature records how persistently and chronically we have wondered about our deeply puzzling selves, our origin and history and destiny. Most of the proposed answers have doubtless been pitifully inadequate. We have evoked above, however, the kind of inquiry—namely, heuristic retrieval of a solution from analysis of the elements of the problem—that culminates in acknowledgement of a historic solution: the phenomenon of Israel which generated the phenomena of John the Baptist and Jesus, Peter and John, James and Paul (all but John martyred).

On the basis of the appearance of the solution in history, our first clues to human destiny bore on "the bread of life." This turned out to be one and the same as the gift that God has made to us of himself in his Son. Already we have seen that the data on human destiny in the New Testament involves a mass of entailments of which there had been not so much as a whispered intimation in the original question. Our brief discussion of eschatological signs of fulfillment, namely, baptism and the eucharist, have already entailed more or less elaborate schemes of meaning. Here we shall spell out some of these entailments more fully.

First, the New Testament schemata bound up with human destiny are mostly elements of apocalyptic or absolute eschatology (as, for example, exhibited by Dan chapters 7-12, ca. 165 B.C.), which tended in the course of the second century to dominate the horizons of Israel. Among its themes were revelation to the wise that beleaguered Israel was on the brink of restoration. Here was a revolution in eschatology due to the new theme of "resurrection," which allowed the eschatologically-minded to think of "the end of the days" *(ʾaḥărît hayyāmîm)* as the very end of history, and of judgment as utterly definitive, with concomitant changes of sense and reference for the themes "new creation, new covenant, new King/Messiah/Man'," etc. We noted above that such eschatological schemata entailed "Adam speculation" and a variety of views of the human dilemma and its intractability. On the latter topic, prophetic and apocalyptic literature took a dark view; the learned elite by the time of Jesus and in later rabbinic tradition took a bright view. (Compare "All Israel has a portion in the age to come" [b.Sanh. 10.1] with "Many [=all] are called, but few [=not all] are chosen" [Matt 22:14]).

Jesus himself offered numerous clues to his view of the human dilemma. The expiatory motif in the ransom-word (Mark 10:45/Matt 20:28) and the eucharistic words (Mark 14:24/Matt 26:28) allows us to infer that an inevitable state of sin and death constituted the human problem. In the word on allowing the dead to bury their own dead (Matt 8:22/Luke 9:50), he left it to be understood that outside the sphere of his own saving mission there was only death and the dead. In alluding to two fatal incidents—the Galileans whose "blood Pilate [had] mingled with their sacrifices" (Luke 13:3) and the eighteen on whom a tower in Siloam had fallen (Luke 13:5)—he converted them into images of judgment looming over all Israel. "Unless you repent, you will all likewise perish" (Luke 13:3). Escape lay only in response to his appeal. Specifically he repudiated the idea that election (Matt 22:14) or even righteous status in terms of Torah observance (Matt 21:31) would preserve Israel from condemnation and perdition, if it turned away from Jesus' climactic and definitive saving mission. See Mark 6:11/Matt 10:4/Luke 9:5; Mark 8:38/Matt 16:27/Luke 9:26; Matt 7:24-27/Luke 5:47; Matt 10:32-33/Luke 12:8-9; Matt 12:41-42/Luke 32-33).

There is no accompanying explanation of the "why" of the human dilemma. It is just there, a given, and liberation from it would come only through response to Jesus. Otherwise the dilemma was universal and lethal. The drama of decision, however, was thought of as taking place only in Israel. Jesus alluded to the question of the Gentiles with little attendant detail. He merely warned that soon the end would come, and the danger exists of the dreadful irony that many from Israel would be lost and many from among the nations saved (Matt 8:11-12/Luke 13:28-29; Matt 25:31-46).

The scenario of the future sponsored by the post-Easter Church was in essence Jesus' scenario modified by the unexpected, advance realization of his resurrection from the dead. The era of the Church or of the world mission extended from the time of the risen Christ to the time of the parousia. In imagery familiar from the gospels and letters, the parousia was to signal the resurrection of the dead, the pilgrimage of the peoples, the judgment, the reign of God. This last expression, the key term in the independent proclamation of Jesus following the arrest of John the Baptist, is a major index to human destiny.

The human being was not made to live briefly and then to be consigned to oblivion. "How far you are from the truth!" Jesus said to the Sadducees; "You know neither the scriptures nor the power of God" (Mark 12:24/Matt22-29). In the scriptures the Lord identified himself to Moses: "'I am the God of Abraham, the God of Isaac, the God of Jacob.' He is not the God of the dead, but of the living!" The Easter Church shared this eschatological view of destiny as involving resurrection from the dead (Mark 12:18-27/ Matt 22:23-33/Luke 20:27-40). It is essentially the same view of the end state sponsored by John the Baptist with its alternatives of heaven and hell. In the Easter Church the accent is overwhelmingly on themes of resurrection, judgment, and paradise. The *hebraioi* maintained the categories and perspectives inherited from Jesus; the *hellēnistai* worked out their own perspectives within the common view of eschatology inaugurated and in process of realization.

We find evidences of Antiochene baptismal liturgy embedded in Pauline texts (e.g., 1 Cor 6:9-10, 14; 2 Cor 4:14; Rom 3:25-26; 8:11). This fund of formulas, though incomplete, is a treasure and allows us (following Ferdinand Hahn)23 to make some judgment on how Antiochene liturgy, Paul, and deutero-Pauline texts (Colossians and Ephesians) are related to one another on the resurrection to come and on human destiny. So far as our present purposes are concerned, however, these distinctions in content and accent are peripheral. They mainly assure us that, while there are traits in Paul which were truly original and distinctive, he was in no sense isolated in his views of human destiny. He stood in a tradition drawing on several sources: his rabbinic education on resurrection; his personal participation near Damascus in the Easter experience; his year long experience in Antioch including thorough acquaintance with the gospel tradition; his mystical experiences as a man of prayer; and the missionary experience of confronting the Hellenistic world with the theme of resurrection.

The theme of coming resurrection/human destiny both in early Christianity in general and in Paul in particular has been a discussion largely mismanaged over the past hundred and twenty years—from Otto Pfleiderer's two-volume pioneer synthesis to today. One constant undertow affecting Pauline texts was Paul's own intense desire to live to greet the parousia. This was a theme that, unlike speculation on the life of the age to come, seemed to have a compelling relevance to the strategies of the world mission. ("Imminent expectation," a topic that we cannot take up here, was bound up with the legacy of eschatological scenarios from John the Baptist and from Jesus.)

Paul's view of human destiny runs through all six of the great undisputed letters (leaving aside Phlm: 1 Thess, Gal, Phil, 1 and 2 Cor and Rom). 1 Cor 15 is a particularly privileged text. It is in Romans, however, that he gives the main lines of his view of the root dilemma; the sin of Adam. In the great passage of 1 Cor 15 there are two references to the motif of Adam's sin. One is in support of Paul's theme, if sin begets death, law begets sin (1 Cor 15:56). The other shows that in Antiochene and Pauline thought the dilemma had infected mankind by the death-dealing act of the first man, and would be resolved only by his antitype:

> for, just as through a man there came death so the more surely
> through a man there shall come the resurrection of the dead.
> (1 Cor 15:21).

Again:

> . . . just as we have borne the image of the man of dust,
> so the more surely shall we bear the image of the heavenly man,
> as well. (1 Cor 15:49).

Eschatological salvation is the creation of a new mankind, "the last Adam a life-giving spirit" (1 Cor 15:45). Elsewhere the writer has attempted to trace the coming to be, as well as the power, of this vision of things. Here it will have to suffice to allow Paul's view of resurrection to stand as typical of early Christian views, whether in Jerusalem or in the Mediterranean mission, of human destiny.[24]

## CONCLUDING PHILOSOPHIC REFLECTION

The philosophic reflection of Jean Guitton on resurrection bore partly on the issue of believability and partly on science as anticipation of the eschatological future. The latter aspect of his thought prolongs a French tradition rooted in Ravaisson (1813-1900), retained and developed in Bergson (1859-1941), and briefly lent contemporary celebrity by the posthumously published works of Teilhard de Chardin (1881-1955). This tradition sought to affirm the reality of spirit by interpreting nature, or matter, as charged with a spiritual teleology. Guitton's reflections on resurrection continue this effort in that he conceives resurrection as the term of natural process (cf. Rom 8:22). "The danger," as Collingwood put it over fifty years ago, "is that a third term, neither mere nature nor genuine spirit, tends to be substituted for both."[25]

Josef Pieper's reflection on resurrection had superior roots in Aquinas's synthesis of the data of faith with the hylemorphism* of Aristotle and, no doubt, superior lasting power. He repudiated every effort of idealist tendency since the Enlightenment (e.g., that of Moses Mendelsohn) to take the sting out of death by glorifying the immortality of the soul.[26] As intrinsically immaterial, the soul is indeed immortal, but the separated soul is *not a human person*. It accordingly exists in a state unnatural to it, that is, in a state of objective violence. Resurrection, therefore, though discontinuous with the limits natural to mortal man, is not only "an intelligible human destiny"; it is the only truly integral solution to the human problem. So in some sense resurrection is the one and only wholly intelligible—though absolutely supernatural—destiny of man.

This way of putting the matter may have already gone beyond Pieper's extremely careful formulation. The following reflection, I believe, will nevertheless correlate with the thought of Pieper on resurrection as the divinely determined, boundlessly blessed fulfillment of fundamental hope, the hope of mankind salvaged, redeemed, remade on the model of Christ, last Adam and life-giving Spirit (1 Cor 15:45). Hope became a theme of investigation and debate among post-World War II phenomenologists positioned to draw on new conceptual resources from Hegel to their own time. Our point of departure, a theme recurrent in Pieper's books on hope, can be summed up in the report of Herbert Plügge, a doctor (cited by Pieper) whose medical anthropology was grounded in treatment of terminally ill patients.[27] Plügge differentiated between everyday hopes

* [Editor's note: The metaphysical doctrine that every natural object is somehow composed of matter and form.]

which Pieper, following Marcel and others—and drawing on linguistic usage, notes are typically plural, *espoirs* and fundamental hope (essentially singular, *espérance*). It lay within the scope of everyday hopes to prolong life, but what struck Plügge was that as everyday hopes faded and failed, fundamental hope was born. Unlike everyday hopes, which were extremely diverse in object, fundamental hope focused on selfhood—not on having, but on being. Finally, its object was invariably beyond the powers and resources of the hoper. (Hence the everyday idiomatic reservation of "hope" for what is beyond our power to create, engender, or control.)

This is what sets hope apart and sets Christianity apart from the massive illusions on self-transcendence and destiny that have dominated the cultural superstructure of the West from Marx, through Nietzsche, to post-modernism. For over a hundred years we have been deluged with hopeless proposals, sometimes urged in the name of hope. Marxism generated *das Prinzip Hoffnung*,[28] Ernst Bloch's celebrated collection of images and slogans celebrated heaven on earth—and carefully dodged any real confrontation with the fact and theme of death. In lieu of honestly facing the fact of death, Bloch has recourse to a weather-beaten sophism that goes back to Epicurus. But what does Bloch's "golden age" have to do with you, or me, or Bloch? Apart from briefly engaging our curiosity about a perhaps possible future, it is superficially cheering but ultimately—like Bloch's whole collection of images—essentially cheerless chitchat.

Nietzsche was obsessed with the need of the theme of cheer—down with Königsbergian grey and let's hear it for *Heiterkeit* (merriment)! On the other hand, the situation of the human being as Nietzsche presents it is far from cheering. The individual cannot be held accountable for his acts, for he is not free. For the herd of mankind generally there is no hope, for to break with the lethal mediocrity of life is reserved to the few, the noble rebels happily free of moral scruple. For all the bright rhetoric of defiance (like the thousand images in Bloch that are a mockery of real hope) the human situation is far from pleasing and few can follow the master in hoping for its eternal recurrence. Thanks especially to the post modernist appeal to Nietzsche, nothing is more persuasively borne in on us than this.

Michel Foucault drew on Nietzsche for oracles to guide his quest of the philosophic life. The quest came down to the effort to get rid of oneself *(se déprendre de soi-même)*.[29] The reference of this phrase tends to fluctuate between transformation and oblivion. Foucault looked for "positive truth" in the "downward fall" of risky experiment. The experiments—anonymous erotic games, drugs, madness—have no discernible role whatever in self-transcendence. As for destiny, even Foucault had little taste for Nietzsche's eccentric insistence on eternal recurrence, except as a parable defanged of its original sense.

What is most striking about characteristic philosophic efforts from the nineteenth century to the present to deal with self-transcendence and human destiny is their abysmal poverty. Rarely are these themes treated in a manner calculated to elicit or sustain human hope. By contrast, human destiny conceived in terms of Christian tradition stands in profound accord with (a) the make-up of the human person as body and soul; (b) the solution to the human problem as identical with the gospel (Rom 3:21-26; 2 Cor 5:16-21); (c) the deepest, most fundamental hope of the human heart—to be (Rom 8:23-30).

## NOTES

1. Jean Guitton, *Un siècle, une vie* (Paris: Laffont, 1988), 202.

2. Josef Pieper, *Hope and History* (New York: Herder and Herder, 1969), 83, 78, 87.

3. Guitton, op. cit, 202.

4. Jean Guitton, *Philosophie de la Résurrection* (Tournai Desclée de Brouwer, 1978).

5. Josef Pieper, *The End of Time* (New York: Pantheon, 1954); *Enthusiasm and Divine Madness* (New York: Harcourt, 1964); *Hope and History*, 77-81; *Death and Immortality* (New York: Herder and Herder, 1969; *On Hope* (San Francisco: Ignatius, 1986).

6. Gregory Dix, *Jew and Greek* (Westminster: Dacre, 1953), 2.

7. Wilmington: Glazier, 1986.

8. Walter Bauer, *Orthodoxy and Heresy in Earliest Christianity* (Philadelphia: Fortress, 1971).

9. Ernst Käsemann, "The Canon of the New Testament and the Unity of the Church," *Essays on New Testament Themes* (London: SCM, 1964), 95-107.

10. James D. G. Dunn, *Unity and Diversity in the New Testament,* 2d ed., Philadelphia: Westminster, 1990).

11, Helmut Koester, *Introduction to the New Testament. II: History and Literature of Early Christianity* (Berlin and New York: de Gruyter; Philadelphia: Fortress, 1982).

12. "Junger le meteore," interview with Ernst Junger in *Construire* (June 2, 1993) [Switzerland], 40-41.

13. Pieper, *On Hope*, 19-20.

14. Bernard Lonergan, *Insight: A Study of Human Understanding* , 2d ed., (London: Darton, Longman & Todd, 1983), 687-730.

15. Pieper, *Hope and History*, 91.

16. The change of language has been proposed by Schürmann, Jeremias, Pesch, Hofius, and others.

17. Peter Stuhlmacher, *Jesus von Nazareth und der Christus des Glaubens* (Stuttgart: Calwer, 1988) 68-69.

18. Otfried Hofius, "The Lord's Supper and the Lord's Supper Tradition: Reflections on 1 Corinthians 11:23b-25," *One Loaf, One Cup: Ecumenical Studies of 1 Cor 11 and Other Eucharistic Texts* (ed. B. F. Meyer (Macon: Mercer University Press, 1993), 75-115, at 113-115.

19. Hans-Josef Klauck, "Eucharistie und Kirchengemeinschaft bei Paulus," *Gemeinde-Amt-Sakrament,* ed. Hans Josef Klauck (Würzburg: Echter, 1989) 331-347, especially 338.

20. Hofius, "Lord's Supper," 103-111, espepcially 108.

21. Joachim Jeremias, *The Eucharistic Words of Jesus,* 3d ed. (London: SCM, 1966) 253-254; Otfried Hofius, "'Bis dass er Kommt' 1 Kor xi.26," *NTS* 14 (1967/68) 439-441; repr. in *Paulusstudien* (Tübingen: Mohr-Siebeck, 1989).

22. Heinz Schürmann, "Die Symbolhandlungen Jesu als eschatologische Erfüllungszeichen: eine Rückfrage nach dem irdischen Jesus," *Bibel und Leben* 11 (1970), 29-41, 73-78; repr. in Schürmann, *Das Geheimnis Jesu* (Leipzig: St. Benno, 1972), 74-110.

23. Ferdinand Hahn, "Taufe und Rechtfertigung: ein Beitrag zur paulinischen Theologie in ihrer Vor- und Nachgeschichte," *Rechtfertigung* ed. J. Friedrich, W. Pohlmann, P. Stuhlmacher (Tübingen: Mohr-Siebeck, 1976), 95-124.

24. B. F. Meyer, "Did Paul's View of the Resurrection of the Dead Undergo Development?" *Critical Realism and the New Testament* (Allison Park, PA: Pickwick, 1989), 99-128.

25. R. G. Collingwood, *The Idea of History*, ed., T. M. Knox (Oxford: Clarendon, 1946; repr. Oxford University Press, 1980), 185.

26. Pieper, *Death and Immortality*,

27. Herbert Plügge, *Wohlbefinden und Missbefinden: Beiträge zu einer medizinischen Anthropologie* (Tübingen: Niemeyer, 1962).

28. Ernst Bloch, *Das Prinzip Hoffnung* (Frankfurt-am-Main: Suhrkamp, 1959; 2d ed., 1970).

29. Michel Foucault, *The Use of Pleasure* (New York, 1985), 8. See James E. Miller, *The Passion of Michel Foucault* (New York: Simon & Schuster, 1993), 34.

# IF MORTALS DIE, WILL THEY LIVE AGAIN?

## The Old Testament and Resurrection

BEN C. OLLENBURGER

Does belief in the resurrection of the dead have a basis in the Old Testament? In what follows, I will try to provide a positive answer to this general question. However, I believe it is important to keep in mind another pair of questions: On the basis of the Old Testament, *how* should we believe in the resurrection? What should we mean by resurrection? It is with these questions in mind that I will turn, after a brief introduction, to the examination of specific texts. Someone has written that, "Ambiguous and unpredictable, details undermine ideology."[1] This is one reason why Christian theology—and Christian ministry—must return, over and again, to the details of its scriptural texts.

### Introduction

In his survey of Old Testament theology, John L. McKenzie notes that Daniel 12:2 speaks of a resurrection from the dead. He then remarks that this "allusion to the resurrection is the only clear allusion to this belief in the entire Hebrew Old Testament, although it is very probable that the belief is reflected in Isaiah 26:19." In any event, McKenzie concludes, this belief "can be proved only for the end of the Old Testament period. . . , and . . . it simply is not a component of the theology of the books of the Old Testament. Any hope of the future is expressed in terms of the enduring group, not of the individual person. . . ,"[2] Hans Küng, in his book, *Eternal Life,* seems to share McKenzie's judgment, claiming that, except for the latest period, "the various Old Testament statements, which [sic] speak of a 'resurrection,' are meant to be *figurative, metaphorical,* and cannot without more ado be taken as real in their imagery."[3] In this essay I want to give "more ado" to those Old Testament statements Küng has in mind.

Let me begin by turning again to McKenzie. In the passage following the one from which I quoted, he states "If one presupposes that the Israelites believed in the resurrection of the dead, one can interpret some passages as expressions of this belief."[4] I am unwilling to have presuppositions serve as the court of appeal for interpretation, nor do I presuppose that "the Israelites"—a diverse group with a long history—always and everywhere believed in the resurrection of the dead. Still, there is something in what McKenzie says. As Christians, we come to this discussion with something in mind. We come with experience in worship and are steeped in liturgical and theological traditions, to all of which the resurrection is of decisive importance—and not just resurrection in some general sense, but in a very particular sense that gains its shape from the New Testament. It is from the New Testament, and especially from what it says about the resurrection of Jesus Christ, that we Christians have learned to be interested in the resurrection, and have leamed *how* to be interested in it. In my view, this learning, along with the worship and theological reflection that have given it substance and nurture, is not to be abandoned when we turn to the Old Testament. To the contrary, what we have in mind by "resurrection" guides our inquiry; it helps us to know what we are looking for. At the same time, it does not *determine* our inquiry or tell us what we must find. Indeed, an honest inquiry into the Old Testament may help us refine or reform those convictions with which we began.

To illustrate, I refer once more to McKenzie. He concludes that, with insignificant exceptions, the Old Testament expresses no belief in the resurrection, and he reaches this conclusion because he defines resurrection in terms of "the individual person," while the Old Testament expresses a future hope only for "the enduring group." But why should we define "resurrection" in just this individualistic way? I shall argue that resurrection has something important to do with the enduring group. More importantly, I hope in this essay to show that, whatever it says or does not say *explicitly* about resurrection, the Old Testament contributes to our understanding of the resurrection of the dead, and I hope to show how it makes that contribution.

## A STORY OF MARTYRDOM

I begin with a text even later than Daniel, 2 Maccabees 7.[5] This is, of course, an apocryphal or deutero-canonical text; moreover, it moves somewhat beyond anything the Old Testament itself says. These considerations may seem to disqualify it from our consideration, especially if we are rigorously Protestant. However, I suggest that 2 Maccabees 7 lends perspective from which to consider earlier Old Testament texts. It tells the story of a woman and her seven sons who suffered and died at the hands of the Seleucid king, Antiochus IV, because they refused to commit apostasy by eating swine's flesh. Their testimony is stirring: they claimed their sufferings as their own ("we are suffering these things on our own account") and attributed them not to the power or the wickedness of the king, but to "our own sins against our own God" (v. 18). In so doing, they suffered with and for their people, not as heroic individuals; and they suffered death, not in resignation, but in confidence and hope. That hope had as its content resurrection from the dead and as its basis the mercy of God. It is their mother who articulates this hope to each of her sons as they die. "I do not know," she says, "how you came into being in my womb." This is not ignorance of biology on her part, but knowledge of God: "It was not I who gave you life and breath, nor I who set in order the elements within each of you" (v. 22). Their lives, as she tells her sons, are not her creation, nor do they rest in her hands or in the hands of the king who is taking them one-by-one; they rest in the hands of their creator, who is also the *world's* creator: "Therefore, the Creator of the world, who shaped the beginning of humankind and devised the origin of all things, will in his mercy give life and breath back to you again, since you now forget yourselves for the sake of his laws" (v. 23). [6]

This woman uses the technical vocabulary of Greek philosophy to express her ancient faith; for her courage, but also for her abilities as a theologian, the narrator in 2 Maccabees says that, of these eight martyrs, "Most remarkable was the mother" (v. 20).[7]

And remarkably, in vv. 28-29 she again joins resurrection with creation, this time in language that the church translated into Latin as *ex nihilo* —creation out of nothing.[8] When they did not exist, God created this mother and her sons, and not only them, but Israel; and not only Israel, but all humankind and everything that is in heaven and earth (v. 28). Trusting in God's mercy, persuaded of God's wrath and God's justice (v. 38), these eight martyrs expect the resurrection of the dead—of their dead bodies and of their family, their community.[9] Just so, they expect what does not now exist, what is being taken from them, because they know that God is the Creator, the King of the universe (v. 9), and merciful. Death will not prevail because God will again be reconciled with his own servants.[10] Reconciliation here is an act of God's creation *ex nihilo* in the form of resurrection from the dead.

Obviously, in 2 Maccabees 7 we have to do with the resurrection of individuals, but it is just as obvious that we have also to do with what McKenzie calls the "enduring group." Their mother does not expect her seven sons to rise from the dead into loneliness, by themselves on, say, the mountains of Ararat. She expects them to be restored to *her* and their resurrection to be the restoration of family. But it is not only this group, this family, consisting of mother and sons, that resurrection restores and continues; it is also that "group" consisting of God and God's servants. God, too, has a stake in the resurrection of the dead.

## DANIEL

The latter half of the book of Daniel, beginning with chapter 7 and then continuing in chapters 8-12, contains a series of visions that move forward in history to the time of Antiochus IV. In other words, these visions reflect the same setting that the story in 2 Maccabees 7 describes. In Daniel's visions, however, that setting of persecution under the Greeks remains future; it is revealed to Daniel and through Daniel to his readers "at the time of the end" (11:40; 12;1).[11] The concluding vision (or apocalypse) begins in chapter 10 and extends through 12:4, with an angelic being—presumably, Gabriel (8:15; 9:21)—describing for Daniel future events that will culminate in the "appointed time" (11:35). These events, in which one empire, the Persian, is followed by another, the Greek, mark a descent into tyranny that has its unprecedented embodiment in Antiochus IV (11:21-45). However, Daniel's vision does not merely predict the future. Rather, it explains to its readers the time in which they live—a time of wrath (*zaʿam*), in which the Jewish community faces the same choice between faithfulness, with likely martyrdom, or apostasy as in 2 Maccabees 7. The vision is preceded in chapter 9 by Daniel's prayer of contrition and supplication. He confesses that the calamity of Jerusalem's destruction and Judah's exile was due to Judah's treachery (9:7, 11-14), and, acknowledging both God's righteousness and Judah's shame, he appeals to God's mercy and forgiveness in asking that God's anger and wrath be turned away from Jerusalem (9:7, 17). Gabriel then interrupts Daniel's prayer in order to give him the wisdom to understand (9:22) that the end—the end for which Daniel is praying—has been decreed (*neḥerāṣâ* 9:27). The events that then transpire, and which chapters 10 and 11 portray, are not only the product of machinations among minor potentates along the Mediterranean shores; they fall within God's determination of the time—the time "to finish the transgression, to put an end to sin, and to atone for iniquity, to bring in everlasting righteousness. . ." (9:24).[12]

According to Daniel, the righteousness of God governs history, and this is a righteousness both to be honored by God's people and to be exercised, as God has determined to do, in the history that God's people suffer in utter dependence on God's mercy (9:18). God's determination of time and history does not rob them of their drama or their conflict, which are played out on a very human stage. However, Daniel does affirm that the mundane drama, with all of its very human suffering, participates in a transcendent conflict among the heavenly princes—the angelic representatives—of the various human parties. History does not simply run its predetermined course; rather, there is struggle in heaven itself, with the angel, or prince, Michael battling on behalf of the Jews (10:13-21). The unprecedented tyranny that Antiochus exercises against the Jews renders this battle precarious and crucial. But the battle with Antiochus is asymmetrical. Antiochus is represented by no heavenly prince, he honors no god—not even those of his people—but bows only to his own might, "the god of fortresses" (11:38), and he recognizes no divinity but his own. As such, Antiochus stands in direct contrast, and in conflict, with "the God of gods" (11:36), whom he imperiously blasphemes. Antiochus is God's rival.

Unlike 2 Maccabees, the book of Daniel does not speak explicitly of creation; even so, it does reflect the Old Testament's consistent interpretation of creation in terms of God's universal dominion—of the world as *God's.*[13] In the earlier chapters of Daniel, foreign kings come routinely to acknowledge this dominion, having failed in their challenges to it. For example, following his descent into madness, Nebuchadnezzar confesses that the rule of the Most High is everlasting, that his kingdom endures endlessly, and that he exercises sovereign disposition over both heaven's host and the earth's inhabitants (4:34-35). Daniel pointed out, to Belshazzar that he had exalted himself *(hitrômamtā̆)* "against the Lord of heaven" (5:23). It is this self-exaltation *(wĕyitrômēm)* against God and against God's dominion that Antiochus embodies in unprecedented measure (11:36). The prerogatives belonging only to God, which Babylonian and Persian kings acknowledge, even if belatedly, are exactly those claimed by Antiochus for himself, the power to do what he pleases (11:36; cf. 8:24) as sovereign over the earth (compare Ps 115:3, 15). And from all earthly appearances, God is unwilling or unable to prevent the abominations of Antiochus or to challenge his arrogant claims to divinity. This puts God's dominion and God's righteousness in question, which puts the world in question.

Traditionally, questions like these, along with efforts to address them, have been gathered under the category of *theodicy.* Apocalyptic literature like Daniel is often placed within this category.[14] I have my doubts about this,[15] but it is true that the book of Daniel does seek to persuade its readers that earthly appearances are neither the truth of the matter nor its end. The goal of Daniel is to encourage the kind of faithfulness that resists—even to the point of death—seduction by forces, so appealing in their success and so terrifying in their power, that claim for themselves what is God's alone. According to Daniel, this kind of faithfulness depends on, and it is characterized by, wisdom and understanding—of the sort that Daniel receives in chapter 9, and of the sort displayed by the "wise" *(hammaśkîlîm)* under the terrible reign of Antiochus (11:33, 35). The wise understand that the time is appointed, that the decisive battle is waged in heaven, and that the righteousness of God will prevail. They also understand that the stories of four young men, narrated in chapters 1-6, are witness to God's capacity to rescue from death: from murderous designs, from a fiery furnace, and from a den of lions. At the outset, these four young men, including Daniel, are described as "wise" (1:4).[16] They are instructive for the book's readers and paradigms for the wise "who give understanding to many" under Antiochus (11:33). Even so, many of these experience, not extraordinary deliverance, but something so ordinary as death at the hands of a tyrant. Granted,

Antiochus will come to his end (11:45), but what of these wise who understood and were faithful, who resisted both seduction and threats, and who fell victim (11:34)?[17]

The answer to this question is, of course, the resurrection. Daniel 12:2 announces, not a general resurrection of the dead, but the resurrection of "many" who sleep in the land of dust, that is, in death.[18] While the verse seems to refer indiscriminately only to some among those who have died ("many who sleep"), we should understand this in light of the two groups who are then specified: those raised to everlasting life, on one hand, and those raised to shame and everlasting contempt on the other. Daniel's point here is, not to define or to delimit the extent of the resurrection,[19] but to extend to the realm of the dead what chapter 9 calls the righteousness of God. This is a resurrection for judgment, and even more for vindication—for the vindication of those whose deliverance is promised in 12:1, namely, those whose names are written in the book (cf. Exod 32:32; Isa 4:3; Mal 3:16). However, the vindication of righteous individuals does not exhaust the point.[20] As under the persecution described in chapter 11, so here, following deliverance and resurrection, the faithful have exemplary leaders, the "wise" *(hammaśkîlîm)*, v. 3). They are described as shining "like the brightness of the sky" and "like the stars forever and ever," and as leading "many to righteousness." We should not take the similes here as implying that the wise are to ascend to an astral sphere, to join the host of heaven; rather, they are exalted precisely in relation to the community to whom and with whom and for whom they are restored.[21] The verbal root here translated "to shine" (*zhr*) more often means "to warn" (e. g., Exod 18:20; Ezek 3:16-21; 33:3-9; Ps 19:11), which is proper to the wise as those who instruct.[22] Warning and instruction are communal functions, and the resurrection of the dead in Daniel 12 is also the restoration of the community. As Robert Martin-Achard summarizes, "The resurrection of the dead implies a *solidarity* . . . between the Yahwists who have died and their people."[23] On the part of the wise, this solidarity—in life, in death, and in resurrection—has transforming power. To express it, Daniel draws on the language of Isaiah's fourth servant song (52:13-53:12), which proclaims the mortally wounded servant's vindication and declares that he "shall make many righteous." The same is true, in both respects, of the wise in Dan 12:1-3.[24]

It would be a mistake, then, to see in Daniel 12 a contrast between the resurrection of individuals and the enduring group. Both are squarely in view, but it is not only an *enduring* group; it is a group, a community, newly constituted after "that time" when Michael, "the great prince, the protector of your people, shall arise" (12:1). This is a modest note, but still an awful one. It introduces a period of unprecedented anguish, "such as never occurred since nations first came into existence;" and it introduces an unprecedented event—a resurrection from the dead—and, with it, a new world where righteousness, not death, prevails.

## PRAISE, LAMENTATION, AND HOPE

The notion of a resurrection seems to violate traditional—perhaps we could even call them orthodox—Israelite or Old Testament conceptions of death.[25] According to one of the most basic of these conceptions, adapted to a contemporary idiom, death happens. It is not that only some die, or that only grievous sinners die, but—ever since Eden—all die, and all *must* die.[26] In this, of course, the Old Testament's conception does not differ from our own. However, another of its orthodox conceptions is that the dead do not simply pass out of existence—they do not simply *die*; instead, they persist in a miserable, shadowy existence, cut off from their community and from communion with God.

Among the saddest statements about death is that of Ps 115:17, which says that the dead, those who descend into silence, do not praise Yahweh. The silence of death, which makes participation in the community's praise of God impossible, marks it off most clearly from life. As Claus Westermann puts it, "Praising and no longer praising are related to each other as are living and no longer living."[27] But the silence of death is to the detriment, not only of the dead, but also of Yahweh, who is, after all, enthroned on the praises of Israel (Ps 22:3).[28] So it makes sense to ask, as Ps 30:9 does, "What profit is there in my death, if I go down to the Pit? Will the dust praise you? Will it tell of your faithfulness?" Or as Ps 6:5 reminds Yahweh, "in death there is no remembrance of you; in Sheol, who can give you praise?" Or as Ps 88:10 asks Yahweh, "Do the shades *(rĕpā'îm)* rise up to praise you?" The ancient Israelites accepted the reality of death, but, especially when it was tragic—when it came by violence or treachery or disease—they saw in death something requiring God's attention.[29]

They also seemed to accept, as another of their orthodox conceptions, that the dead *remain* dead, consigned to their shadowy, isolated existence in Sheol. In St. Paul's idiom, death reigns. Job expresses this conception in chapter 14 contrasting the fate of mortals with that of a tree: a tree has hope, even if it is cut down, that it will sprout again from its roots (vv. 7-9). By contrast, mortals die: they "lie down and do not rise again; until the heavens are no more, they will not awake or be roused out of their sleep" (v. 12). Notice that Job here expressly denies what Daniel affirms: that those who sleep will awake *(yāqîṣû)*. Daniel 12, like 2 Maccabees 7, departs from the orthodox conception and promises what that conception seems to deny, a resurrection. How should we understand this?

I do not ask this as a question in the history of religions. If that were our question, as it quite legitimately could be, perhaps we could point to Persian religion, to Zoroastrianism, and show how its expectation that Ahura Mazda would raise the dead influenced the development of similar beliefs among Jews in Babylon.[30] If this is what happened, knowing more about it could perhaps aid our understanding; indeed, I will later suggest that knowing something about Canaanite mythology aids our understanding of a crucial Old Testament text. But I am here asking a slightly different question. How can we understand the resurrection of the dead as an authentic part of the Old Testament's witness, if it is in tension with the Old Testament's own, orthodox conceptions about death? That Zoroastrian religion may have helped to bring about the tension does not yet answer our question, which concerns the coherence of the Old Testament's witness. Neither is this a question about how to harmonize the Old Testament's diversity by eliminating its tensions or reducing them by resorting to either proof texts or abstractions.[31] It is, finally (to return to my introduction), a question about how to understand the resurrection of the dead.

In discussing 2 Maccabees 7 and Daniel, I have already hinted in the direction of an answer. 2 Maccabees depends explicitly on creation theology, to which it gives a particular twist. Daniel depends, similarly, on an understanding of God's universal dominion at war with divine and human assaults against it. However, to pursue this direction further, and profitably, I think we have to take seriously Israel's orthodox conception of death. Moreover, I think we have to acknowledge that this conception is close to our own. We may not believe—I suppose it is safe to say that we do *not* believe—that the dead continue a shadowy existence in the earth's dust, but we do believe that the dead remain, whatever else, firmly dead. As did the ancient Israelites, we have excellent reasons for this belief. When Job says that the dead do not awake, we can hardly disagree.

Nothing in our experience suggests that Job is wrong. Death *does* reign, and we routinely acknowledge that it does; and yet in our prayers and our liturgies and our theologies we affirm that *God* does. Job's problem is not materially different from our own.

Job wants desperately to put his case directly before God, but he expects that this will happen only after his death. Then,a redeemer will represent him before God, whom Job's eyes will behold (Job 19:23-27).[32] Job expects only the opportunity, after his death, to be vindicated before God. He does not expect a resurrection of the dead, but he does entertain the possibility. In chapter 14 he poses the question, "If mortals die, can they live again?" (v. 14). If so, then it may be that death—that a mute and otherwise hopeless existence in Sheol—could provide him temporary shelter from the oppressively constant, judging presence of Yahweh. And then it may be that Yahweh, separated from Job by death, would eventually long for the work of his hands—for Job, his creation (Job 14:15b; 10:8).[33] Job is exemplary in that he does not deny what his tradition teaches him and what his experience (like ours) everywhere confirms, but also and especially in that he points to the tensions within his tradition which render his experience thoroughly ambiguous. As a mortal, Job expects to die and he accepts death, but he cannot deny that *his* death—including the divinely sanctioned series of otherwise unwarranted deprivations that amount to the same thing, or worse—raises profound questions about and against God. In chapter 26 Job acknowledges that, regardless the breadth of death's realm and the extent of its power, before God the creator—before the one who imposed order, creation, on all the forces of chaos—Sheol is naked (26:6).[34] In other words, just in case God is *God* the curtain shielding the realm of the dead, Sheol, is both transparent and permeable to God's action. For Job, this is not an answer to the problem of suffering and death; rather, it is the very basis on which Job's case stands. Since God "makes peace in his high heaven" (25:2) and makes life on the earth possible by subduing those powers that would sink it in chaos (26:12-13)—and since Sheol itself cannot hide from God's power—how is it that mortals are consigned to death's dust? If God reigns, how can death reign?

Job is not alone in raising this question. In Psalm 22, the Psalmist asks, "My God, my God, why have you forsaken me?" (v. 1). And he goes on to remind God, who is enthroned on Israel's praises and has been the object of Israel's trust, that God's abandonment exposes him, not only to death, but to scorn. It also exposes God to scorn: "'Commit your cause to the Lord,' the mockers say, 'let him deliver—let him rescue the one in whom he delights!'" (v. 8). In this case, God does deliver, and the Psalmist turns to praise (vv. 21b-24). However, his praise does not end with thanksgiving for his own deliverance; in vv. 27-31 it expands to include the whole world. It announces that the world, everyone, will "remember and turn to Yahweh, and all the families of the nations shall worship before him" (v. 27). The Psalm does not say what will bring about this universal worship of Yahweh, but it does cite the basis for this announcement: "For the kingdom belongs to Yahweh, and he rules over the nations" (v. 28).[35] Remarkably, Yahweh's kingdom extends; not only to the farthest reaches of the earth, but also to its depths—to that alien and awful realm of the dead. "All who sleep in the earth bow down; before him shall bow all who go down to the dust" (v. 29).[36]

We should be cautious about describing Psalm 22's concluding announcement as a resurrection of the dead. But, as Hans Wildberger has written, "with reference to the problem here under discussion, it is clear that with the world-encompassing *mlwkh* [kingdom] of Yhwh, the problem of the dead—and of death in general—must become explicit. . . . If the *mlwkh* [kingdom] seriously belongs to Yahweh, then he must also be Lord over death."[37] If God reigns, then death's kingdom is invaded.

## EZEKIEL'S VISION

Even if Psalm 22 drives us to this confession—the confession that God's kingdom does not reach its limit at the gates of Sheol—even if Job entertains the possibility of a resurrection, and even if the Psalms attest a tension in death's irreversible termination of the praise that Yahweh seeks, death remains a reality of such indisputable constancy and permanence that the resurrection never becomes, anywhere in the Old Testament, an article of faith, or even a belief with a fixed content. Ezekiel had no such belief. When the spirit of Yahweh brought him to a valley full of bones (37:1), Ezekiel brought with him no expectation that those human bones—very dry bones (v. 2)—would live. But Ezekiel *did* have some experience at being moved around, in more than one sense, by the spirit of Yahweh.

In the book's first eleven chapters, Ezekiel sees Yahweh's chariot-throne, a symbol of Yahweh's glory and dominion. It appears in the first chapter, and in chapters 10 and 11 it departs the sanctuary—Yahweh's sanctuary and abode in Jerusalem—which is to say that Yahweh abandons his royal residence, but not his dominion.[38] This is an utterly improbable turn of events, and so is Ezekiel's experience in the meantime. The spirit of Yahweh transports him from Babylon to Jerusalem and back again, while Ezekiel receives his commission. It is an awful and improbable commission, but, given what he has seen and where he hasa been, Ezekiel is in position to contest it. By the time the spirit again transports Ezekiel, years later, to the valley (cf. 3:22)—a valley this time filled with very many, very dry bones (37:2)—Ezekiel realizes that he is in no position to assess what is probable, or possible, and what is not.[39] So, when Yahweh puts to him the pertinent question, "Can these bones live?" (v. 3), Ezekiel answers appropriately, "O Lord God, you know"—a response as brief as it is profound. Walther Zimmerli says that Ezekiel's "You know"

> has two sides to it: the admission of the powerlessness of [humankind], who faced with such an irrefutable victory on death's part, is incapable of saying anything about the possibility of life for these dead bones; at the same time, however, the knowledge that he is replying to the God whose abilities are not curtailed by [humankind's] lack of abilities . . . this response reveals that the period of Ezekiel, exactly like Job 14:14, knows nothing of a general eschatological resurrection of the dead, but does not wish, either, to deny to Yahweh the possibility of awakening, thanks to his power as creator, some time the dead to life again.[40]

Ezekiel brings with him no belief in the resurrection, but neither does he contest the improbable commission Yahweh gives him: to prophesy to the bones that they will live (37:5).

Zimmerli's reference to Yahweh's "power as creator" may seem gratuitous in relation to Ezekiel 37, but the prerequisite of the dry bones' living is the "breath" that Yahweh will cause to enter them (v. 5), just as in Gen 2:7: God breathed "the breath of life" into the first creature, and he "became a living being." The word for breath in Ezekiel 37 *(rûaḥ)* is different from that in Genesis, but the allusion to the first creation is clear.[41] Moreover, Ezekiel plays on the flexibility of this word, whose range of meanings also includes "wind" and "spirit." Thus, in v. 8 Ezekiel notices that the bones, which have come together and are supplied with sinews, flesh, and skin, still lack breath (and, hence, life). In v. 9, Yahweh tells Ezekiel to instruct the "breath" to come from the "four winds" (the whole world's breath, as it were) and to breathe on the bodies so they may live. And in v.

14, through Ezekiel Yahweh promises the people, "I will put my spirit within you, and you shall live." In each case, "breath," "wind," "spirit" translates *rûaḥ*. However, by the end of the vision it is clear that, not just an impersonal breath or the four winds, but precisely the spirit of Yahweh is the source of life—and, as we may say, the power of the resurrection. It is also, and for the same reason, the life-sustaining power of creation. Psalm 104, a creation hymn, makes this explicit. When Yahweh hides his face and takes away breath *(rûaḥ)* from the earth's creatures, they die and return to the dust (v. 29). But, v. 30 declares to Yahweh, "When you send forth your spirit *(rûaḥ)*, they are created (brʾ); and you renew the face of the ground." *All* of God's creatures, and the earth on and in which they live, depend for their life and their creation, their renewal, on the spirit of Yahweh. In Ezekiel 37, creation takes the form of resurrection.

But is this really a resurrection? Is not Ezekiel rather talking about the "enduring group?" Is he not talking about the restoration of Israel? Quite clearly, and explicitly, he *is* talking about Israel's restoration, and specifically their restoration as a people in the land of Israel (37:12, 14). There can be no disputing this, in which case perhaps we should admit that Ezekiel 37 is an instance of what Hans Küng calls figurative and metaphorical talk about resurrection, not to be taken as "real" in its imagery.[42] Perhaps, but what would we gain from such an admission? Ezekiel is talking about Israel, but can there be any doubt that he is talking about Israel as *dead*, and that he means us to take this as, however metaphorical or figurative, still in every important respect *real* death? He sees bones, which Zimmerli describes very well: "The bones have been lying about for a long time, naked, already picked clean by the birds of the sky, stripped of their skin and flesh and sinews, bleached and dried out by the heat of the day." As Ezekiel inspects the scene, "there is to be impressed upon him the idea that this is not simply a symbol of death but death in all its fullness—the great death."[43] It is death so utterly real that, shifting the imagery, the people are in graves, which only Yahweh can open (37:12). They know that they are "cut off completely" (v. 11). As Psalm 88 attests, to be "cut off" is the fate of the dead—"the slain that lie in the grave. . . . those whom you remember no more, for they are cut off from your hand" (v. 5; cf. Isa 53:8). In Ezek 37:11, the dead know that their hope is lost, that it has perished ( *bd*).

If you have any experience as a pastor, or just as a human being, you know that not every death is accompanied by a burial; not everyone who dies is memorialized in a funeral; not every corpse is laid to rest. We are taught that, where there is life, there is hope. But a body—an individual body, or a corporate one, even a congregation or a community or a nation—entirely bereft of hope and severed from life is dead. Bereft of hope, empty of breath, stripped of flesh, utterly cut off, Israel was really and truly dead. Not only was it devoid of life, but it lacked any potential for life, any possibility that it might have actualized, any power that it might have exercised. Israel's restoration to life, its passage from death to life, depended entirely on an improbable, utterly surprising action of God—"resurrection" seems the best word for it—fittingly compared with God's initial act of creation.

As we have seen, Ezekiel makes this comparison by referring to the "breath" of life, which he identifies, finally, with the spirit of Yahweh. This is the same spirit who has been moving Ezekiel around from the beginning. Indeed, just as the spirit entered Ezekiel and set him on his feet in the valley (3:22, 24; cf. 2:2), so the spirit enters the new Israel, in the valley of dry bones, and sets them, resurrected, on their feet (37:10). The glory and dominion—the power—of Yahweh that, thanks to the spirit, Ezekiel witnessed in his inaugural visions, visions that portended judgment and destruction, is the same power and dominion that, through the same spirit, restores, resurrects, a dead Israel.[44] It is also the same spirit that is the promise of Israel's new life in the chapters surrounding chapter 37. In 36:26-27, Yahweh promises Israel a new heart and a new spirit—a heart of flesh to replace their heart of stone and Yahweh's own spirit. And in 39:29, Yahweh promises to pour out his spirit on the house of Israel.[45] But intervening between chapter 36 and the end of chapter 39 is not only the promise of resurrection, but also Ezekiel's vision of a terrible apocalyptic battle in which the international powers of chaos and death, symbolized by Gog, of the land of Magog, wage a cataclysmic war against a defenseless Israel, to be thoroughly and finally defeated by Yahweh. Like the resurrection of the dry bones (37:13), and the transformation of the land to resemble Eden (36:35-36), Yahweh's triumph over Gog and Magog will display Yahweh's glory (39:21), so that Israel and the nations, the whole world, will *know* that "I am Yahweh." Ezekiel does not envision resurrection to things as they have always been, but to a new order. It is a new world order, in which defenseless villages are secure from the insolent powers of greed and violence, and it is a new order of life. In praising the creator, Psalm 104 says that the hiding of Yahweh's face brings death, while the sending of his spirit creates life again (vv. 29-30). In Ezek 39:29, Yahweh says, "I will never again hide my face from them, after I have poured out my spirit on the house of Israel."[46] Yahweh's spirit—the spirit of creation—brings life, new life, and Yahweh's face protects it against death.

Ezekiel did not emerge from his visions with a doctrine of the resurrection of the dead. However, as we have seen to be the case in other Old Testament texts, what Ezekiel does know of God, and what he has been shown and commissioned to say, hardly permit him to avoid the conclusion that Yahweh is Lord also over death. For Ezekiel, too, this has to do with vindication—not the vindication of a righteous individual, and certainly not of Israel, but of Yahweh. As the Psalms of lamentation protest that death is to Yahweh's detriment as well—it robs Yahweh of praise—so Ezekiel knows that Israel's death is to Yahweh's detriment in that it profanes Yahweh's name. In announcing his intention to enter into a decisive conflict with the powers who make their own, rival claims to sovereignty, Yahweh says, "I will not let my holy name be profaned any more; and the nations shall know that I am Yahweh, the Holy One in Israel" (39:7). The resurrection—and precisely the resurrection of Israel—is integrally part of Yahweh's self-revelation, because Yahweh is the God of Israel. Not *only* of Israel, but if not of Israel, to whom he has made promises and staked his name, then not of the nations, either.

## ISAIAH'S APOCALYPSE

Ezekiel recognizes that Yahweh's self-revelation involves conflict, because it is the revelation of Yahweh's unrivaled sovereignty. Yet Yahweh has rivals. A collection of texts in the middle of Isaiah, chapters 24-27, attest that death is one such rival, or enemy, and stands in the way of resurrection.[47]

Virtually nothing in Isa 24-27 is perfectly clear, unfortunately including the crucial verse, 26:19.[48] This verse announces that "your dead shall live," but it is not clear who is speaking to whom. Contributing to this unclarity is the next part of the announcement, "and my body [*nĕbēlātî* ("corpse")] shall arise."[49] However, if we assume that Isaiah is here addressing Yahweh, which he began to do in v. 7, then Isaiah equates his "corpse" with Yahweh's dead.[50] In that case, Yahweh's dead are Israel, with whom the prophet identifies. Yahweh's salvation of Israel is here interpreted as a resurrection from the dead, and it responds to the hopelessness and futility of which Isaiah complains in 26:16-18. Isaiah is confident that Yahweh will ordain peace *(šālôm)* for Israel (v. 12), and he points to what Yahweh has done in the past, former enemies are dead and no longer remembered (v. 14), and the nation's borders have expanded (v. 15). Even so, present circumstances provoke lamentation. Isaiah says little about those circumstances: he refers only to the wicked (v. 10) and Yahweh's adversaries (v. 11). However, he understands Israel's situation to be the consequence of Yahweh's discipline (v.16),[51] and he compares his community with a woman who endures the pain of childbirth but bears only wind (v. 18). "So the lament ends in total resignation."[52] As in Ezekiel 37, resignation is answered by resurrection.

In the second half of 26:19, Isaiah addresses Yahweh's dead directly: "O dwellers in the dust, awake and sing for joy!" This instruction, in language familiar from Dan 12:2, is consistent with the announcement in the first half of the verse, and it depends on what the prophet says next: Yahweh's dew is "a radiant dew" (v. 19b). This is a curious statement, but it seems to refer to the life-giving power of the morning dew;[53] this is consistent with the result, described in the last line of the verse: "the earth will give birth to those long dead"—that is, to the "shades" *(rĕpā'îm)*. This is a fitting response to the last clause of the lament in v. 18: "no one is born to inhabit the world." Joined with the image of giving birth only to wind in v. 17, this suggests that the land (with its expanded borders, v. 15) suffers from a lack of population. Similarly, Isaiah's later chapters portray Zion as barren and bereft of children, hence of population, because of Yahweh's past judgments, and they describe Zion's exaltation as the reversal of that condition (49:14-21; 54:1-3).[54] Further, Isa 24:6 complains that the inhabitants of the earth have dwindled, "and few people are left." It is unlikely that only a lack of population prompts the lament in Isaiah 26; it stands as a symbol of the desperate circumstances, the desolation, to which resurrection is an answer: The life-giving dew, granted by God, prompts the earth to give up its dead, its "shades."[55]

Certainly, this refers to a national restoration, which is achieved through what looks very much like a resurrection.[56] But that is not the end of the matter. The promise of resurrection is based on an event that is announced with solemn warning in 26:19-20 and then summarized in 27:1. This summary promises that Yahweh will punish Leviathan and kill the dragon that is in the sea. Many other Old Testament texts refer to Leviathan, to the dragon *(hattannîn)*, or to mythological beasts, symbols of chaos, going by other names (Job 26:12-13, which I mentioned earlier, is one such text). Even so, the appearance of Leviathan here in Isa 27:1 is striking, not least because its description matches so closely that in Canaanite texts of centuries earlier. These describe Leviathan as a "wriggling serpent, the tyrant with seven heads," as the "dragon," and as a "slippery serpent," using terms *(ltn, tnn, 'qltn, brh)* whose cognates appear here in Isaiah.[57] In the Canaanite texts, Baal destroys Leviathan in a struggle for cosmic order; the victor in Isaiah is Yahweh, but the results are not less significant. Neither is Leviathan the only foe.

The Canaanite texts portray Baal as encountering two principal enemies, the first of which is Yam, a god who threatens the world with chaos and whose name is the common Northwest Semitic term for "sea," where Isa 27:1 says the dragon lives. Baal is victorious over Yam and scatters his body (cf. Isa 51:9-10; Ps 74:13-14). Baal's second enemy is the god Mot, whose name is the common Northwest Semitic term for "death," and who threatens exactly what his name implies. Baal succumbs to Mot, whose maw embraces everything: he has "a lip to the earth, a lip to heaven. . . . Baal must enter his innards and go down into his mouth." In Mot's own words, "I made him [Baal] like a lamb in my mouth and he was carried away like a kid in the breach of my windpipe."[58] As Alastair Waterston accurately summarizes the episode, Baal "is swallowed up by death."[59]

This mythological background helps us, I believe, to understand the announcement in Isa 25:7 that Yahweh "will swallow up death forever." This is an exact reversal of the Cannanite myth.[60] However, it is a direct consequence of what Isa 24:21-23 says will happen "on that day"—presumably, on the same day that 27:1 has in mind. The latter text says that Yahweh will punish Leviathan and kill the dragon, while 24:21-23 promises that Yahweh will punish the "host of heaven in heaven, and on earth the kings of the earth," but especially, and more positively, that Yahweh of hosts will reign on Mount Zion and in Jerusalem. . . . " It is on this mountain, where Yahweh will reign as king, that Yahweh will will make a feast for all peoples—not only for Israel, but a feast for us all—replete with red meat and fine, aged wines (25:6). And it is on this mountain that Yahweh will swallow up death forever, and "wipe away the tears from all faces"—tears that are, as everyone knows, the inevitable accompaniment of death (Ps 116:8).

Isaiah 24-27, Isaiah's apocalypse, is constrained to speak of resurrection and of the end of death's ultimately futile but still terrible reign, because it envisions a future in which all of God's rivals, whether in heaven or on earth, are defeated. It envisions a future when the order of creation corresponds to the rule of the creator, which extends even into Sheol and to the "shades." With respect to Isaiah 24-27, a distinction between the resurrection of individuals and the enduring group is not helpful, nor is a distinction between metaphorical and real. Everything we know and everything Isaiah says suggests that death is not only real but a power, whose representatives and agents continually tempt us, and with good reason, to see greater realism in the story of Baal than in the promises of God. It is not for nothing that Isaiah 26 counsels trust (v. 4), which is a synonym of faith, whose object is not seen.

## IN PLACE OF A CONCLUSION

Finally, it seems to me that the mother and sons in 2 Maccabees 7 are perceptive interpreters of the Old Testament and authentic witnesses, martyrs. They base their hope of resurrection on faith in God the sovereign creator—who is also faithful and merciful—consistent with what we have found in the Old Testament. They point to something else as well in speaking of God's reconciliation with the dead. In 2 Maccabees, this reconciliation is limited to God's faithful servants, God's martyrs, in Israel. But even here, and in Isaiah's vision of a great feast for all peoples when God swallows up death, and in Job's dream that God may long for him after his death, and in the Psalmists' hope that God would not allow death to end the communion between them and God—in all of these is at least a small basis for hoping that God will not forget, that God will keep and does keep solidarity with the dead.[61]

In Daniel, as in 2 Maccabees, the promise of resurrection is powerful motivation for unwavering faithfulness to God, even in the face of death. That point is worthy of emphasis. Even so, it is too limiting to think of resurrection as our own personal guarantee of life after death, even a glorious life. To believe in the resurrection of the dead is also to join with God in solidarity with the dead—to hope for the reconciliation of us all, living and dead, with the God who is our maker. This hope gains strength in the resurrection of Jesus Christ.[62]

## NOTES

1. I cannot cite a precise source, but the statement comes from an old issue of *The New Yorker*.

2. *A Theology of the Old Testament* (Garden City, NY: Doubleday, 1974), 307-308.

3. *Eternal Life: Life After Death as a Medical, Philosophical and Theological Problem* (Garden City, NY: Doubleday, 1984), 83. The italics are Küng's. On the general topic, see Wendell W. Frerichs, "Death and Resurrection in the Old Testament," *Word and World,* 11 (1991): 14-22.

4. *A Theology of the Old Testament*, 308. He adds, "If one presupposes that they did not so believe, the passages make excellent sense, but a different sense."

5. Judah Goldstein dates 2 Maccabees between 78 and 63 B. C. E., which would be about a century later than Daniel. Goldstein, *II Maccabees* AB (Garden City, NY: Doubleday, 1983) .

6. Unless otherwise noted, all quotations of the Bible follow the NRSV.

7. This is Judah Goldstein's translation, in *II Maccabees*, 290. On the mother's use of philosophical vocabulary, see 312-13.

8. Goldstein (307-11) argues that the Vulgate's *quia ex nihilo fecit illa Deus et hominum genus ita fit,* inadequately translates οὐκ ἐξ ὄντών ἐποίησέν αὐτο ὁ θεός καὶ τὸ τῶν ἀνθρωπών γένος οὕτω γίνετι which he renders, "it was not after they existed that God fashioned them, and in the same manner the human race." I accept his argument; still, the Latin text, if it is not interpreted materialistically, makes a legitimate claim.

9. George W. E. Nickelsburg, Jr., stresses the mother's expectation that her sons would be restored to her (vv. 23, 29). As he puts it, "There is a restoration of community." *Resurrection, Immortality, and Eternal Life in Intertestamental Judaisim* (Cambridge, MA: Harvard University Press, 1972), 107. 2 Macc 12:39-45 also expresses this solidarity with the dead, extending them atonement for sins.

10. V. 33: καὶ πάλιν καταλλαγήσεται τοῖς ἑαυτοῦ δούλοις.

11. John J. Collins discusses the different nuances of "the end" (*qeṣ*) in Daniel, in "The Meaning of 'the End' in the Book of Daniel," *Of Scribes and Scrolls* (ed. H. W. Attridge, J. J. Collins, T. H. Tobin; (Lanham, MD: University Press of America, 1990), 91-98. The word occurs fifteen times in Daniel, all of them in chapters 8-9 and 11-12.

12. The composition and date of Daniel 9 are complicated matters that need not detain us. For discussion, see Louis F. Hartman and Alexander A. DiLella, *The Book of Daniel,* AB 23 (Garden City, NY: Doubleday, 1978), 245-54; André Lacocque, "The Liturgical Prayer in Daniel 9," *HUCA* 47 (1976): 119-42; John J. Collins, *Daniel. With an Introduction to Apocalyptic Literature* , FOTL 20 (Grand Rapids: Eerdmans, 1985), 89-96. I understand the chapter, in its biblical form, to provide a framework for reading the chapters that follow.

13. I have tried to show this, in "Isaiah's Creation Theology," *Ex Auditu* 3 (1988): 54-71.

14. G. Tom Milazzo, *The Protest and the Silence: Suffering, Death, and Biblical Theology* (Minneapolis: Fortress, 1992), 66-103. Milazzo claims that "The theodicy question serves as a focal point" for what he calls "apocalyptic reflection" (p. 78). Cf. Küng, *Eternal Life*, 88.

15. See Nickelsburg's remarks, in *Resurrection*, 23. Terrence W. Tilley argues that we should have doubts about theodicy itself, in *The Evils of Theodicy* (Washington, D. C.: Georgetown University Press, 1991).

16. The material in Daniel 1-6 is composite: chapters 2-6 bring together earlier stories, some of which circulated independently before being associated with Daniel. Chapter 1 provides a framework for reading them as one story with several episodes.

17. André Lacocque frames the questions left unanswered in Daniel 11, in *The Book of Daniel* (Atlanta: John Knox, 1979), 234.

18. The term *ʾadmat ʿāpār* ("land of dust," or "dust of the earth," NRSV) is difficult, but it clearly refers to the realm of the dead, Sheol. Lacocque, *Daniel*, 241.

19. The precise meaning of *wĕrabbîm mîyyĕšēnê . . .yāqîṣû* is disputed. Most interpreters take it to mean that only some will awake (see Nickelsburg, *Resurrection*, 23), while Lacocque takes

it as referring to all faithful Israelites who have died *Daniel*, 244-45. The logic of the text favors the latter view; its grammar (so far as I can see) the former one.

20. Nickelsburg has stressed the character of Daniel 12:1-3 as a "judgment scene," *Resurrection*, 27; see also Pheme Perkins, *Resurrection: New Testament Witness and Contemporary Reflection* (Garden City, NY: Doubleday, 1984), 39-42. Collins's cautions about this are worth heeding, *Daniel*, 100-101.

21. John J. Collins has argued that the resurrected "wise" join the angelic host in heaven, *The Apocalyptic Imagination* (New York: Crossroad, 1984), 90-91; *The Apocalyptic Vision of the Book of Daniel*, HSM 16 (Cambridge, MA: Harvard University Press, 1977), 133-38. Collins also assumes that the wise who will shine like stars include the dead as well as the living, *Apocalyptic Imagination*, 91. My interpretation more closely resembles that of John E. Goldingay, *Daniel*, Word Biblical Commentary 30 (Waco: Word, 1989), 308-309.

22. Nickelsburg, *Resurrection*, 26 suggests the possibility of a play on words. In order to avoid cluttering the text, I wiil cite the Psalms and other texts according to English versification only, even in cases like Psalm 19, where Hebrew versification differs.

23. "Trois rémarques sur la résurrection des morts dans l'Ancien Testament," *Permanence de l'Ancien Testament* (Geneva: Revue de Théologie et de Philosophie, 1984), 183. The italics are his.

24. Nickelsburg, *Resurrection*, 24-26.

25. These are described in most Old Testament theology handbooks and Bible dictionaries, and especially in four monographs: Robert Martin-Achard, *From Death to Life: A Study of the Development of the Doctrine of the Resurrection in the Old Testament* (Edinburgh: Oliver and Boyd, 1960); Lloyd Bailey, *Biblical Perspectives on Death* (Philadelphia: Fortress, 1979); Christoph Barth, *Die Errettung vom Tode in den individuellen Klage- und Dankliedern des Alten Testamentes* (Zürich: Theologischer Verlag, 1987); Hans Walter Wolff, *Anthropology of the Old Testament* (Philadelphia: Fortress, 1974); Leonard. J. Greenspoon provides a brief but very helpful survey, which he draws mainly from Wolff, in "The Origin of the Idea of Resurrection," *Traditions in Transformation*, ed. Baruch Halpern and Jon D. Levenson (Winona Lake, IN: Eisenbrauns, 1981), 247-321.

26. Horst Dietrich Preuss, *Theologie des Alten Testaments* Vol. 2: *Israels Weg mit JHWH* (Stuttgart: Kohlhammer, 1992), 158.

27. *Praise and Lament in the Psalms* (Atlanta: John Knox, 1981), 159.

28. Hans-Joachim Kraus follows Greek, Latin, and Syriac versions in repunctuating the verse and amending "praises" to "praise," so that it reads: ". . . you are enthroned as the Holy One, you Praise of Israel." Kraus, *Psalms 1-59 A Commentary* (Minneapolis: Augsburg 1988), 290-92.

29. See Samuel Balentine, *The Hidden God* (Oxford: Oxford University Press, 1982).

30. Bernhard Lang argues this way in "Street Theater, Raising the Dead, and the Zoroastrian Connection in Ezekiel's Prophecy," *Ezekiel and His Book*, ed. J. Lust; *BETL, 74;* (Leuven: Leuven University Press, 1986), 297-316.

31. For example, we could observe that Enoch did not die (Gen 5:24) and that both Elijah (who did not die either) and Elisha were empowered to restore the dead to life. 1 Kgs 17:17-24; 2 Kgs 4:32-37. We could also refer to Mitchell Dahood's controversial translation and interpretation of certain Psalms and other texts as referring to an afterlife (*Psalms III*,, AB 17A (Garden City, NY: Doubleday, 1970), XLI-LII.

32. See Norman C. Habel, *The Book of Job* , OTL (Philadelphia: Westminster, 1985) 302-309; Hartmut Gese, "Death in the Old Testament," *Essays on Biblical Theology* (Minneapolis: Augsburg, 1981), 47-49.

33. Marvin Pope, *Job , AB* 15 (Garden City, NY: Doubleday, 1973), 108. Pope points for comparison to Amos 9:2-4, which portrays the wicked trying to hide in, among other places, Sheol.

34. It is common, for reasons I accept, to assign parts of Job's speech in chapter 26, including the verse I have cited, to Bildad, whose speech begins in chapter 25 (representative is Habel, *The Book of Job)* 366.

35. *NRSV* has "dominion" instead of "kingdom," as a translation of *hammĕlûkâ*, from the root *mlk*, "to reign," or "to be king." On the basis of this announcement in Jerusalem's traditions, see Kraus, *Psalms 1-59*, 300; Ben C. Ollenburger, *Zion, the City of the Great King, JSOTSS* 41; (Sheffield: JSOT Press, 1987).

36. The text and translation of the last line in the verse, which I have omitted, are in doubt. With most others, including *NRSV*, I emend *dišnê* ("fat ones"), in v. 29, to *yĕšēnê* ("ones who sleep").

37. *Jesaja, Kapitel 13-27, BKAT* 10/2; (Neukirchen-Vluyn: Neukirchener Verlag, 1978), 964.

38 There are differences in detail between the vision of chapter 1 and that of chapter 10 and questions about what those differences mean. See Moshe Greenberg, *Ezekiel. 1-20,* AB 22; (Garden City, NY: Doubleday, 1983), 51-59, 192-205.

39 On Ezekiel's "throne visions" as background to chapter 37, see Thomas Krüger, *Geschichtskonzepte im Ezechielbuch, BZAW* 180; (Berlin: de Gruyter, 1989), 426-38.

40. *Ezekiel 2,* Hermeneia (Philadelphia: Fortress, 1983), 260.

41. Referring to Ezekiel 37, Preuss, too, notes that resurrection has to be understood as "new creation." *Theologie des Alten Testaments* , 2, 161.

42. *Eternal Life,* 83. So far as I know, Bernhard Lang is alone among Old Testament scholars in maintaining that Ezekiel expected "that Israelites *would* rise from the dead." "Street Theater," 308.

43. Zimmerli, *Ezekiel 2,* 259-60.

44. Krüger, *Geschichtskonzepte* 432.

45. Zimmerli says in this regard, " . . . one must think beyond the mere revivification of corpses to the promise of the spirit in 36:27 (39:29), by which also the inner transformation of the people comes about." *Ezekiel 2* , 263.

46. I am following Zimmerli's translation. *Ezekiel 2,* 295.

47. Leonard. J. Greenspoon holds that Yahweh's battle against his rivals is the origin of the idea of resurrection. See his article cited in n. 25

48. Otto Kaiser provides an inventory of interpretive possibilities in *Isaiah 13-39,* OTL; (Philadelphia: Westminster, 1974), 215-20. See also Hans Wildberger, *Jesaja, Kapitel 13-27,* 994-98; Dan G. Johnson, *From Chaos to Restoration, JSOTSS* 61 (Sheffield: Sheffield Academic Press, 1988), 79-81.

49. *NRSV* eases this difficulty by reading "their corpses," with the Syriac version.

50. In v. 9 the prophet refers to his "soul" and his spirit and in v. 20 to his people. I will call the prophet "Isaiah" for convenience.

51. On the text and translation of this difficult verse see John N. Oswalt, *The Book of Isaiah: Chapters 1-39,* NICOT (Grand Rapids: Eerdmans, 1986), 483-84.

52..Wildberger, *Jesaja, Kapitel 13-27,* 994.

53. Note Mic 5:6 and especially Hos 6:3, to which John Day draws attention in "*tlʾōrōt* in Isaiah 26:19,"*ZAW* 90 (1978) 265-69. The second person pronoun in 26:19b must refer to the people; even so, the dew comes from Yahweh.

54. Johnson, *Chaos to Restoration* 78-79. Johnson assumes that passages from Isaiah 49, 54, and 66 refer to an initial return from exile; on this basis he dates most of all of Isaiah 24-27 prior to 538. This seems to me unlikely, though I have no alternative date(s) to propose.

55. Isa 26:19 stands in a certain tension with the general and otherwise indisputable observation of v. 14: "The dead do not live; shades do not rise." However, the general observation is there given a specific basis. It is because Yahweh has punished them that these dead, Israel's old enemies, do not live or rise.

56. Leonard J. Greenspoon insists that Isa 26:19 expressly promises resurrection, not just restoration. "The Origin of the Idea of Resurrection," 285.

57. These Ugaritic texts are conveniently transliterated and translated in J. C. L. Gibson, *Canaanite Myths and Legends,* (Edinburgh: T. & T. Clark, 1977), 50, 68. William R. Millar has especially stressed the mythological background, Canaanite and Mesopotamian, to Isaiah 24-27, in *Isaiah 24-27 and the Origin of Apocalytic, SBLDS* (Missoula, MT: Scholars Press, 1976).

58. The quotations, omitting text-critical sigla, are from Gibson, *Canaanite Myths,* 69 and 76.

59. "Death and Resurrection in the A. B. Cycle," *UF* 21 (1990) 425-34, quoting from 431. It is interesting in this regard that, in Jer 51:34, the personified Zion (Jerusalem) laments that Nebuchadrezzar "has devoured me. . . , he has swallowed me like a monster (tannîn)."

60. Other scholars have noticed this. See Klaas Spronk, *Beatific Afterlife in Ancient Israel and in the Ancient Near East , AOAT 219;* (Neukirchen-Vluyn: Neukirchener Verlag, 1986), 304.

61. Solidarity with the dead is the theme of Helmut Peukert's *Science, Action, and Fundamental Theology* (Cambridge, MA: MIT Press, 1986).

62. I would like to thank Professor Walter Michel for his vigorous and insightful response to my paper when it was presented to the symposium on The Theological Interpretation of Scripture at North Park Seminary. Shortages of time and ability prevent me from incorporating many of his suggestions.

# THE RESURRECTION OF JESUS AND THE RESURRECTION OF THE DEAD*

PETER STUHLMACHER

In the early part of 1993, Rainer Riesner and I led an exegetical-archaeological study course in Jerusalem for pastors of the Protestant Church of Württemberg. The purpose of this course was to study the New Testament narratives of the passion and resurrection of Jesus at those places where the events actually took place. All participants were deeply impressed by the fact that the locations where Jesus had been during his last visit to Jerusalem can still be found today. The recent excavations at the temple and in the upper city of Jerusalem, sensational finds such as the discovery of the grave and bone coffin of the High Priest, Caiaphas, the results of archaeological investigation in the Church of the Holy Sepulcher, and a detailed study of the history of construction in Jerusalem do indeed make it possible to follow the footsteps of Jesus between Palm Sunday and Good Friday. Coming from Bethany, he entered Jerusalem through the City of David. By way of the southern outside staircase and the double Hulda gate he gained access to the temple, and there in the so-called Royal Hall of Columns the cleansing of the temple took place, an act by which he extremely provoked the priests responsible for the temple. He taught in the temple and held the Last Supper with his twelve disciples in the upper room upon the (Christian) Mount Zion. He proceeded from there to the Garden of Gethsemane, passing through the Kidron Valley. There he was arrested by the group which Judas had led to Gethsemane. The men brought Jesus to the palace of the High Priest in the upper city. Annas and Caiaphas interrogated him there and found him to be a messianic blasphemer. The next morning Jesus was led from the palace to Pilate in the praetorium (possibly directly next to the palace of the priest). The Roman governor interrogated Jesus and condemned him to die on the cross. After the scourging, the Romans took Jesus through the so-called Garden Gate leading him to a stone mound in an abandoned quarry before the city walls called Golgotha and nailed him to the cross together with two other rebels. The Roman inscription above him on the cross gave the charge which led to his condemnation: "The King of the Jews" (Mark 15:26). After the (relatively) quick death of Jesus, Joseph of Arimathea asked Pilate for the body of Jesus and placed it in his own (individual) tomb cut out of rock, which was just a stone's throw from Golgotha. Today, the Church of the Sepulcher in Jerusalem encloses this tomb of

---

* Translated by Jonathan M. Whitlock, Tübingen

rock and Golgotha. Anyone in Jerusalem reading the gospel story of the passion and burial of Jesus can literally retrace the steps described in the narratives and can thereby make a discovery, which, although often denied or forgotten, is of great importance. The biblical reports bear witness to the story of the suffering and death of Jesus which had been handed down with such accuracy that the stones begin to scream when people remain silent or think they are better informed than the texts (cf. Luke 19:40). We have before us in the story of the passion and burial of Jesus, not late Christian fiction, but historical reports which are dependable, even down to the details of topography.

This is also of considerable import for our topic. Instead of making the texts the object of arbitrary interpretation, we can and must proceed from the supposition that they provide a dependable witness to events, even with regard to their historical details. It is therefore unacceptable to immediately or even only ask what we can do with the texts and what we cannot. Rather, we are called upon to hear the witness of the texts first and consider what they want to do with us. Instead of seizing control over the text by interpreting it, we should try—as the Gernan poet, Rainer Maria Rilke so well put it—"to house" ourselves in the text as men and women for whom Jesus suffered death and was raised again by God.

## AN OVERVIEW OF THE ACCOUNTS

If we approach the reports of the burial of Jesus given by the four Gospels and Paul (cf. 1 Cor 15:2) with these presuppositions and this intention, then the following features of their reports are striking:

1. Mark, Matthew ard Luke report that the women close to Jesus, the names of which were known to the early Church, had observed his burial. This means they knew where the tomb of Jesus was (cf. Mark15:47).

2. Mark and Luke agree in their report that Jesus had received at first only a quick burial. Therefore, the women started out very early on Easter morning in order that they might prepare him for his final rest in accordance with Jewish custom: to anoint him wlth good smelling oil and wrap his body with cloth impregnated with myrrh and spices so as to neutralize the odor of the decaying corpse (cf. Mark 16: l; Luke 24:1).

3. Only Matthew (Matt 27:62-66) mentions that Roman soldiers watched over Jesus' grave, and according to him the women went out only "to see the sepulcher" (28:1).

4. Contrary to the first three Gospels, the Gospel of John reports that the burial of Jesus was already completed by Joseph of Arimathea and Nicodemus in the late afternoon of Good Friday before the beginning of the Sabbath and that the place of burial was a new rock tomb located in a garden near Golgotha (cf. John 19:38-42). On Easter morning Mary of Magdala went to the tomb only to mourn for Jesus, who lay there (cf. John 20:1-18 and Matt 28:1)

5. According to all four Gospeils, on the third day after the crucifixion of Jesus the women found the tomb of Jesus to be empty. The large stone blocking the entrance to the tomb had been rolled away, the body of Jesus had dsappeared, and the cloth strips which had been wrapped around him were lying to the side.

6. According to all four Gospels, the women were at a loss to explain their discovery. None among them had observed the resurrection of Jesus nor had any other human being. For this reason, Mary of Magdala thought at first that someone had taken the body of Jesus and placed it somewhere else (cf. John 20:2,13,15), and the Jewish opponents of the early Church could hold the view that the disciples of Jesus had come in the night and taken his body away (Matt 28:13).

7. Only through the message from the angel (or angels) and the encounter with Jesus did the women correctly interpret the empty tomb. God had raised Jesus bodily from the dead, they were therefore not to search for the living Christ among the dead but were to tell the disciples that the tomb is empty and Jesus is risen (cf. Mark 16:6-7; Matt 28:1-10; Luke 24:1-12; John 20:11-18).

These different reports share the same core. The rock tomb of Jesus was found opened and empty in the early morning of the third day after the crucifxion by several women who were close to Jesus. This discovery engendered amazement and doubt both within the circle of Jesus' followers and outside of it, a doubt which could and can only be removed through the appearances of the risen Jesus and the message of Easter preached in divine authority.

In pondering this shared core and the different reports individually, one is immediately confronted with a critical paradigm explaining them. The reports about the women who had remained true to Jesus finding the empty tomb on Easter morning are up to the present day judged to be late Christian apologetic legends which were used to demonstrate to sceptical people that Jesus indeed was resurrected bodily. This paradigm of interpretation presupposes that what really transpired is something other than that to which the Gospels bear witness. It is assumed that Jesus' tomb remained closed as do the tombs of other human beings, that, faced with the sealed tomb of Jesus, the disciples developed the belief that death was unable to conquer Jesus and that which he came to accomplish, and that the Easter message is to be understood as the expression and bearer of this conviction.

If one examines more closely this widely held critical view regarding the credibility of the reports concerning the discovery of the empty tomb, it becomes quickly evident that only modern readers find this view convincing and that it is historically a failure. The archaeological findings and the construction history of the Church of the Holy Sepulcher in Jerusalem alone are enough to render such a critical view of the reports of the empty tomb untenable. Those who criticize the New Testament texts fail especially to recognize that these reports from the witnesses of the early Church in no way made the preaching of the resurrection any easier apoogetically. The very opposite is true; they made it much more difficult! In old Jerusalem, no Jew would have seriously objected if the followers of Jesus had done with their dead master as had the disciples of John the Baptist with their prophetic teacher, who had been beheaded by Herod Antipas. They could have buried Jesus and then have revered him as a dead and martyred (messianic) prophet lying in his grave. It was generally believed that, because of their meritorious death, Jewish martyrs were certain candidates for the resurrection of the dead in glory at the end of time, as described in Dan 12: 2-3. The remains of the dead were allowed to rest in the grave, but the souls of the martyrs were believed to have already been removed to the divine realm (cf. so Rev 6:9-11). For this reason, the martyrs were called upon to intercede in heaven for those still living, and a martyr-cult developed around the martyrs' graves. The followers of Jesus could have done so with their crucified Lord, and this would have been considered "normal" by the Jews. The discovery of the empty tomb by the women made it impossible for the disciples of Jesus to stay with the normal Jewish view. They were suddennly forced to interpret the amazing and offensive phenomenon of the empty tomb, and the key impulse for an interpretation came from the appearances of Jesus. Because of these appearances, it was possible to counteract the polemical Jewish charge of grave-robbing and to see in the empty tomb three signs from God: first, a sign that God here and now in Jerusalem had raised Jesus bodily from the dead (cf. Mark 16: 6-7 par; John 20: 17-18); second, a sign that the crucified Jesus was more than a martyr—

he was the messianic Son of God whom God had lifted up (in accordance with 2 Sam 7:12-16; Ps 89: 28 and 110:1) and placed at his right hand as "Son of God in power" (cf. Rom 1:3-4); and third, a sign that with the bodily resurrection of the Son of God, the eschatological resurrection of all the dead had been promisingly initiated (cf. 1 Cor 15:4.20-22; Col 1:18; Rev 1:5).

If this function of the empty tomb as a threefold sign is taken seriously, and if the evidence found in the Church of the Holy Sepulcher in Jerusalem is not ignored, then it is impossible to consider the New Testament reports of the empty tomb to be fictive stories of a later period. One must rather come to the conclusion that the empty tomb confronted the early Christian witnesses as an historical phenomenon. It did not make the preaching of the Gospel, which went out from Jerusalem, any easier but made it more difficult, because it gave new dimensions which were offensive both for Jews and Gentiles alike (and remain so).

## THE APPEARANCES OF THE RISEN LORD

With this we have anticipated some of our results and must now attempt to approach that which has been said step by step. The New Testament does not hide the fact that the empty tomb was only a sign which was disputed between Christians and Jews. The sign could be interpreted in various ways, and it alone was not enough upon which to base the message of Jesus' resurrection from the dead. This message came about only through the Easter appearances of Jesus. The essential witnesses to these appearances are listed by Paul in 1 Cor 15:5-8: First Cephas (Peter), then the Twelve, then more than 500 of the brothers at the same tlme, then James, the brother of the Lord, then all the apostles and finally he himself.

The text indicates with the formulation "he appeared" appearances before the chosen witnesses (Acts 10:41) of the exalted Jesus "from heaven," who is at God's right hand (cf. Acts 9:13, 22:6). Mary of Magdala saw on Easter morning the Lord who had risen from his rest in the grave, but had not yet gone up to the Heavenly Father. It is for this reason that he commands Mary not to touch him and keep him from returning to his Father (cf. John 20:17). Although Mary of Magdala is indeed a witness to the resurrection and Jesus' departure to his Heavenly Father, she is not an Easter witness in the sense used in 1 Cor 15:5-8. The same seems to be true for the women mentioned in Matt 28:8-10, whose encounter with the risen Christ is different from that described in Matt 28:16-20, and it is for the reason that no names of woman appear in the list of witnesses in 1 Cor 15:5-8.

There are four circumstances which characterize the appearances of the exalted Jesus (from heaven): they happened at different places and at different times; they occurred to a variety of different people, they had an unobjectifiable character, and they engendered faith in those who experienced them. It is advisable to look at these circumstances individually.

1. That the appearances occured at different places and at different times can be concluded by comparing the reports of these appearances as recorded by the Gospels according to Matthew, Luke and John as well as by Acts. The three Gospels tell of appearances of Jesus in Jerusalem (e.g., Matt 28:9; Luke 24: 36-49; John 20:19-29), in Emmaus (Luke 24:13-35), but also at the Sea of Tiberias (John 21:1-23) and upon a mountain in Galilee (Matt 28:12-20). In addition, Acts mentions several times that Paul was surprised by an appearance of the exalted Lord on the road to Damascus (Acts 9:3-9; 22:6-11; 26:12-18). Paul considered himself to be the last Easter witness both with regard to time and to im-

portance (1 Cor 15:8). The great variety in times and places of the appearances makes it difficult to hold all the reports of appearances to be legendary.

2. Those experiencing the appearances were also so different that one is unable in one sweeping judgment to dismiss the Easter appearances as pious delusions. Among those who witnessed such appearances were not only the women and men who had followed Jesus before Easter, such as Peter, the Twelve and Mary of Magdala, but also men like James, the brother of the Lord, and Paul. If Mark 3:21 and John 7:5 are to be believed, James did not belong to the followers of Jesus when he was on the earth, but distanced himself in unbelief from his brother. It was the appearance of the risen and uplifted Christ which first made him into a respected member of the church in Jerusalem and, after Peter's departure, to its (second) head. In 62 C. E. he was stoned by the Jews as an alleged transgresser against the law. Paul had even violently persecuted the church of Jesus and became the greatest of all apostles only after being surprised by the appearance of Christ to him on the road to Damascus. In view of the completely different nature of the witnesses to the appearances, it is necessary to assume that the Easter appearances were true religious experiences.

3. The nature of these appearances of Jesus is described differently in the various texts. While the risen Jesus, according to John 20:19-29, went through locked doors and offered to let the unbelieving Thomas touch his wounds, he disappeared from the view of the disciples in Emmaus as soon as they recognized him by the way he broke the bread (cf. Lk 24:31). According to Luke 24:42-43, Jesus ate a piece of baked fish in the presence of his disciples, while in John 21:1-13 he only helped the disciples, who had returned to their Galilean home to catch fish, in a miraculous way and mysteriously offered them a meal of bread and fish. Paul, in Gal 1:15-16 and 2 Cor 4:5-6, describes the appearance of the Son of God which he experienced as an act of divine revelation in which the inner light of the true knowledge of Christ shone upon him, and the popular version of his conversion in Acts (see above) confirms this. For those who witnessed appearances all of the senses seem to have been involved in the experience. At the same time, the nature of the appearing Christ is not easily compared to a specific mode of being in our world. His new existence touches our world, but at the same time points beyond it.

4. Of course, all of the reports of the appearances mentioned do concur on one point. The risen Christ appeared to these women and men so that they could recognize him as their Lord, and that he, having gone beyond the abyss of his death on the cross and despite their failure and resistance, met them in a very personal way. This encounter and the greetings of peace connected with it in some of the texts conveys forgiveness and (re-)acceptance to those experiencing it (cf. Matt 28:9-10; Luke 24:36; John 20:16, 19, 26; Acts 9:4-5; 22:7-8; 26:14-18). Those women and men to whom it had been granted to experience such an appearance could, therefore, understand it to be the establishment of a new fellowship which Jesus granted to them in his divine authority.

Having been moved by this very experience of forgiveness and having been confronted with the astounding report of the empty tomb, these women and men learned to interpret the whole event in a way which Jesus had already suggested as they travelled toward Jerusalem. His Heavenly Father would deliver him up to die (on the cross), but would not surrender him over to eternal destruction. Rather he would raise his son from the dead, exalt him to his right hand and invest him with the honor due to the messianic Son of Man (cf. Mark 8:31 par; 9:31 par,10:33-34 par, 14:61-62 par). Through the Easter appearances and the empty tomb of Jesus the witnesses gained the insight and courage to confess, "God has raised Jesus Christ from the dead" (cf. Acts 3:15; 5:30-31; 10:40; Rom 10:9), or, "The Lord is risen indeed and hath appeared to Simon," (Luke 24:34); or "Christ died for our sins according to the Scriptures, and he was buried, and he was raised on the third day according to the Scriptures, and he appeared to Cephas, and then to the Twelve" (1 Cor 15:3-5).

All of these sentences are confessional statements and not descriptions of an objective fact, the truth of which both believers and unbelievers could in the same way be convinced. According to the biblical witness, Jesus' resurrection from the dead did not occur before any human eyes, but remained a divine mystery, the truth and reality of which can only be confessed in faith. Acts 10:41 states also that Jesus "was not seen by all the people, but by witnesses whom God had already chosen." Thus, the Easter appearances remain enclosed in a shroud of divine mystery. Christians can speak of Easter and of Jesus' resurrection only by following the witnesses and by doing this with hearts aflame and in courageous faith. Such witness of faith remains subject to the doubt and criticism of unbelief until the day of the final appearance of Jesus. This must be said so clearly, because, since the second century, the unfortunate Christian habit of calling the resurrection of Jesus an "objective fact" has prevailed. In more modern times many like to add that—if the technical possibility had then existed—not only the empty tomb, but also the risen one could have been photographed. This may be a pious thought, but it is an audacious false interpretation of the situation. It began with the apocryphal *Gospel of Peter* (35-42), which portrays Jesus rising on the eve of Easter before the eyes of the Romans guarding the tomb and before the Jewish elders, and, as mentioned, is still with us today. It tries to understand God's actions on that Easter eve, which go beyond the limits and standards of that which is earthly, better than the Bible, and in this attempt it reduces them to the extent that they fit within the limited horizon of that which modern people can consider free of doubt. This pious false interpretation also fails to take seriously the agonizing doubt and earnest questions of those people who struggle with their faith in view of the Easter message. For the sake of the truth of the Easter message and the truthfulness of a missonary dialogue with our contemporaries, we should forgo the claim that the Easter events are "objective facts," and better speak of events in space and time which are not objectifiable.

## THE JEWISH AND OLD TESTAMENT FOUNDATION OF RESURRECTION FAITH

The Christian confession of the one God, "who raised Jesus our Lord from the dead" (Rom 4:24) leads from Easter back to Jesus. In his argument with the Sadducees over the resurrection of the dead, he coined the classic saying, "the God of Abraham, Isaac and Jacob is not the God of the dead, but of the living" (cf. Mark 12:27 par). With this confession, Jesus places himself on the side of the Pharisees in this question and directs his followers attention to the Holy Scriptures of the Old Testament. A closer look at this matter quickly makes evident that the whole Christian expectation of the resurrection of the dead and the daring interpretation of the resurrection of Jesus are unthinkable without the ancient Jewish confessional tradition. The Christian Bible does not consist of Old and New Testament by accident; they are inextricably bound together. It is also no accident that the Bible witnesses to the history of God's saving acts for Jews and Gentiles, which began long before us with the creation of the world and the election of the patriarchs and which stretches on to a time beyond our lifetime to the last coming of Jesus Christ, the salvation of all Israel, and the final establishment of the Kingdom of God.

1. As Jesus' confrontation concerning the resurrection in Mark 12:18-27 par documents, at the time of Jesus and the apostles, it was still a matter of debate among the Jews whether the expectation of a resurrection of the dead was a genuine part of the Jewish

faith tradition or only an augmentation to the teaching contained in the five books of Moses. The Pharisees assumed the former to be the case, while the Sadducees held the opposing viewpoint. Jesus agreed with the Pharisees on this point. Twice a day they prayed the Jewish prayer, the Eighteen Benedictions, which is still in use today. The second benediction reads:

> Thou art mighty, who bringest low the proud, strong, and He that judgeth the ruthless, that liveth for ever, that raiseth the dead, that maketh the wind to blow, that sendeth down the dew; that sustaineth the living, that quickeneth the dead; in the twinkling of an eye Thou makest salvation to spring forth for us. Blessed art Thou, O Lord, who quickenest the dead! (Translation: E. Ferguson, *Backgrounds of Early Christianity*, 1987, 459)

This benediction shows clearly that the resurrection of the dead according to Jewish belief was the work of God alone; only he, in his creation power, can cause the dead to rise. The individual phrases of this benediction are reminiscent of Hanna's song of praise in 1 Sam 2:11-10 or of its New Testarnent counterpart in Luke 1:46-55, the Magnificat of Mary. Moving from the concluding word of praise "Blessed art Thou, O Lord, who quickenest the dead!" to the confession of the Christians, it becomes evident that the Jewish confession of the one God who, being the Lord over life and death, brings the dead to life is the basis for the Christian confession. The one God who brings the dead to life is the very God who—as Rom 4:24 puts it—"raised Jesus our Lord from the dead." Paul in Rom 4:17 and 24 virtually points out this inextricable connection between the two confessions. It is not a fortuitous mood which motivates Paul to do this, but results from his conviction that the inspired word of God, which is the Old Testament, teaches the Christians how they should think about God, his Christ, and about the future of the world. This view of things is not restricted to Paul; rather all of the apostolic teachers of the early Church viewed the—for them sometimes puzzling—fate of Jesus, his cross, his burial, the discovery of the empty tomb, and Jesus' appearances upon the background of the Old Testament, expecting that God would through this word teach them how Jesus' suffering, death, and appearances from heaven were to be interpreted. The early Christian confession that the one God, who, being the creator and he who raises the dead, had raised his son Jesus Christ from the dead is the result of this method of interpretation.

2. If we consider the exact wording of this early Christian confession more closely, we find that the connection between the resurrection of Christ and the resurrection of all the dead becomes completely clear. The one God who makes the dead to live has made the crucial beginning to the final resurrection of the dead by raising Jesus Christ from the dead here and now. Jesus, therefore, has become the risen "firstfruits" of those who have fallen asleep who are to be resurrected, the "new Adam" through whom the resurrection of the dead will be achieved (1 Cor 15:20-22), or, also, the "firstborn from among the dead" (Col 1:18; Rev 1:5). As Heb 1:6 shows, this daring talk of Christ being the "firstborn from among the dead" is suggested to the early Church by Ps 89:28. Upon the background of this divine promise, the resurrection and exaltation of Jesus appeared to be his designation as the "firstborn" from among the dead who at the end of time is appointed to be the ruler over the whole earth. His bodily resurrection is an unparalleled sign of hope for all mortals and for all who already rest under the earth.

3. If we go one step further, we recognize that the Old Testament texts inform the New Testament witnesses and all Christians how their hope in resurrection is to be understood. I would like to give four examples.

3.1. The Old Testament was and is the Holy Scripture for Christians too, and the idea should not be entertained for one second that the New Testament in any way replaces the Old. On the contrary, the Christian may and should read the Old Testament in the same way as the early Church, who followed the example of Jesus and the apostles; that is, as the voice of the living God, who is the Father of Jesus Christ. As far as the resurrection of the dead is concerned, there are stirring expressions of trust to be found in the Psalms and in Job which helped Jews and Christians learn to depend on the one God who raised Jesus from the dead, even in extreme affliction and mortal danger. The language of Ps 73:23-36 ("Yet I am always with you. . .") and Job 19:25-27 (". . . I know that my redeemer lives. . .") reach up into the very heavenly world from which Jesus appeared to the chosen witnesses (Acts 10:41) and from which he will appear anew to transform—as Paul writes in Phil 3:21—"our lowly bodies so that they will be like his glorious body," and that "by the power that enables him to bring everything under his control."

3. 2. In Isa 26:19 the people of God are promised that their dead will live again and shall be born anew. New discoveries in the Qumran texts document that in ancient Judaism the fulfillment of this promise was expected to coincide with the messianic age of salvation (cf. 4Q521). According to Matt 11:5 and Luke 7:22, Jesus considered the resurrections of the dead attributed to him to be the fulfillment of this expectation, and it is from him that this expectation was taken and added to the treasure of Christian hope. The resurrection is initiated at baptism in the life of every Christian (cf. Eph 5:14), and when the Kingdom of God is completely manifest at the end of days, the resurrection of believers will be completed also (cf. Rev 20:2).

3. 3. In Deut 32:39; 1 Sam 2:5; Wis 16:13 and Tob 13:2, the Old Testament confesses that God is the Lord over life and death. After the early Church had learned to identify the Christ exalted to the right hand of God with the messianic "firstborn" from among the dead whom God had appointed to be ruler of the world, it possessed the boldness to accord to the risen Christ the divine power over life and death. The clearest witnesses for this are found in Revelation and the Gospel of John. In Rev 1:17-18, Christ in heaven speaks to John in a vision: "I am the First and the Last. I am the living One. I was dead, and behold I am alive for ever and ever! And I hold the keys of death and Hades." The Fourth Gospel explains how God's own creation power is related to the mission of his Son in the last days. In John 11:25-26 Jesus says: "I am the resurrection and the life. He who believes in me will live, even though he dies; and whoever lives and believes in me will never die." And John 5:19-27 tells what gives Jesus the right to speak in such a way. The Heavenly Father has given his Son the authority to raise the dead and, as the Son of Man, to judge the world. In the much puzzled-over word in John 5:28-29, Jesus adds the following explanation: "Do not be amazed at this, for a time is coming when all who are in their graves will hear his voice and come out—those who have done good will rise to live, and those who have done evil will rise to be condemned."

3. 4. In order to understand this sentence one must look at Dan 12:2-3. The expectation is expressed here for the first time that the dead are not just allowed to rise but must rise and that this resurrection has a twofold result: the righteous will be clothed in the light of God's glory and may inherit everlasting life, while the godless will be rejected and experience shame and everlasting contempt (cf. Isa 66:24). Jesus unfolds the same view in his parable of the great judgment in Matt 25:31-46, and it is unfurled as well in Rev 20:11-15. In agreement with this, according to John 5:28-29, Jesus is selected by God to judge, he being the messianic Son of Man, and he is to bring about the twofold resurrection of the dead at the end of time. The twofold resurrection corresponds to a double dimension of death in the Old Testament. There is, on the one hand, the natural death,

which every person must suffer after his allotted years have passed, but beyond this death lies the terrifying prospect of the second death, which excludes the godless from eternal life before and with God (cf. Rev 2:11; 20:6,14). Once again being based on the Old Testament and in agreement with it, both Paul and John emphasize that God's reign will be completely manifested only when death with its twofold dimension has been forever destroyed (cf. 1 Cor 15:26, 54-55; Rev 21:2 with Isa 25:8).

Without the Old Testament and the Jewish conviction of faith that God raises the dead, the Easter message could not have been verbalized, and there would be no Christian hope of resurrection.

## FUTURE RESURRECTION

A twofold question was already being asked by the churches of Paul. It ran as follows: "How and when will the dead arise? The answers which Paul gave to this question set the standard for the future.

In taking up this question, we must be sure to consider one circumstance which, though taken for granted by the apostle, causes problems for the interpretation of his letters. The recipients of Paul's letters were Christians, and Paul only answers their specific question: "How and when will we and our brothers and sisters who have already died arise?" Paul hardly mentions in his letters the more basic question, treated in Dan 12:2-3, as to the how and why of the resurrection of all the dead. Whoever seeks an answer to this basic question cannot take the Pauline statements to be the whole picture, but must go beyond Paul's letters and consult the whole of the Bible.

1. Paul addressed the question of how the resurrection of the dead will happen in 1 Cor 15, because, apparently, a part of the church in Corinth had trouble imagining what a bodily resurrection of the dead might mean. They had been brought up with the common Greek view that the earthly body was only an outer garment. (Some Greeks even said that the body was the tomb of the immortal soul or also of the eternal spiritual self). These ideas were brought into the churches. For Paul, this way of thinking is tantamount to denying the resurrection completely. It contradicts, according to his (common Jewish) convictions, not only the concept of God as creator and the bodily resurrection of Jesus, but also does injury to the singularity of the individual before God. In response to the question of the mockers about how the bodily resurrection might be accomplished, he wrote in 1 Cor 15:38-49: "Just as God has given each creature an earthly body, so will he also give each who is raised in glory a new spiritual body." Since the Christians are, on the one hand, descendants of the old Adam, on the other, redeemed by the new Adam, Christ, the following principle is valid for them: ". . . as in Adam all die, so in Christ all will be made alive" (1 Cor 15:22). This means with respect to the resurrection: "As was the earthly man, so are those who are of the earth; and as is the man from heaven, so also are those who are of heaven. And just as we have borne the likeness of the earthly man, so shall we bear the likeness of the man from heaven" (1 Cor 15:48f). According to Paul, every Christian during his whole lifetime may and should praise God with his body (1 Cor 6: 20; Rom 12:1-3). In the final judgment he will be required to give an account of all bodily deeds to his creator and redeemer (2 Cor 5:10; Rom 14:10). Through the grace of God, however, he is destined to enter, with Christ's help, into the Kingdom of God and there to rejoice in the glorious freedom of God's children; and this the Christian does with a new heavenly body, within a creation redeemed from all perishableness (Rom 8:18-30).

What Paul writes in 1 Cor 15 about the bodily resurrection of Christians is born out of an assurance of faith that all people who believe in Christ will be acquitted in the final judgment because of the intercession of their crucified and resurrected Lord so that they may participate in the heavenly glory (cf. Rom 8:28-39). Thus, Paul views the bodily resurrection as an act of salvation. When we speak in the modern version of the third article of the Apostolic Confession of the "resurrection of the dead," this is not referring to this act of salvation. As the original Latin text shows, it concerns the *resurrectio carnis,* that is the "resurrection of the flesh." Of this the apostle never speaks. It is not by accident that he introduced the teaching in 1 Cor 15:50, "flesh and blood cannot inherit the kingdom of God." The concept of the "resurrection of the flesh" appears in its full formulation for the first time in Justin Martyr (*Dial* 80:5) and means the resurrection of all the dead, which places them before the tribunal of the last judgement. According to Dan 12:2-3, it will have a twofold result: some will inherit eternal life, while the others will be overcome by eternal destruction (see above).

2. Paul was first asked the question: when the resurrection would take place by the Christians in Thessalonica, and they posed it because of anxiety over the possibility that the church members who had died before the final appearance of Christ—which at that time was expected to happen in the near future—might not be able to have a part in the redemption and the glorious freedom of the children of God in God's kingdom (see above). The answer which Paul gave to the (again specifically Christian!) inquiry has remained the standard answer to this day. The apostle proceeded from the assumption that God made possible a participation of all believers in his everlasting reign through the saving death and resurrection of Jesus Christ. Therefore, for those who believe in Jesus Christ, there is in view of their crucified and resurrected Lord no "died too soon!" or "lived too late!" but only the assurance that in and through the one, all may participate in the glory which he has already inherited. When the Lord appears to pass judgment and to establish the reign of God, God will lead all believers who died, from the realm of the dead to life in glory, and those believing in Christ who are still alive will be transformed into the glorious light of the children of God. In Paul's words, "We believe that Jesus died and rose again and so we believe that God will bring with Jesus those who have fallen asleep in him" (1 Thess 4:14). In 1 Cor 15:15-55 he impresses this upon the Christians in Corinth as well. He is of the conviction that Christians, having faith in their Lord, can confidently leave the question about when the resurrection will take place to God's care.

## THE RELEVANCE OF RESURRECTION FAITH

The biblical statements concerning Jesus' resurrection and the resurrection of the dead are an important part of the testimony of Holy Scripture, and this testimony has its foundation in God's saving act for the sake of Jews and Gentiles in Jesus' passion, burial, and exaltation on the third day. The historically unambiguous traces of this saving act are to be seen in the Church of the Sepulcher in Jerusalem. In view of these traditions which have come down to us, it cannot be our objective to sort out the texts dealing with the resurrection according to modern standards, considering only those things to be valid which are agreeable to us and marking through the unpleasant remainder. Were we to proceed in this way, we would be taking it upon ourselves to in novel fashion arrange and define according to our own discretion the saving act of God in Jesus' death and resurrection. In attempting this, we would inevitably destroy the foundation of the assurance of faith which the biblical Easter message intends to make accessible to the reader. Considering the nature of this message, the question should be turned around. Where do we find ourselves written in the biblical texts, and in what way do they not only relate to the Christians of the first hour but also to us and to the coming generations? These questions can be best answered in three steps.

1. It is undeniable that Jesus' passion and the events of Easter were played out almost two thousand years ago and that the biblical testimony to these events is almost as old, but this does not mean that they have nothing to do with the coming generations. The women who found the tomb of Jesus empty on the third day, the apostolic witnesses of Easter, and the biblical authors lived in the first century of our Christian calender, but they formulated their testimony in such a way that all Christians could and should join in and confess with them, "Christ died for our sins according to the Scriptures, and he was buried, and he was raised on the third day according to the Scriptures, and he appeared to Peter, and then to the Twelve" (1 Cor 15:3-5). Or even more concise: "We believe in the God who raised Jesus our Lord from the dead" (Rom 4: 24). What is true for the Easter confession, is also true for the Jewish word of praise from the second of the Eighteen Benedictions, "Be thou blessed, Lord, who makes the dead alive," and it is no less true for the expressions of assurance in Ps 73: 23-26; Job 19: 25-27, the promise from Isa 26:19, and the announcement in Dan 12:2-3. All of these texts invite us to repeat and to join in with them. Without the biblical language, the testimony to the resurrection is out of reach, but with it, this testimony is retained in such a way that by learning this language we participate in the assurance of faith which fills the texts. The biblical testimony concerning the resurrection of Jesus and the resurrection of all the dead is intended for us in that it invites us to join in with the first Christians in their confession.

2. There is no doubt that the biblical witnesses experienced the world in which they lived, the people with whom they lived, and life in general in some ways much differently from what we do today. However, this is no reason to consider their way of thinking and of expressing themselves to be antiquated. When the ancients thought about God and of Christ who had been exalted to his right hand, they looked up towards heaven and expressed the hope that the Son of Man would come with the clouds of heaven to establish redemption upon the earth. They buried their dead in the earth and expected God would raise them up at the Last Judgment and would lead them through Christ to redemption. They assumed that the living were closest to God when they led a life of righteousness and in reverence of God. Nevertheless, even in biblical times, people were surrounded by doubters and enemies who held God for a figment of the imagination, the hope in eternal life for an illusion, the fear of God for superstition, the attempt to achieve righteousness for uselessness, and the body merely for a perishable thing. In the depths of our heart, we think and feel no differently today than did the ancient witnesses, and the problem of faith presents itself no differently to us than it did to them. When we try ourselves to imagine and to tell our children where God lives, then we point to the heavens above. When we lay the dead to rest in the earth, there remains only the hope that God will do with them what only he has the power to do. And when looking for the meaning of life, we still seek it in peace, joy, and righteousness. In those things which really matter, the conceptual world of the Bible is not outdated at all. The truth is rather that if we remain at home with the biblical language, then we gain words with which we can express our experiences, and we will be able to speak and to think when many of those around us have become speechless. Thus it is not backwardness, but a true gain for our religious life to be able to join in with the Bible in speaking about God, about Jesus' death and resurrection and, about the future of the whole creation.

3. The extent to which this gain in language can make a difference is taught in the example of Christians who have died trusting in the God who makes the dead to live and who raised Jesus our Lord from the dead. Death was bitter for all of them, but they faced death knowing that Jesus Christ is stronger than death. I would like to give two exam-

ples.

When Dietrich Bonhoeffer received the order on April 8, 1945 to prepare himself to be taken to his execution, he called to an acquaintance, "That is the end—for me the beginning of life." At dawn on April 9th, according to the report of the prison doctor (who did not know at the time that Bonhoeffer was before him), after an intense prayer at the gallows, he died in a state of such complete surrender to God that the doctor could not remember having seen anyone die that way.

Three years ago, before he had to undergo an operation from which he would not awaken, my late faculty colleague, the Old Testament scholar Hans Peter Rüger, instructed that in case of his death the funeral service should carry the stamp of Psalm 31. This is the Psalm which, according to the Gospel of Luke, Jesus himself prayed on the cross and in which the following can be read: "Into your hands I commit my spirit; you have redeemed me, Lord, you faithful God" (Ps 31:5; cf. with Luke 23:46.)

When it is possible to face death in this way, then the Easter message is by no means outdated. Rather it belongs to the words of everlasting life, words which will endure until Judgment Day.

# RESURRECTION: WHAT KIND OF BODY?

TED PETERS

One of the things we expect the future to bring is our own death. Despite all the advances in medical science, the death rate for human beings is still running at 100%. Thus the question regarding the possibility of life beyond the grave is still on people's minds. Polls consistently show that nearly three out of four Americans answer "yes" to questions asking about belief in life after death. A recent Gallup poll reports that 67% of teenagers believe in life after death, including 91% affirming that there is a heaven where the good are rewarded and 76% that there is a hell where the wicked are punished.[1] This kind of data prompts Andrew Greeley to remark that "we are born with two incurable diseases: life—always fatal, and hope—never curable. The critical question is whether hope is revelation or deception."[2] The Christian faith affirms that it is revelation and not deception. Further, the specifically Christian vision of life beyond death affirms with the Apostles' Creed belief in the "resurrection of the body and the life everlasting." Now, what does this mean?

Our task here will be to clarify just what we mean by life beyond death understood in terms of resurrection, and we will pursue this task by comparing the biblical view with some alternatives. The alternatives we will entertain here are four: (1) modern naturalism; (2) immortality of the soul; (3) absorption into the infinite; and (4) astral projection.

## ALTERNATIVES TO THE BIBLICAL VIEW

### *Modern Naturalism*

The first possibility we will dub the position of modern secular naturalism which in effect says, "when you're dead you're dead!" Death is the natural conclusion to life. It is the end, pure and simple. Naturalism assumes and asserts that the natural world constitutes the whole of reality. There are no windows that open out into another reality. There is no supernature. Life is fundamentally physical in character, and there is no spiritual reality to which we can escape the inevitable terminus that death brings. Living is only a physiological process with only a physiological meaning, argues Joseph Wood Krutch. Novelist Jack London goes on to describe our desire for immortality in terms of a delusion.

> All these baffling head-reaches after immortality are but the panics of souls frightened by the fear of death, and cursed with the thrice-cursed gift of imagination. . . .[The human person] is compounded of meat and wine and

> sparkle, of sun-mote and world-dust, a frail mechanism made to run for a span, to be tinkered with by doctors of divinity and doctors of physic, and to be flung into the scrap-heap at the end.[3]

The naturalist position must conclude that not only do individual human beings die, but knowing the scientific projections for the future of the cosmos, that all the achievements of civilization must also pass into oblivion. Moving from the personal scrap heap to the cosmic scrap heap, Bertrand Russell draws out the nihilistic consequences:

> . . . all the labor of the ages, all the devotion, all the inspiration, all the noonday brightness of human genius is destined to extinction in the vast death of the solar system, and that the whole temple of man's achievement must inevitably be buried beneath the debris of a universe in ruins—all these things, if not quite beyond dispute, are yet so nearly certain that no philosophy which rejects them can hope to stand.[4]

"If that's all there is," once sang Peggy Lee on the U.S. Hit Parade, "then I'll just go on dancing."

The diagnosis of modern secular naturalism is that death is incurable. The patient will die completely and stay dead. The next three alternative views, however, all believe they can save the patient through a surgical procedure in which they extract a nonphysical selfhood from the physical body. By performing what we will here call a "soulechtomy," they believe the patient can live on even though the physical body will die.

*Immortality Of The Soul*

The first soulechtomy we wish to mention is that performed by the great philosophers of the Platonic tradition in ancient Greece. The Greeks began by noticing how the ideas of the mind *(psyche)* seemed to be immune to the deteriorations of the body. Even though individuals would die, their ideas could be passed on from generation to generation unchanged. Perhaps certain ideas are eternal, the Greeks thought. If so, then the task of philosophy would be to discern which ideas are eternal and then try to train the mind to ponder only the eternal thoughts, so that the mind— which is identified with the true self apart from the body—would cut itself free from all temporal concerns. Free from temporality it could then leave the body and enter the realm of strictly disembodied and hence everlasting reality. With this scheme in mind, death became thought of positively because it would release the soul from temporal concerns and permit greater concentration on what is eternal. Thus Socrates says to Phaedo just before drinking the hemlock that will put his body to sleep forever:

> The body and its desires are the only cause of wars and factions and battles; for all wars arise for the sake of gaining money, and we are compelled to gain money for the sake of the body. We are slaves to its service. And so, because of all these things, we have no leisure for philosophy. But worst of all is that if we do get a bit of leisure and turn to philosophy, the body is constantly breaking in upon our studies and disturbing us with noise and confusion, so that it prevents our beholding the truth, and in fact we perceive that, if we are ever to know anything absolutely, we must be free from the body and must behold the actual realities with the eye of the soul alone. . . . when we are dead we are likely to possess the wisdom which we

desire and claim to be enamoured of; but not while we are alive.[5]

What we need to notice here is the direct competition between the mind or soul, which is the suprasensible self, and the body in which it is trapped. Plato says the soul "is imprisoned in the body like an oyster in his shell" and it seeks to escape from it through death. There is no concept here of a transformation or renewal of the physical world which would put body and soul into harmony, as one would find in Christianity. Nor does death cause Socrates to tremble with the fear of annihilation, because he seems confident that his true self is leaving a forsaken world to enter a blessed one.

Not everyone who dies becomes blessed, however. According to the Platonic scheme human souls are confronted with a judgment beyond the grave that determines where they will spend eternity. Following the ways of God and embodying justice are the criteria. Plato writes, "he who has lived all his life in justice and holiness shall go, when he is dead, to the Islands of the Blessed *(eis makaron nesous)*, and dwell there in perfect happiness out of the reach of evil; but that he who has lived unjustly and impiously shall go to the house of vengeance and punishment, which is called Tartarus."[6] Then after a millenium (1,000 years) the souls of both may be reincarnated and return to life on earth, the souls of those never having seen the truth returning in the form of animals while those who have sought eternal ideas will return as humans. But the soul of the philosopher has wings with which after three millenia it can fly to the heavenly throne of God and there enjoy the eternal beatific vision.[7]

Plato's version of the soulechtomy has been partially integrated into Christian thought. The Fifth Lateran General Council of 1513 filtered Plato's view through Aristotle and then pronounced it Christian dogma, condemning and rejecting all those "who assert that the intellectual soul is mortal or one soul common to all. . . "[8] The Westminster Confession combines immortality of the soul with resurrection by placing them in sequence.

*Question 37:* What benefits do believers receive from Christ at death?

*Answer:* The souls of believers are, at their death, made perfect in holiness, and do immediately pass into glory; and their bodies, being still united to Christ, do rest in their graves till the resurrection.

*Question:* What benefits do believers receive from Christ at the resurrection?

*Answer:* At the resurrection, believers being raised up in glory, shall be openly acknowledged and acquitted in the day of judgment, and made perfectly blessed in the full enjoying of God to all eternity.

John Newport is uneasy with this. He writes, "The biblical view teaches that human persons are in no way created to be or to become immortal by their nature. Rather, persons created in the image and likeness of God live within the limits of human nature bounded by mortality and dependent upon God for the gift of immortal life through resurrection from the dead. . . . Thus we see that the Greek idea of the innate immortality of the soul is alien to the teaching of the Bible, even though such ideas have become mixed in with Christian doctrine at various times in the centuries since Plato."[9]

### *Absorption into the Infinite*

What Plato propounded is quite similar to what Brahman seers in India believed. In the ancient Asian version of the soulechtomy—the Asian version precedes Socrates and Plato by half a millenium—we find the same basic competition between what is physical and what is mental; we find a similar version of metempsychosis or reincarnation; and we find that salvation is also understood as escape from the physical realm. But a certain accent appears during the age of the Upanishads in India that distinguishes it somewhat from the Greek doctrine of body-soul separation, namely, salvation understood as absorption into the infinite. Thus, although there is considerable overlap, we will think of this as a third alternative way to view life beyond death.

In Sanskrit one's true self, *atman,* is suprasensible or spiritual in nature and is in essence at one with the ultimate and comprehensive reality, *Brahman.* It is life amidst the cares of the body within the finite constraints of time and place that prevent ordinary human consciousness from realizing this transcendental oneness. We think of ourselves as separate and unique individual selves even though we are not. Our problem then is one of ignorance, of living in an illusion. To find the truth we must transcend the cares of our physical existence by penetrating the depths of the mind until cosmic unity is apprehended. Rather than ponder a group of eternal ideas as Plato suggested, in ancient India one seeks to get beyond all ideas whatsoever to the undifferentiated and meta-intellectual unity of all things. To do this one is not supposed to study philosophy but rather meditate—that is, practice yoga.

Should one fail through meditative yoga to free the atman from the body before one's physical death, then karma—the karmic triad of desire, thought, and action—will cling to the soul and force it back into rebirth. Ordinary death can not produce the liberation which Socrates was expecting. Between death and rebirth the disembodied soul can experience great truth, but once it reenters the new mother's womb it returns again to ignorance and must start again to walk the long path toward enlightenment. The ultimate objective of Upanishadic Hinduism is to achieve liberation, moksha—that is, to get off the wheel of rebirth and dwell forever in the disembodied oneness of atman and Brahman.[10] To achieve this liberation our finite consciousness must be absorbed without remainder into the infinite, into eternal oblivion.[11]

As various strands of Asian mysticism have begun to dangle amidst the loosely knit fabric of Western culture, interest has begun to grow for both meditation and for reincarnation. But the connection is not regularly made. Meditaion is pursued by middle class professionals for the purpose of overcoming stress and gaining self-control, not necessarily to lose oneself in the infinite. Reincarnation, curiously enough, is often taken to be a good thing, as an opportunity to gain another chance at terrestrial living and to refute the pessimistic naturalists. It becomes an object to be sought in the West. This is almost comical because at home in India it is something from which the truly spiritual souls seek to escape. There is a deep cleavage between European culture and Indian-based religion that often goes unnoticed. What the Eastern heirs to the Upanishads view as the equivalent to eternal life, namely, the escape from ego existence into the oblivion of the infinite, appears to those of us in the West with our strong egos and essentially materialistic disposition as eternal death.[12]

### *The Astral Body*

A fourth mode of conceiving life beyond death is that of the astral body or etheric double, a version of the soulechtomy employed especially in the contemporary occult. It may have roots in certain ancient conceptualities such as the Egyptian *ka,* the detached part of the personality which plans and acts for the rest of the person. The ka is born with the individual as an identical but immaterial twin, accompanies one through life as a sustaining and constructing force, and then effects existence in the world beyond death. Pictured on the walls of the early pyramids, this etheric double has one's human shape and shadows one's profile in a fashion that leads German archaeologists to dub it a *Döppelgänger*. The distinctive characteristic here is that even though the ka is supraphysical in character it assumes one's physical shape.

The actual name "astral body," however, means "star body" and connotes a form composed of light and deriving its existence from the heavens. It is an exact copy of the flesh and blood body—that is, the earthly body—but is made of a finer supraphysical material and has a shining and luminous appearance. Among the magicians of the West Indies, people of either sex called "hags" are said to be able to release themselves from their physical bodies and travel about astrally. The release is effected through the singing of charm songs while sitting naked and alone in the woods at night.

At death the astral body sleeps for a period of three or four days in a half-conscious state sometimes dubbed "hades." During this time the cords that bind it to physical life are being cut. Then the astral being awakens to find itself in a world so much like the one it left that at first it may be difficult to realize that death has taken place. Sometimes the new world appears as a beautiful land where illnesses and infirmities are healed. Other times it is purgatorial in nature where selfish souls mourn their loss rather than find new delights. But this world has an illusory character to it because it still reflects memories of life on earth.

Today's occult reflects the ancient spiritualist cosmos constructed with seven planes or spheres of existence. We start out on the lowest, at the level of physical life on earth. Immediately after death, when released from the physical realm we travel upward in our astral bodies to hades. This is followed by the world of illusion. Eventually one advances to the higher planes of supraphysical existence: the planes of color, flame, light, and finally union with God.

Philosophers of a naturalistic bent have for some time looked upon claims regarding astral travel and spiritualist ascent with light-hearted skepticism. But recent anecdotal testimonies of involuntary out-of-the-body experiences have raised new scientific interest in the whole question of a suprasensible self and survival beyond death apart from one's body. We will return to this modern development following a brief detour through a premodern view of soulechtomy.

## IS SOULECHTOMY FOREVER?

The three versions of soulechtomies just discussed—immortal soul, absorption into infinity, and astral body—all seem to presuppose not only that the self can be extracted from the body, but that in its disembodied form it is potentially, if not actually, eternal. Is it always the case that disembodied existence is thought to be everlasting? No, not necessarily. It is conceivable that the supraphysical self can pass out of existence.

Let us turn to the Akamba people who, like most all traditional African religious cultures, work with a dualism. According to Akamba tradition, the human person is made up of at least two parts: the physical part which at death is put into the grave or otherwise disposed of and the non-physical part which survives and bears one's selfhood into the hereafter. Hence, physical death for the Akamba does not mean annihilation, but a departure to the world of the *Aimu*, of the departed spirits. Each human being has a spirit *(veva)*—that is, he or she has, but is not, a spirit. At death his or her personhood moves to the spirit world where it receives another body which is identical with the body left in the physical world. This new body belongs to the Aimu world, not ours. There is no doctrine of reincarnation here, but we do have another case of soulechtomy.

When someone dies to the physical world, say the Akamba, he or she begins a process towards disintegration and disappearance into the past. The new member of the living-dead comes back on occasion to visit former relatives, usually appearing to one or two and asking about the welfare of the others. The new initiates to the Aimu realm may serve as guardians in our physical world and may even influence the birth of new children. Shamans receive instructions on medicine and the cure of diseases from their deceased predecessors. Some hostile disembodied souls take possession of various individuals, causing injury and epileptic fits. Thus, there is communication between the living-dead and their survivors, but it is not a full fellowship because they do not share meals, chores, and the joys of life.

But this communication does not go on forever. It dissipates. As long as one's name can be remembered, the living-dead may remain present. But after three to five generations when it is difficult for the survivors to remember, the loss of the name signifies the loss of existence. The living-dead slip away into the forgotten realm of nonbeing. "The individual finally disappears," writes John Mbiti, "melts away into the existence without personal names and hence without personality, deprived of the totality of being. God does not enter into the picture in this process of evaporation to reintegrate, recondense the vapour of human being into a new whole, a new persona, a new nameable thing.'[13]

In their own way, then, the Akamba believe there is an interim period between physical death and final disposition. During this interim period the living-dead function as nonphysical or spiritual beings who, as long as their survivors remember their names, continue to bear their own identities and personhood. The annihilation of the self does not occur at the moment of physical death, then. As with the Greeks and Hindus the true self disengages itself from the physical body and continues on. Annihilation only comes later, gradually. In contrast to Christian eschatology, there is no anticipated ultimate future when the God and creator of all things will recreate us and establish for us an everlasting life. Once the dead past is dead for the Akamba, it stays dead.

## LIFE-AFTER-LIFE

As one more sign that the ediface of modern naturalism and materialism is showing cracks and losing some of its mortar, the recent and widespread fascination with out-of-the-body experiences (OBEs) or near death experiences (NDEs)—sometimes dubbed near death out of body experiences or NDOBEs—reveals the double mind with which we approach natural science. On the one hand, the naturalistic philosophy that so often accompanies modernity seems too restrictive, too insensitive to our deeper feelings and aspirations, too inflexible on the question of human immortality. So when witnesses from the beyond tell us of another reality, we are ready to listen. With a marked tone of iconoclastic relish we like to think that the narrow restrictions of science have been exceeded, that the chains of the modern mindset have been broken. On the other hand curiously enough, we are not ready to listen to the witness of religious faith in this matter. It is important for the public to think that "scientists are working on this question," because we assume it can become fully believable only when it can be proved empirically. So what we end up with is a phenomenon which commands great interest and which allows us to express a love-hate relationship to scientific truth.

At the eye of the hurricane we find the journalistic work and reflection of Raymond A. Moody during the 1970s. Moody scrupulously studied the reports of out-of-the-body experiences of three groups of people: (l) those surgical cases where the patient was pronounced "dead" in the clinical sense of the word and then rescusitated; (2) those who came close to death but remained alive; and (3) those who died and who told others of their experience while in the process of dying. With numerous peripheral variants, a fascinating and significant core pattern has emerged. The core pattern can be discerned in his first person account of someone undergoing surgery.

> I heard the doctors say that I was dead, and that's when I began to feel as though I were tumbling, actually kind of floating through this blackness, which was some kind of enclosure. There are not really words to describe this. Everything was black, except that, way off from me, I could see this light. It was a very, very brilliant light, but not too large at first. It grew larger as I came nearer and nearer to it.
>
> I was trying to get to that light at the end, because I felt that it was Christ, and I was trying to reach that point. It was not a frightening experience. It was more or less a pleasant thing. For immediately, being a Christian, I had connected the light with Christ, who said, "I am the light of the world." I said to myself, "If this is it, if I am to die, then I know who waits for me at the end, there in that light."[14]

The core elements found in many similar reports include the darkness usually described as a tunnel, the bright light which grows larger as one approaches, the lack of fear if not feeling of well-being, the sense that the light not only symbolizes truth, but is also compassionate and accepting. It is also interesting to note how, in this case, the party undergoing the OBE does not actually see the profile of Jesus. What is seen is light, obviously the light of truth. Knowing that Jesus is the truth as well as the way and the life, the patient connects the two at the level of interpretation.

People who undergo such experiences usually report that upon return to normal day to day living they now have a deeper sense of the meaning of life. Their values change. No longer do they wish to put off to tomorrow what is important today. Material possessions lose their worth and intense appreciation of human relationships and spiritual truths free them from the obsession to obtain money or status. Finally, they say they no longer have a fear of death.

The light-hearted skeptics among us have sought to identify such reports with Jungian archetypes or to explain the tunnel-light phenomenon as an imaginary recapitulation of one's birth and the emergence into the world from the mother's birth canal. Psychiatrists working at the Menninger Foundation do not believe that the souls of these people actually leave their bodies, but that we should look for some "parapsychological explanation." Moody himself speculates that what is being reported may look at first like Plato's immortal soul, but upon closer examination it comes closer to the idea of the "spiritual body" reported by Paul in 1 Corinthians 15. It is my judgment that most of the cases Moody cites come closer to fitting the idea of the astral body, although not all of the testimony is easily corralled into a single theoretical idea. Regardless of which model it fits better, we have here another form of soulechtomy.

We will not tackle the scientific veracity of personal testimonies of OBEs.[15] But I believe that for the time being we must grant them hypothtetical status—that is, we must grant the possibility that there is some validity to what is reported. We must note further that there seems to be continuity between these reported life-after-life experiences in our own modern world and similar reports in ancient times that may or may not have fed into the construction of religious beliefs. The tale of Er reported in the closing pages of the *Republic* has a curious or anomolous character to it, but Plato is able to refashion it to support his overall vision. Similar accounts are reported by Augustine and the Venerable Bede. In the *Tibetan Book of the Dead (Bardo Thodol)* and in Chinese *Buddhist Sutras* we find accounts of souls passing from one incarnation to the next through darkness, experiencing light, and even seeing one's future mother and father in the act of conception which will bring the soul back to the physical plane.

Now let us simply observe a couple of things about our original four options. First, there is a significant difference between modern naturalism and the various soulechtomies. The revival of soulechtomy on contemporary operating tables right beneath the hands of the paradigm of the modern mind—the medical scientist—marks a point at which current consciousness is challenging the modern naturalistic worldview for its narrowness. Second, none of these four positions point toward the path we should follow if we wish our evangelical explication to draw out faithfully what Christians mean by "resurrection of the body and life everlasting." We need now to turn to the specifically theological understanding of the significance of death and its relationship to what has been accomplished in the work of Jesus Christ. Then we will return to an analysis of soulechtomy to determine just how much—if any—complementarity there can be. We will begin by stepping back into the Garden of Eden where all this death stuff began.

## D EATH AS THE DESTRUCTION OF EVIL[16]

The Garden of Eden story in Genesis 2-3 introduces us to the tension between knowing that we must die yet imagining life without dying. The fall into sin that subjects us to mortality was precipitated by the violation of God's command to avoid the knowledge of good and evil. Reacting to this disobedience God threw Adam and Eve out of the garden and placed the cherubim at the gate with a flaming sword, preventing the man and woman from returning. Why such a dramatic reaction on God's part? Was it due to a divine temper tantrum? Could God claim temporary insanity, claiming that it was blind rage that drove him to pull the trigger leading to the death of Adam and Eve? No, the explusion from the Garden expresses the same abiding love of God that leads to redemption and salvation.

Why then did God expel them? The answer has to do with the second special tree. Although Adam and Eve had eaten the fruit from the tree of the knowledge of good and evil, they had not yet tasted fruit from the tree of life. This is important. Had they eaten fruit from the tree of life, then they would "live forever" (Gen 3:22). What we know as the fall introduced into God's otherwise good creation such things as enmity between humans and wild beasts, the sweat of the brow by which a living must be wrested from nature, pain in childbirth, and all manner of suffering. None of us, not even God, wants the items on this list to go on forever. It is redemptive love, then, that motivates God to separate Adam and Eve from the tree of life. In its own way death becomes a gift of divine grace; it marks the point at which the consequences for sin come to an end. There is no suffering in the grave. Death is the door that God slams shut on evil and suffering within his creation.

Paul said that "the wages of sin is death" (Rom 6:23). What does this mean? We may interpret this negatively to mean that death is the appropriate penalty for disobedience.[17] We may think that just as serial killers should be punished in the electric chair or gas chamber, so also is eating forbidden fruit similarly punishable. Death is a sign of the deserved loss of divine grace. Yet, it may not be quite so simple. We may offer a long range positive interpretation as well. Might we say that in light of Genesis 3 and in light of Easter that death plays an important role in the divine plan of salvation? Is death a necessary step down the path toward resurrection to new life, to a new life immune from the sufferings of this fallen world? Perhaps we can interpret death according to either the Law or the Gospel. According to the Law it is our just desserts for acting sinfully. According to the Gospel, it is a gift that opens the door to an everlasting life free of the sufferings we undergo in this life.[18]

If this is the case, then we need to emphasize the totality of death. The Bible really believes that we humans are mortal. We really do die and cease to exist. There is no salvation by heroic soulechtomy. The understanding of sin with which we work is that sin is a cancer which eats away at the totality of human existence, leaving no organ, whether physical or spiritual, uninfected. The resulting death means true extinction.

Does this sound like modern naturalism? It should. Death, theologically understood, puts an end to all that we are and have on this side of mortality. It puts an end to all evil. It also puts an end to all that is good, mortally good. We do not possess an intrinsically good immortal soul that is somehow exempt from the disease of sin so that it can simply shed the body like a shelled oyster and go on to a higher plane of existence in the great sea of eternal ideas. And certainly there is no room for an evil immortal soul that similarly sheds the body so that its evil existence will continue on everlastingly. Whoever and whatever we are dies totally and completely. Death symbolizes that end, the termination.

## THE DEATH AND RESURRECTION OF JESUS

This applied to Jesus. He was born a mortal and died a mortal and he knew it. There are many things in common between the death of Socrates and the death of Jesus. But there are some notable differences which are relevant to our discussion here. Jesus did not live with the comfort Socrates had regarding the immortal soul and the bliss of philosophical speculation. The death of Socrates, as described by Plato, is a beautiful death. It is free of anxiety and terror. Like shedding one's coat, Socrates rids himself of his body and slips quietly off into a better existence.

This is not the case with Jesus. Death for him was the end. In Gethsemene he was "greatly distressed and troubled," saying to his disciples, "my soul is sorrowful, even to death" (Mark 14:33-34). In agony Jesus prayed "with loud cries and tears" (Heb 5:7), "his sweat became like great drops of blood falling down upon the ground" (Luke 22:44). The contrast with Socrates is vivid. Socrates took the cup of hemlock calmly and voluntarily; but Jesus, in contrast, petitioned God: "remove this cup from me" (Mark 14:36). "Jesus is afraid," writes Oscar Cullmann. "He is afraid in the face of death itself. Death for him is not something divine; it is something dreadful. . . . Here is nothing of the composure of Socrates, who met death peacefully as a friend."[19] Note how Socrates went out drinking the hemlock in sublime calm, whereas Jesus cried from the cross, "my God, my God, why have you forsaken me?" (Mark 15:34). This is not a death of liberation, but death in all its frightful horror. It is genuinely the "last enemy" of God (1 Cor 15:26).

This is by no means to picture Jesus as a coward. His courage was stalwart. Despite his petition in the Gethsemene prayer that he not have to drink the cup of death, he still concluded his prayer, "yet not what I want, but what you want" (Mark 14:36). And despite his agonizing sense of abandonment on the cross, he still uttered, "Father, into thy hands I commit my spirit" (Luke 23:46). Death is terrible, but Jesus' faith was strong.

The death Jesus died on Good Friday is the death of Adam, the death of us all. Yet, this is not the end of the story. On Easter God raised the dead Jesus to new and everlasting life. Jesus died a mortal, but God the creator of the old creation acted with the power of the new creation. God bestowed new life. And this new life is different from the old life which Jesus gave up. The new life is no longer subject to sin, suffering, or death. It is this that makes Jesus' resurrection salvific. In this regard we can contrast Jesus' Easter resurrection with the resurrection miracles such as the widow's son at Nain (Luke 7:11-17), Jairus' daughter (Mark 5:21-43), and Lazarus (John 11:38-44). In these miracles we find a resuscitation of a corpse. Three persons were raised, but they were not raised to immortality. They were simply returned to normal life. They would all have to face death again just like the rest of us. But Jesus' corpse was not merely rescusitated, not merely restored to ordinary life. No one expected Jesus to return to Nazareth to resume his duties as a carpenter. Jesus' resurrected existence had become eschatological. Jesus will not have to die again. When those who enjoyed fellowship with the risen Jesus reported what they saw, they did not say, "wow, the Nazarene is back!" Rather, they reported that they had seen "the Lord" (Luke 24:34; John 20:18).[20]

Easter opens the gate so that as we share in Jesus' resurrection we pass through to a new and everlasting life. As we turn and look backward, we see Jesus' death standing like the angel with the flaming sword at the Garden of Eden, preventing suffering and death from following us into the new creation.

## THE SPIRTUAL BODY

Let us ask about the nature of resurrected existence.[21] In introducing his great discussion of resurrection, Paul speaks of heavenly bodies *(somata epourania)* with their *doxa* —connoting glory or radiance or luster—and identifies them with the resurrection of the dead (l Cor 15:40-42). Does this indicate that he has something like the ka or astral body in mind? After all, does not occult thinking affirm that we have a star body, a body of light immune to the decay of more physical things? For the occultist, the body of glory simply sheds its physical body and goes on, maintaining continuity between this world and the next on the basis of some built-in radiance principle. There is no genuine death or destruction in alleged astral existence. An element of the person abides. Is this what Paul means? No. Glory here does not refer to a body with radiance or any other such quality. "Rather, this reflects Jewish eschatological language for the future state of the righteous."[22] For Paul there is no abiding life force at all that perdures through death. "Between 'is sown' and 'is raised' lies an infinite gulf which the body cannot span."[23] If there is resurrection, it is new creation. Therefore, the resurrected body of the New Testament must be something different from the astral body as ordinarily understood.

That there is total death and total new life is indicated by Paul's appeal to the image of the seed sown in the ground. The flower or tree that grows up looks quite different from what had been planted. However, in order to guard against any possible misinterpretation in terms of soulechtomy, he exploits the deadlike appearance of the typical seed to say, "What you sow does not come to life unless it dies" (l Cor 15:36). This analogy is delicate. Paul wishes to affirm continuity and discontinuity between the present and future realities. Resurrection is not exactly creation out of nothing, but creation of something out of something else. A dead seed is sown, but what is harvested is new life.[24]

Paul describes this eschatological harvest in terms of four complementary contrasts.

> So it is with the resurrection of the dead. What is sown perishable (corrupt, *phthora)* is raised imperishable (incorrupt, *aphtharsia).* It is sown in dishonor

> *(atimia);* it is raised in glory *(doxa).* It is sown in weakness *(astheneia);* it is raised in power *(dynameis).* It is sown a physical body *(soma psychikon);* it is raised a spiritual body *(soma pneumatikon)* (1 Cor 15:42-44).

For Jesus or for us to be raised "imperishable" is to be raised to everlasting life.[25] One's body is not resuscitated for the purpose of simply returning to one's daily toil. *Doxa,* which in reference to the heavenly bodies usually means luster, here means we are raised in honor. The power into which we will be raised, *dynamis,* is the same power by which miracles of healing are performed (l Cor 12:28).

Of these four antitheses, the most interesting is the contrast between the earthly and the spiritual bodies. Pertinent to our discussion here is the fact that Paul does not describe the earthly body as one of flesh *(soma sarkikon),* as one might have expected. Rather, Paul describes the earthly body as a "psychic" body *(soma psychikon).* Literally this is the ensouled body with which we would associate the Greek philosophical tradition.[26] For Paul, the soul dies. And as if to rub it in, Paul says it is not the *psyche* which we find in the resurrection, it is the *soma.*

The resurrected body is a "spiritual body." Other writings of Paul indicate that he probably intended to contrast this spiritual body with the fleshly body as well as the ensouled body. When depicting the tension which characterizes Christian existence, Paul frequently portrayed it in terms of a war between the flesh *(sarx)* and the spirit (Gal. 5:13-26). Flesh is the power of sin that leads to death. The spirit is its great antagonist; it is the power of creation and new creation. Both powers attempt to invade and control us. It is important to discern here that when Paul used these terms he did not intend to make metaphysical statements regarding human nature—that is, flesh and spirit are not distinct ontological components of each human being. This is not another version of the Greek body-soul dualism. Rather, flesh and spirit are proclivities or forces which contend for domination of the whole person, body and soul included. Oscar Cullmann goes a bit too far when he hypostasizes them, describing flesh and spirit as "two transcendent Powers" which can enter us from without. But he is correct in saying that "neither is given with human existence as such."[27] With this background, we can see why Paul might say, "flesh and blood cannot inherit the kingdom of God" (1 Cor 15:50).

Nevertheless, the concept of flesh as that which corrupts cannot be separated from its milder designation of the physical body which simply decays, and both meanings seem to be present in 1 Corinthians 15. Hence, there is overlap between flesh *(sarx)* and body *(soma),* although some scholars such as Cullmann try to drive a wedge between them. That there is room for some interchangeability is evidenced by the writings of the Greek fathers such as Justin Martyr, who could use the phrase "resurrection of the flesh" and declare that because flesh was created by God it must be deemed valuable by God.[28] Early versions of the Apostles' Creed rendered part of the third article as "I believe in the resurrection of the flesh." This upset Cullmann, who complained that this is "not biblical". Instead of "flesh" it should read "body," he said. Well, contra Cullmann, it appears quite biblical. This is clear from Luke 24:39, especially as interpreted by Augustine who affirms that even in our resurrected spiritual bodies the term 'flesh' may apply just as it did to the post-Easter Jesus.[29] Perhaps Cullmann's problem is that he wanted to deal with the issue strictly as a matter of word choice without looking at the conceptuality being conveyed. Paul and Luke paid less attention to vocabulary choice than Cullmann would approve of.

One attempt to get at Paul's underlying conceptuality here is to think of the *soma* as the form which can exist with one or another substance, either flesh *(sarx)* or spirit *(pneuma* or *doxa).* Following the earlier work of Lietzmann, Hans Conzelmann advocated this form-substance theory and contended that there is no such thing as a *soma* all by itself. *Soma* always exists in a specific mode of being, either as *sarx* or as *doxa.* The form is always related to its concrete mode of being. It is always either heavenly or earthly. It does not constitute the individual human being as such. It exists on its own only as an abstract concept.[30] Although Conzelmann helps us here, this theory is not careful to show just how his idea takes account of the fact that Paul's contrast is actually between a psychic body and a spiritual body, not between a fleshly and a glorified body.

It seems to me that the spirit is not simply one substance interchangeable with others. The spirit is the power of God whereby reality itself is determined. The *soma pneumatikon* is the resurrected body which is determined by the Holy Spirit. It is the reality which we will be, because God will have created us—re-created us—in this form. And because it is an eschatological reality belonging to the new creation, and because we still live amidst the old creation, we cannot expect to apprehend clearly just what this means. Now we can only look through a mirror dimly, and Christ is that mirror reflecting the light of future glory amidst our present darkness. What we can say with confidence is that there will be a resurrection of the human self.[31] What we cannot say at this point is precisely what that resurrected mode of existence will look like.

To my reading Paul seems to be thinking this out for the first time in his dialogue with the Corinthians.[32] He is not simply reiterating an already existing set of ideas that previously belonged to the Jews, the Gnostics, the Corinthians, or any other group about which we know. He is not proposing one theory of immortality among others. Paul here is struggling to explicate the Gospel, to apply what he knows about the resurrection of Jesus to our promised resurrection. Paul has already confronted the Gospel and is now trying to represent it to an audience which probably believes the material body is inimical to the spirit. The readers of his letter in Corinth, probably heavily influenced by the Greek intellectual tradition, have misunderstood what the significance of the Gospel is for human mortality and eternal life. We today do not know exactly how Paul thought of the Gospel before explicating it to the Corinthians, so for us this letter serves as a primary stage of thinking through the implications of a Gospel that begins with the Easter announcement, "he is risen."

The final point I wish to make in this treatment is that neither the resurrection of Jesus nor your or my individual resurrections stand, alone. They play roles in a much larger drama, namely, the consummation of God's redemptive work for the whole of the cosmos. Resurrection and eschatology belong together. Before turning to the tie between the resurrection body and the cosmic scope of the new creation, however, we need to pause to ask about the interim state.

## THE INTERIM STATE

A question which theologians have been compelled to ask in every generation since the close of New Testament times down to the present is, What happens to us between the time of our death and the time of Christ's return in triumph? This question is already asked by the Thessalonians. In responding, Paul speaks of the dead as "asleep," but tells us not to worry. Hope does not die with us. In fact, those who are alive at the advent of the eschaton will not precede those already in their graves. "The dead in Christ will rise first" (1 Thess 4:16). But, we might still ask, what happens to the dead prior to that resurrection?

There are different theories. Jerome believed that dead matryrs cannot be kept "shut up in a coffin," and if the devil and demons can wander the streets; so can the souls of these holy ones.[33] Augustine certainly rejected the idea that the spirits of the dead live on to influence actively the course of normal events.[34] He said that during the interim between one's individual death and the cosmic consummation "the soul dwells in a hidden retreat, where it enjoys rest or suffers affliction in just proportion to the merit it has earned by the life which it led on earth."[35] Thomas Aquinas went further, saying that "as soon as the soul is set free from the body it is either plunged into hell or soars to heaven."[36] Even though both Augustine and Thomas insisted that resurrection consists in the transformation of our bodies which will occur at the consummate end, they were satisfied that in the meantime our souls are capable of leaving the body and going to a place where they will be occupied with either pain or pleasure. Calvin objected here. He objected not to the idea of a disembodied soul, which he approved, but to the excessive speculation of these earlier theories. He contended that "it is neither lawful nor expedient to inquire too curiously concerning the soul's intermediate state."[37] He failed to follow his own advice, however, and proceeded to argue that during the interim state the faithful exist in the presence of Christ, while the reprobate suffer the torments they deserve. Calvin differed from Thomas only in that he did not specifically locate these interim activities in heaven or hell. In our own time Karl Rahner stated unequivocally that the doctrine of the immortality of the soul and the interim state of disembodiment are not mere speculations but full articles of Catholic faith.[38]

Oscar Cullmann, who expressed more than a little distaste for the Greek notion of a disembodied soul, tolerated none of this. He followed Calvin in reiterating the ban against too much speculation regarding the interim state. And like Calvin he spoke of the faithful as enjoying a "special nearness to God" even though they are "still in time" while fast asleep.[39] Such an interim of sleep should not bother us, he argued, because having died in the faith we will continue to exist within the grasp of the Holy Spirit until raised. Though asleep, we are not abandoned. Behind Cullmann is a long tradition of invoking the image of Abraham's bosom in Jesus' parable of Dives and Lazarus, according to which the faithful dead lie restfully in the bosom of Christ until awakened by the trumpet blast on the last day. They will not experience the lapse of time during their nap, and when they awaken on the last day it will seem like just a moment beyond their own death.

The Cullmann position has the virtue of being theologically consistent. Thomas Aquinas' position, in contrast, is less consistent. Thomas worked strenuously to defend the doctrine of the resurrection of the body, and in so doing he appealed to Aristotle's allegedly convincing argument that the soul cannot exist separated from its body.[40] Once he has convinced the reader with Aristotle's help of the impossibility of a disembodied soul, he then proceeds with his own theological surgery to sever the soul from the body at the moment of death and to send it off temporarily to heaven, hell, limbo, or purgatory. In short, Thomas wants both immortality of the soul and resurrection of the dead, and the concept of the interim state permits him to have them in sequence. The only price is inconsistency. Cullmann avoids the inconsistency because he is willing to stick with the implications to be drawn from understanding just how seriously Paul meant it when he said that "what you sow does not come to life unless it dies" (1 Cor 15:36) What this means for us at this point in time is that the naturalists are right: when you're dead, you're dead!

But what about widespread belief systems that claim existence for disembodied souls of those who are dead? What about those we discussed earlier who claim to have had an out-of-the-body experience? Before proceeding further down the path which our theological logic would like to direct us, let us pause to observe and assess some of these potential claims to the contrary. It is not necessarily helpful to march lockstep down the road of doctrinal reasoning without looking occasionally from side to side at common human experience. If we do, it will not be long before we will look back and wonder why no one is following us. In the case of what we have been calling the 'interim' and what other people normally think of as the time 'after death.' there are some amazing things to consider. Most of the peoples of the world do not accept the naturalist position that when you're dead you're simply dead. It is important to know this if for no other reason than our pastoral ministry will be ineffective if we do not take this into account. And what is important for our study here is that we are responsible for explicating our theology in light of this.

The particular question we are concerned with is, During the interim state do disembodied spirits exist and do they have social intercourse with those of us who are still alive? We have already noted that the Akamba—and this is true for both Christian and non-Christian Akamba alike—see the Aimu when they appear. They claim that the Aimu appear less often now than they did before Europeans arrived, but the appearances have by no means ceased altogether. We have also discussed OBEs, where people claim to be able to perceive what is going on in the physical world even if they are unable to affect it themselves while in their disembodied state.

Augustine wrestled with this issue while formulating his own position. He told of the case of a man named Curma in the town of Tullium, who had the equivalent of an OBE while he lay "all but dead for several days." While engaged in astral-like travel he met up with other previously deceased souls as well as living people in geographically removed locations. He also approached the gates of paradise, but there he was told that he should return to his earthly body and become baptized. Augustine was skeptical about Curma's account, but he wished to examine it with care rather than dismiss it out of hand. He wished to handle with equal gingerness the more widespread claims that dead people have at times either in dreams or in other ways appeared to their living descendents and communicated astonishing information. Then he raised the question, Is there really social intercourse taking place between disembodied souls and those of us who still live corporeally? Augustine answered negatively. But rather than dismiss these anecdotal reports, he speculated that perhaps these appearances of the dead are due to the work of God-directed angels who wish to communicate with us mortals.[41] Rahner asked the same question and, while affirming that the dead still live and denying that we can communicate with them, said that our posture should be one in which we "open our hearts to the silent calm of God himself, in which they live."[42]

The problem which we face is that our evangelical explication of Paul's discussion of resurrection of the body seems either to ignore or preclude the possibility of supraphysical personal existence after death. Yet, there exist many philosophies of soulechtomy, and there are widespread claims that people have experienced communication from just such disembodied beings. Have we come to a point of showdown where the Christian view is either right or wrong? Or is there any hope of merging horizons to form a larger more comprehensive integration of views?

## PARA-ESCHATOLOGY

In working our way through this problem, two resources can aid us: first, the observation that the Bible in general gives no sign of conflict between belief in disembodied spirits and eschatology; second, John Hick's helpful concept of pareschatology for organizing our thoughts.

Contact with the spirits of the dead through witchcraft is simply assumed to be possible when the frustrated Saul asks the medium at Endor to raise the dead Samuel so he can consult with him (l Sam 28), although the Old Testament in general outlaws necromancy and divination (Exod 22:18; 1 Sam 15:23; 28:3; Micah 5:12). The New Testament seems to assume the existence of numerous supranatural beings such as cosmic rulers, *archontes* (l Cor 2:6, 8; Eph 2:2), powers, *dynameis* (Rom 8:38; 1 Peter 3:22), authorities, *exousiai* (Eph 3:10; Col 1:16; 2:15), elemental spirits, *stoicheia* (Gal 4:3,9; Col 2:8,20), along with various and sundry demons and unclean spirits (Matt 9:33; Mark 1:23, 27, 34; 3:11; 1 Cor 10:20f) and even Satan himself (Matt 4:1-11; Rom 16:20; 1 Cor 5:5). Then, of course, there are the angels, whom we will be like in the resurrection (Matt 22:30). There may be a difference between some supraphysical beings and the souls of the deceased however. Demons and unclean spirits, for example, can enter a person and establish possession. In Jesus' parable of Dives and Lazarus, in contrast, it appears that dead people are not permitted to leave their abode to return and influence the course of ordinary events (Luke 16:26). In short, there is no shortage of background presence of supraphysical beings in scripture. Had there been an intrinsic antipathy between belief in disembodied spirits and the eschatological vision one would expect that it would have surfaced already within the New Testament. But such a tension does not seem to exist.

Thus we might consider the merits of the concept of pareschatology introduced by John Hick. Hick begins by affirming that the Christian doctrine of resurrection refers to the final or ultimate state of human existence. It does not refer to what happens immediately upon death. This opens the door to speculation regarding the interim state. Hick considers the various possibilities we have been discussing here and finds no intrinsic conflict between disembodied existence immediately after death and a final eschatology of the Christian type. Our discussion of what happens in between he dubs "pareschatology." The term appears to prefix 'eschatology' with the preposition 'para,' mening 'along side of.' Whereas eschatology deals with 'last things,' pareschatology permits us to deal with the 'next-to-last things.'[43] As with 'parapsychology' and 'paranormal' we now have a category for dealing with relevant material which hitherto has fallen outside the confines of the discipline.

This category is helpful. The essential commitment of Christian theology is to the explication of the concept of resurrection as it is associated with ultimate destruction and new creation. What the category of pareschatology does is leave open—theologically speaking—considerable room for debate regarding the experience of death and what happens immediately thereafter.

It leaves it open to scientific reflection and discussion, however, not to religious dogma. By this I mean we should attend honestly and forthrightly—as a scientist would attend to an experiment—to the evidence. This is not the same thing as accepting the beliefs of occultists or Tibetan Buddhists as true on the basis of their traditional authority. Nor is it the same thing as accepting the assertions of modern naturalism, because this "ism" is really a form of unfounded ideology which is attached to science but not essential to science. If by 'science' we refer to an open-minded appraisal of possible explanations for experience, then this should be our approach in this matter. If the evidence is strong enough to make the naturalist case that when a person dies he or she remains dead, then we will have to accept it. If, on the other hand, reports of life-after-life experiences prove to be unassailable, then we will have to assess this theologically. At present, the jury is still out.

In the event that the jury returns with a convincing verdict in behalf of some form of soulechtomy, we need to ask what this could mean? The preliminary answer I suggest is that whatever the make-up of this disembodied post-mortem existence, it still belongs to this order of creation. It belongs to the old aeon. It is still subject to further destruction and new creation. If death does not occur when the body dies, it still will. Whenever claims are made that the nonphysical realm to which the disembodied self goes looks like life on this side—that the living-dead continue their anxieties over the welfare of their descendents, or that in this new realm we find punishments for previous sins and rewards for virtue—then we know that things have not changed much. Postmortem experience is in too much continuity with premortem experience. Death has not yet done its job of annihilating the curse of evil. In other words, should the evidence compel us to affirm the existence of the living-dead now, then we must still anticipate that the living-dead like the rest of us will be subject to destruction at a later time. The Akamba provide us with an example of how we might conceive of soulechtomy occuring at the point of physical death, but annihilation occurring later. Thus, the thought is not without some precedent.

One of the difficult tasks conceptually is to coordinate the great divergence of opinions regarding what happens to the self once it is disengaged from the body at death. Does it hang around as a ghost so that we can communicate with it through a medium? Does it proceed gnostic style up the planes of existence toward some sort of perfection? Does it go immediately to a place of happiness or torment, as Plato or Thomas would suggest? Does it become reincarnated? These are open questions which we will simply leave open at this point. What needs to be affirmed here is that our theological method can and should be open to participating in a discussion of such matters.

## THE COMING NEW CREATION

Let us turn to our final point and central thesis: human destiny is inseparable from cosmic destiny. One element in common among the four theories of immortality (or nonimmortality in the case of naturalism) as well as interim state speculations is that they all deal with the question of human destiny in partial isolation from that of cosmic destiny. One's own soul may exercise its philosophical wings and fly to heaven and there enjoy the beatific vision, or through strenuous meditative effort one might attain enlightenment and realize oneness with Brahman, but the affairs of this mundane world will simply go on as a matter of course without these now departed human souls. Not so with the Christian vision. What happens to us depends on what happens to the cosmos. The resurrection to a spiritual body can only occur at the advent of the eschaton. If there is no cosmic transformation, then there is no resurrection, and if there is no resurrection then our faith is in vain and we of all people are most to be pitied (1 Cor15:14,19).

Resurrection is indispensably tied to the eschatological parousia—the second coming of Christ. Paul suggests an order to things. First comes Christ, the first fruits (1 Cor 15:23). This probably refers to Easter. Then at his coming "the dead in Christ will rise first, then we who are alive" (1 Thess 4:16-17). He "will transform the body of our humiliation that it may be conformed to the body of his glory" (Phil 3:21; see Rom 8:29). "Then comes the end, when he hands over the kingdom to God the Father, after he has destroyed every ruler and every authority and power. . . . The last enemy to be destroyed is death" (1 Cor 15:24, 26).

The key to understanding the resurrected body is placing it within the broader horizon of God's promised new creation. As the creation is transformed, so are we. Salvation is creation wide, our bodies included. This leads Gordon Fee to comment:

> The transformed body, therefore, is not composed of 'spirit'; it is a body adapted to the eschatological existence that is under the ultimate domination of the Spirit. Thus for Paul, to be truly pneumatikos is to bear the likeness of Christ (v.49) in a transformed body, fitted for the new age.[44]

Augustine's works provide us with a logical direction for drawing out implications of these New Testament commitments. In the final sections of his *City of God*, Augustine asked whether everybody will be raised. Yes, he said, and the resurrection will even include aborted infants. Will we get our own bodies back or will we be issued new ones? He said that the actual physical elements which composed the first body will be retrieved for the new one. What condition will our physical bodies be in? Every blemish and infirmity will be removed. How old will we be? The age at which we die? No. We will be at our healthiest mature age. This Augustine guessed is about thirty, about the final age of Jesus.[45] Will some of us be bigger and stronger than others? No, we will all have the same stature. Will there be two sexes in heaven? Yes, but "we shall enjoy one another's beauty without any lust."[46] Will we remember our past tragedies and sufferings? Yes, we will remember them intellectually, but we will no longer feel the pain.

Augustine did not have apodictic knowledge. He was speculating. But, then, that is what theologians are supposed to do. On the basis of the witness of scripture to the Gospel we try to construct reasonable answers to questions which may not have been directly posed and answered within the pages of the Bible. What Augustine said is a carefully thought out explication of the New Testament. His thoughts regarding the great transformation have been quite widely accepted in subsequent centuries. This is a mysterious area, of course, and many questions almost defy a coherent answer.

## CONCLUSION

Despite the mystery, the Christian faith has medicine appropriate to humanity's two diseases: life that is always fatal and hope that is never curable. The latter is medicine for the former. Yet, his hope is not a generic drug for a vague expectation that there might be more beyond the grave. Rather, it is prescription for hope based upon God's promise for the transformation of creation, for the new world to come into which the godly in the present world will be resurrected for everlasting life.

## NOTES

1. George H. Gallup, Jr., and Robert Bezilla, *The Religious Life of Young Americans* (Princeton: The George H. Gallup International Institute, 1992), 22-23.
2. Andrew Greeley, *Death and Beyond* (Chicago: Thomas More Press, 1976), 49.
3. Jack London, *John Barlycorn* (New York: Signet, 1990), 218-219.
4. Bertrand Russell, "A Free Man's Worship," *Mysticism and Logic* (New York: Doubleday, 1957), 44.
5. Plato, *Phaedo*, 66.
6. Plato, *Gorgias*, 523.
7. Plato, *Phaedrus*, 249-250; *Republic*, X:614-621.

8. Cited by Karl Rahner, ed., *The Teaching of the Catholic Church As Contained in her Documents* (Staten Island, NY: Alba House, 1966), 124.

9. John P. Newport, *Life's Ultimate Questions* (Waco, TX: Word, 1989), 277.

10. Three broad paths or *margas* make up the complex history of Hinduism: the path of ritual action *(karma marga);* knowledge *(jnana marga);* and devotion *(bhakti marga).* The second, the path of knowledge, most emphasizes the ultimate identlty of the self *(atman)* with the All *(Brahman).* See Thomas J. Hopkins, "Hindu Views of Death and Afterlife," in *Death and Afterlife: Perspectives of World Religions,* Hiroshi Obayashi, volume editor, Number 33 of *Contributions to the Study of Religion,* Henry Warner Bowden, series editor (New York: Greenwood Press, 1992), 143-156.

11. Some nondualist theists within Hinduism claim to stop short of oblivion. "Moksha for the nondualist (advaitin) does not mean that the self merges into Brahman as a river merges into the sea, but that the self realizes itself as it eternally exists; i.e., in perfect identity with the Absolute. Hence liberation is not a state to be newly attained, but is the very nature of the Self become conscious of its identity with the All-One." Mariasusai Dhavamony, "Death and Immortality in Hinduism," in *Death and Immortality in the Religions of the World,* Paul and Linda Badham, editors (New York: Paragon House, 1987), 106

12. In another work I attempt to show that the Western interest in reincarnation as we find it in New Age spirituality is due to the conflation of the notion of karma with that of trauma in psychotherapy and its use in so-called reincarnation therapy. See Ted Peters, *The Cosmic Self: A Penetrating Look at Today's New Age Movements* (San Francisco: Harper, 1991), 71-74.

13. John S. Mbiti, *New Testament Eschatology in an African Background* (Oxford: Oxford University Press, 1971), 139.

14. Raymond A. Moody, *Life after Life* (Atlanta: Mockingbird Books, 1975 and New York: Bantam, 1977), 48; see *Reflections on Life after Life* (New York: Bantam & Mockingbird, 1977) and Elizabeth Kübler-Ross, *Death, the Final Stage of Growth* (New York: Macmillan, 1975). Ordinarily interpreters of NDEs speak modestly about subjective survival beyond physical death. On a much more grand scale, however, Kenneth Ring connects NDEs with UFO experiences, sees both as initiation rites into a cosmic reality, and then projects a near eschatological vision of a new level of evolutionary development. He says "the world of the dead and the world of the living are ones between which there may eventually no longer be a sharp distinction. Veils will be lifted from the face of the nonphysical, and we ourselves will become diaphanous beings, with bodies of light." Kenneth Ring, *The Omega Project: Near Death Experiences, UFO Encounters, and Mind at Large,* (New York: William Morrow, 1992), 239.

15. John Newport summarizes critical assessments of NDOBE claims such as attempts to explain them physiologically as hallucinations created by the brain due to the trauma of approaching death. *Life's Ultimate Questions,* 289. Questions of authenticity lead to controversy. Author Betty Malz published a book, *My Glimpses of Eternity* (Grand Rapids: Zondervan, Chosen Books, 1977) which has sold nearly a million copies, describing her alleged 1959 death of 28 minutes on a hospital operating table, her OBE, plus her trip to heaven and back. The doctors involved—H. Clark Boyd, Henry Bopp, James Bopp—reported to *Christianity Today* investigator Lorna Dueck, however, that Betty Malz nee Upchurch did not die as she claimed. They describe what she writes as "almost a complete fabrication" and say "this didn't happen." Her editor defends her by saying that, whether actually dead or not, Betty Malz has "a marvelous ministry." Ken Sidey, "Doctors Dispute Best-Selling Author's Back-to-Life Story," Christianity Today, 35 (July 22, 1991): 40-42.

16. This expands a discussion begun in my book, *GOD—the World's Future: Systematic Theology for a Postmodem Era* (Minneapolis: Fortress, 1992), 310-316.

17. Over against the neo-orthodox theologians for whom death belongs naturally to human finitude, evangelical theologians hold that human death is the result of human sin. John Newport writes, "humans were created with contingent or conditional immortality. They could have lived forever, but it was not certain that they would. Upon sinning, they lost this status." *Life's Ultimate Questions,* 296.

18. By adding this role of death in the plan of salvation I move a bit beyond the interpretation of John Newport who writes, "we must experience physical death simply because it has become one of the conditions of human existence." *Life's Ultimate Questions,* 296.

19. Oscar Cullmann, "Immortality of the Soul or Resurrection of the Dead?" in *Inmortality and Resurrection*, ed. by Krister Stendahl (New York: Macmillan, 1965), 14-15.

20. "The post-resurrectional confession is not simply 'We have seen Jesus' but 'We have seen the Lord' (John 20:18; 25; 21:7; Luke 24:34). Since 'Lord' is a christological evaluation of Jesus, the evangelists are teliing us that the witnesses enjoyed not only the *sight* of Jesus but also and even primarily *insight*." Raymond E. Brown, *Virginal Conception and Bodily Resurrection of Jesus* (New York: Paulist, 1973), 112 (italics in original).

21. I am particularly indebted to Patricia Codron, my research assistant, for her aid in thinking through the issues associated vith the spiritual body.

22. Gordon D. Fee, *The First Epistle to the Corinthians*, in *The New International Commentary on the New Testament*, F. F. Bruce, general editor (Grand Rapids: Eerdmans, 1987), 785.

23. Roy A. Harrisville, *I Corinthians* in *Augsburg Commentary on the New Testament* (Minneapolis: Augsburg, 1987), 276.

24. Roy Harrisville notes that Paul's seed analogy emphasizes the discontinuity between death and resurrection. "But in neither instance is the move from agronomy to Christian existence, but exactly the reverse. The analogy is warped to what it serves, and here it is made to fit the assertion of discontinuity, the contention that there is no resurrection unless 'from the dead'. What that warping and twisting of the figure to serve its topic means is that there is, after all, no analogy in nature to the activity of God envisioned here, but only a refraction; no possibility of inferring the 'wisdom of God' from what can be observed in the world." *I Corinthians*, 274-275.

25. My assumption is that the Easter body of Jesus is the prototype of the eschatological bodies of the faithful. John Newport, however, is reluctant to make the equation. He drives a wedge between the body of Jesus immediately after Easter and Jesus' ascended reality which comes later. "Our resurrection body will be like Jesus' present body, not necessarily like the body he had between his resurrection and ascension. We will not have those characteristics of Jesus' postresurrection earthly body which appear inconsistent with our resurrection bodies, which the apostle Paul calls 'spiritual bodies' (1 Cor 15:44). The characteristics we will need will not necessarily include physical tangibility and the need to eat." *Life's Ultimate Questions*, 305-306. I gather this means that in heaven there will be no Big Mac Attacks.

26. "The idea that the soul is naturally immortal, deathless by definition, is at home in much of Greek thought but not in the New Testament. . . . The New Testament has a unique idea of immortality: The whole person will become immortal by resurrection." Leander E. Keck, "Death and Afterlife in the New Testament," *Death and Afterlife*, 84. This seems to be the consensus. Thomas Deidun sees Paul as refuting a presupposed dualism of spirit and body among the Corinthians and proposing in contrast to see the resurrection and transformation of the body as the completion of God's work of salvation. "The *soma* is to be eschatologically changed by God's *power*. It will become *soma pneumatikon*. Yet it remains *soma*—the substantial point of *continuity* between now and then." Deidun proceeds to argue that this affirmation of the body in resurrection has an impact on sexual morality, because "the mutual love of sexual union is capable of eschatological transformation without losing its deepest significance." "Beyond Dualisms: Paul on Sex, Sarx, and Soma," *The* Way, 28:3 (July 1988): 203. Brendan Byrne similarly argues that affirmation of bodily resurrection has an impact on morality: "Paul derives from the heart of the gospel an eschatology of resurrection that endows bodily life with lasting moral value." "Eschatologies of Resurrection and Destruction: The Ethical Significance of Paul's Dispute with the Corinthians," *The Downside Review*, 104 (October 1986): 295.

27. Cullmann, 25. Walter Wink would tend to agree with Cullmann in dubbing sarx a transcendent power. The transcendent power in Wink's case has to do with fallen social-psychological structures, not necessarily a supernatural power. "Life lived 'according to the flesh' *(kata sarka)* denotes the self externalized and subjugated to the opinions of others. It is the self socialized into a world of inauthentic values, values that lead it away from its own centeredness in God. . . . 'Fleshly' or 'carnal' refers to a life that has abandoned the transcendent and become fixated on personal satisfactions. . . . The best paraphrase I can render for *kata sarka* is 'dominated existence' . . ." *Engaging the Powers* (Minneapolis: Fortress, 1992), 62-63.

28. Justin, *On the Resurrection*, II and VII in ANF, I:194 and 297.

29. Augustine, *Enchiridion*, Chapter 91 in NFNF, 1st: 266.

30. Hans Conzelmann, *I Corinthians* (Philadelphia: Fortress, 1978), 282.

31. Resurrection will include a dialectic between transformation and continuity. Our personal identity cannot be obliterated completely; otherwise transformation would consist of simple destruction. Something subjective and identifiable must continue. Newport reminds us that this continuity is a gift of divine grace, however, not a natural propensity. "Our personal identity is not a predication we can make based on our creaturely nature. Rather, it is predicated upon the initiative of God, who addresses us and upholds us as the persons we are before him and with each other." *Life's Ultimate Questions*, 303.

32. A panoramic view of the Pauline writings shows no special apologetic preoccupation in the presentation of the resurrection of Jesus. However, on the relatively few occasions when the question came up, Paul did have to come to grips with the problem of the risen body and with the law of conformity to Christ in all aspects of his life and destiny." Giuseppe Ghiberti, "Contemporary Discussion of the Resurrection of Jesus," in *Problems and Perspectives of Fundamental Theology*, edited by René Latourelle and Gerald O'Collins, translated by Matthew J. O'Connell (New York: Paulist, 1982), 231.

33. Jerome, *Against Vigilantius*, vi.

34. Augustine, *On Care to be had for the Dead*, 12,18.

35. Augustine, *Enchiridion*, 109.

36. Thomas Aquinas, *Summa Theologia*, III:Q,69:A,2.

37. John Calvin, *Institutes of the Christian Religion*, III:6.

38. Karl Rahner, *On the Theology of Death* (New York: Crossroad, 1973), 16; and "The Life of the Dead" in *Theological Investigations* (21 Volumes: New York: Crossroad, 1961-1988), IV:352.

39. Cullmann, "Immortality of the Soul or Resurrection of the Dead?" 39. A similar position is taken by Paul Althaus, *Die Letzten Dinge* (Gutersloh: Bertelsmann, 8th ed., 1961), 155-157.

40. Thomas Aquinas, *Summa Theologia*, III:Q,75:A,l; Aristotle, *On the Soul*, II:2 (414a,12).

41. Augustine, *On Care to be had for the Dead*, 12-15.

42. Rahner "The Life of the Dead," 353-354.

43. John Hick, *Death and Eternal Life* (New York: Harper, 1976), 22.

44. Fee, *First Epistle to the Corinthians*, 786. Ben F. Meyer asks if corporeal participation in the final salvation is ruled out. Then he answers, "No; the issue is not 'body versus spirit' but body in the present age—be it the flesh and blood of the living or the decayed body of the dead—versus body transfigured and immortal in the reign of God." "Did Paul's View of the Resurrection of the Dead Undergo Development?" *Theological Studies*, 47:3 (Summer 1986): 381.

45. Augustine, *City of God*, XXII:15.

46. Augustine, *City of God*, XXII:24.

# RESURRECTION AND ETHICS IN CHRYSOSTOM

STANLEY SAMUEL HARAKAS

It is my intention in this paper to examine the relationship of the resurrection of Jesus Christ, the resurrection of human beings, and the moral life in the writings of St. John Chrysostom, the fourth century exegete, preacher, and moralist of the Christian Church. I approach this material as an Eastern Orthodox theologian in a tradition that counts Chrysostom as one of the most significant guides to understanding the scriptures and the tradition of the Church and explicating its normative meaning and practical significance. Chrysostom's writings are closely related to the sphere of fourth century Cappadocian theology which serves as the theological anchor of Eastern Orthodox Christianity. So to discuss Chrysostom's approach to any question is at once to be examining critical foundational sources of Eastern Orthodox Christianity.

Before approaching the writings of Chrysostom that express his approach to the topic of resurrection and ethics, however, in a most brief and inadequate way I will address two issues in the current discussion on the resurrection that bear directly on Chrysostom's approach to ethics. The first is concerned with the current discussion on the historicity of the resurrection of Christ on the one hand and the approach of Eastern Christendom to it. The second is the issue of the place of the resurrection of Christ as a source for Christian ethics.

## THE HISTORICITY OF THE RESURRECTION

In his study *Biblical Exegesis & Church Doctrine,*[1] the well known Roman Catholic biblical scholar Raymond E. Brown discusses the historical-critical approach to the scriptures. He is in the mainstream of most contemporary historical and critical approaches to the scriptures. Insisting that the historical-critical approach is a valid and necessary way of approaching the biblical texts, on the one hand, he marks out for himself a mediating position between those whom he calls the "ultraconservatives" who reject all historical study of the sacred texts and the "liberals" who magnify the importance of the historical-critical approach so that it seems to displace all other approaches and perspectives.

He presents what he would hold is a "balanced view" in two respects. He both affirms the importance and value of the historical-critical approach, but does not accord it an absolute position in determining the doctrine of the Church.

> No other method has been devised that will answer purely historical questions better; and we are on dangerous ground when we decide that historical answers (even when they are disturbing) are irrelevant or must be changed precisely because they upset our outlook. Once again, I am not saying that historical answers need tyrannize our views so that our views of present realities are incorrect because they do not agree with past views of reality. I am insisting that our views will be stronger and more persuasive if we have not sought to bend the past to suit us, but have entered into dialogue with past contributions to the total picture.[2]

Brown's *via media* represents the majority of biblical scholars in the Roman Catholic tradition; I believe that it is also reflected among a large number of Protestant scholars, as well. Yet, even this moderate approach to the biblical resurrection accounts presents them as beyond the pale of historicity. According to C. F. D. Moule in his introduction to an important collection of German essays on the resurrection, the accounts are based on statements which "cannot now be taken literally."[3]

As a nonspecialist and an Orthodox theologian who is aware of the need for a historical understanding of the texts, I have long sensed an unease with the way the historical-critical approach is handled by different practitioners of the art. Moule completed the phrase quoted above in the following manner:

> . . . scholars evidently see in the statement that the tomb was empty, even if it cannot now be taken literally, at least a way of affirming that the resurrection of Jesus was not independent of or detached from time-space events.[4]

I believe we have come to the point of recognizing that under such an idea of the "historicity" of events it is almost impossible to identify anything that is described in the scriptures as historic in the strictest sense. Yet, in the face of the claimed objectivity of the historical-critical method, we live at a time when the quantum theories of physics have gone a long way in dispelling any claims to the "objectivity" of observation in an absolute sense.

I also sense unease over the working judgments of historians as to what can or cannot be assumed as possible in the determination of what is genuinely historical. Thus, in the volume edited by Moule, one sees a radically different ordering of criteria and equally radically different conclusions among the participants of the debate (Bultmann, Barth, Marxen, and Pannenberg). The final chapter by Hans-Georg Geyer illustrates this weakness very clearly. Especially useful is his summary of the survey on pp. 132-135.

In his work, Raymond Brown introduced the concept of Jesus' "non-corruptive" resurrection. By this the resurrection of Jesus is perceived as a forerunner of the resurrection of the dead by the subsequent tradition of the Church and understood as a valid "drawing out" from an earlier perception (though not strictly historical) of the resurrection of Christ.[5]

Consequently, I continue to have persistent questions regarding aspects of this approach while still affirming the necessity for historical research in the texts. First, it must be observed that the literary witnesses to the tradition are clearly subsequent to the beginnings of the tradition itself. The Eastern Christian approach to the scriptures sees them as part of the living and experienced revelatory act rather than as a unique source that stands alone. The scriptures, Orthodox theology holds, are a part of the tradition of revelation, though a part that is uniquely privileged. I have sought to describe this position in an article on the concept of "tradition" in a recent issue of *The Christian Scholar*.[6]

Second, there seems to be a rationalist reductionism to varying emphases in the tradition that causes complementary views to be seen as contradictory. A less reductionist and rationalistic, but more "aesthetic-image" approach would provide a wholistic framework for understanding and working with the tradition of the resurrection of Jesus Christ.

Third, this approach clearly flies in the face of the self-identity of the Christian community at it earliest stages, as expressed by Paul's judgment on the centrality and fundamental importance of the very concept of resurrection for the Christian faith in 1 Cor 15.

On the other hand, were the historical critical method to "prove" the historicity of the resurrection of Jesus Christ, it would present the Church with another, even more problematic issue. Faith in Christ's redemptive work would then become an issue of intellectual coercion. An historically proven resurrection would require belief in the resurrection of Christ, not as an act of freely chosen faith, but as a matter of intelligence. Rejection of the saving and redeeming work of Christ would not be unbelief, but an act of stupidity. In the larger context of the biblical call to faith, perhaps it is better that the historical method does not serve to verify the historicity of the resurrection of Jesus Christ!

Nevertheless, the early Church's beliefs in the factuality and the ultimate significance of the resurrection of Jesus Christ are expressed by the patristic tradition and remain as fundamental and essential dimensions of the life and worship of early Christianity and Eastern Christianity today. In the case of the relationship of the resurrection of Christ, the resurrection of believers and non-believers alike, and the impact of the resurrection on ethical reflection and norms, we observe strong affirmations of their interrelatedness both in the exegetical and other works of St. John Chrysostom and in the theology, worship and ethical teaching in the Eastern Orthodox tradition.

Among contemporary Eastern Orthodox scholars, we cite two contemporary scripture scholars for whom the resurrection of Christ is the linchpin of Orthodox Christian theology, but who also deal with it as a real event, experienced by the prescriptural Church, and witnessed to not only in scripture, but in the contemporaneous experience of the apostolic tradition.

Old Testament scholar Paul Tarazi, in exegeting the message of 1 Corinthians 15 in the context of a discussion of preaching, expresses a belief both in the historicity and the significance of the resurrection.

> The resurrection of Jesus, then, is so central to the *kerygma*, that it actually reflects the whole of the proclamation. The preacher should, therefore, be aware that, although the resurrection took place at the tomb near Jerusalem, both its presence and its effects cannot be limited to the place.
>
> Saint Matthew tells us that the apostles experienced it in Galilee (Matt 28:10,16-20) while Saint Luke reports in the Book of Acts that it encountered Saul at the gates of Damascus (Acts 9.1-19/22.5-16/26:9-18).
>
> In other words, it is not sufficient merely to refer to the resurrection. It is the preacher's duty to change his hearers with the reality of the resurrection here and now.[7]

Similarly, New Testament scholar Theodore Stylianopoulos in the same preaching context affirms that the reality of the resurrection is at the heart of the preaching of the early Church. The resurrection of Christ influenced every aspect of the prescriptural and subsequent experience of the Church to which the New Testament scriptures in numerous and varied ways attest. As a New Testament scholar, Stylianopoulos is able to distinguish varied emphases between the Matthean and the Pauline understandings of the resurrection, but he does not find these to be properly understood as contradictory. His is a wholistic approach that finds in these two approaches complementarity and not contradiction. Thus, Stylianopoulos affirms

> . . . despite the fact that in eariest times (such as in Paul's mission) the heart of the *kerygma* was the death and resurrection of Jesus, the total witness of the early Church includes in the *kerygma* the entire ministry of Jesus, his person, birth, baptism, teaching, exorcisms, miracles, death, resurrection and the hope for his glorious return. Furthermore, the entire ministry of Christ, proclaimed in the *kerygma,* was viewed from the standpoint of the resurrection. A secure consensus in New Testament scholarship today affirms the position that the Gospels themselves narrate the ministry of Jesus from a resurrectional perspective.[8]

Like Tarazi, Stylianopoulos affirms that the heart of this proclamation is "a resurrectional saving reality experienced and proclaimed by faith in the present." He adds the opinion that this resurrectional reality "can be described by many terms such as new covenant, salvation, redemption, justification, forgiveness, reconciliation, righteousness, sonship, new creation, new life and the like."[9]

The ethicist can then locate in such a comprehensive understanding of the resurrection the ethical dimensions of salvation, perhaps focused on some aspects of this description of the resurrectional faith as encapsulated in terms such as "covenant," "forgiveness," "righteousness," "new creation," and "new life."

The East, of course, is not alone in this perception. Among evangelicals, Oliver O'Donovan has focused on the resurrection of Christ as a source for Christian ethics. This is a move away from the more philosophical trends which have tended to dominate the approaches of much of both Roman Catholic ethical theory and mainline Protestantism, as well as from the more legalistic understanding of some fundamentalist and evangelical Protestants. In his book *Resurrection and Moral Order: An Outline for Evangelical Ethics,* O'Donovan argues that the resurrection of Christ "carries the promise of ethical illumination," and that in fact a distinctly Christian ethic "depends upon the resurrection of Jesus Christ from the dead." He sees "the resurrection as our starting point because it tells us of God's vindication of his creation, and so of our created life."[10]

I have tried to show in my book on the theory of Eastern Orthodox ethics that Eastern Orthodox theology does not limit itself to only one aspect of the Orthodox faith in building a foundation for Christian ethics.[11] Rather, it wholistically draws on the whole panoply of the Christian faith, seeing ethics as a derivative of the faith as a whole. But one would have to be blind not to see as one of its most important and pivotal elements the crucial place of the resurrection of Jesus Christ in the total scheme of the Christian faith tradition.

Few in the Eastern Christian tradition express the importance of the resurrection of Jesus Christ and the resurrection of created human beings for ethics as does the premier Eastern patristic scriptural exegete St. John Chrysostom. To his contributions to reflections on resurrection and ethics we now turn.

## CHRYSOSTOM: RESURRECTION AND ETHICS

For Chrysostom there is no doubt about the historicity and factuality of the resurrection of Jesus Christ. But he recognized that there were many of his time who accepted neither the bodily resurrection of Jesus Christ nor that of human beings. He repeatedly set himself the task of seeking to convince these people of its truth.

His arguments in support of the empirical reality and historicity of the resurrection were based almost exclusively on the inner coherence (rather than diversity) of the biblical accounts and upon appeals to reason. Thus, Chrysostom argued that both the cross and the resurrection of Jesus Christ are predicted in the Old Testament through mainly typological interpretations.

An example of this view is found in his work *Against Marcionites.*[12] Chrysostom first called on intrabiblical witnesses to the resurrection of Christ. In the text, for example, of his eighty-eighth homily on Matthew commenting on Matthew 28:8, he wrote,

> "And they departed from the sepulchre with fear and joy." Why could this be? They had seen a thing amazing, and beyond expectation, a tomb empty, where they had before seen Him laid. Wherefore also He had led them to the sight, that they might become witnesses of both things, both of His tomb, and of His resurrection. For they considered that no man could have taken Him, when so many soldiers were sitting by Him, unless He raised up Himself. For this cause also they rejoice and wonder, and receive the reward of so much continuance with Him, that they should first see and gladly declare, not what had been said only, but also what they beheld.[13]

Such arguments in support of the facticity and reality of the resurrection abound in Chrysostom's exegetical and homiletical works. This passage argues from internal scriptural evidence. In another commentary on Matthew he argued more speculatively that the resurrection of Christ took place precisely so that the fact of Christ's death might be believed, thus, reversing the epistemological argument. Commenting on the parallel made by Jesus reported in Matthew 12:39-40 between Jonah in the belly of the whale and the three days of the resurrection,[14] Chrysostom wrote:

> And for this intent too did He allow three days, that the fact of His death might be believed. For not by the cross only doth He make it certain, and by the sight of all men, but also by the time of those days. For to the resurrection indeed all succeeding time was to bear witness; but the cross, unless it had at the time many signs bearing witness to it, would have been disbelieved; and with this disbelief would have gone utter disbelief of the resurrection also.[15]

But most importantly for an ethical discussion of the resurrection is how Chrysostom more often than not equated resurrection with life after death and the moral implications of life after death for the kind of life and the behaviors either encouraged or discouraged in the present life. There are numerous such passages. Let only one serve to illustrate this perspective at this time. Describing his attitude when he was abducted by Eutropius to be tried, he presented his hearers with his own personal example that did "not fear any present terrors." Death is presented as "not terrible: for we speedily reach the unruffled haven." Neither, he said is the loss of material possessions, nor exile, nor false accusation, for as the Lord promises "great is your reward in Heaven." The passage continues in a characteristically Chrysostomian rhetorical mode, not only identifying the resurrection with eternal life, but also concluding with an equally characteristic ethical judgment involving sin and the integrity of conscience within this context of the understanding of the resurrection.

> I saw the swords and I meditated on Heaven; I expected death, and I bethought me of the resurrection; I beheld the sufferings of this lower world, and I took account of the heavenly prizes; I observed the devices of the enemy, and I meditated on the heavenly crown: for the occasion of the contest was sufficient for encouragement and consolation. True! I was being forcibly dragged away, but I suffered no insult from the act; for there is only one real insult, namely sin: and should the whole world insult thee, yet if thou dost not insult thyself thou art not insulted. The only real betrayal is the betrayal of the conscience: betray not thy own conscience, and no one can betray thee.[16]

For Chrysostom, the eschatological framework of the Christian faith is rooted in the facticity of the resurrection of Jesus Christ, and it is the source of the resurrection of all. This emphasis on resurrection, rather than on a naturally understood "life after death" or on the philosophical concept "of an immortal soul," has been noted by several scholars as characteristic of the Eastern Christian understanding of life after death, the most important of whom among the Orthodox is John Romanides in his volume on original sin.[17] As we shall see below, the anticipation of the resurrection (not the belief in an immortal soul) becomes a powerful motivating force and foundation for ethical reflection in the writings of St. John Chysostom. In some ways, Chrysostom anticipated not only O'Donovan's emphasis on the resurrection for the moral order, as noted above, but also, provided a "resurrection" argument for the need of a moral universe, anticipating Kant's Practical Reason by fourteen centuries.

## RESURRECTION AND ETHICS IN CHRYSOSTOM'S EXEGESIS

Chrysostom, without question, was not only a superior exegete of scripture, but is also reflective of the mainline Eastern Christian approach to ethics. He drew his ethical teaching directly from the canon of faith of the Christian tradition. While there is a sense of a low-level natural law undergirding human society in Chrysostom, this too is biblically and doctrinally based.[18]

Chrysostom functioned with an understanding of the economy of salvation that retains a significant place for human decision making and responsibility. Fully aware of the fallen human condition that can only be redeemed by the death and resurrection of Jesus Christ, he understood that human beings appropriate that saving work not simply by an affirmation of faith that justifies in an essentially forensic manner, but by a belief that also requires a life marked by continuous repentance, an ascetic discipline of renunciation of the works of the "old man" and a struggle freely chosen to realize the image and likeness of God as the "new man" in Christ, expressed in the practical sphere of life. This approach affirms at once the full adequacy of the redemptive work of Christ, but also reflects a biblical view of the human element in the appropriation of the saving work of Jesus Christ in the life of each human being. In later theological parlance, this "cooperative" approach to the redemptive actions of God would come to be called the doctrine of "synergy," (*sunergeia*).[19] A good description of Chrysostom's "synergistic" approach to the Christian life and its ethical corollaries is found in George W. Forell's discussion of Chrysostom's ethics in his well known history of ethics in the Christian tradition. Forell describes Chrysostom's understanding of his teaching ministry as follows:

> . . . it is the task of the preacher to encourage men and women to use their power as free moral agents to choose righteousness. For this reason he added a moral application at the end of his sermons. Again and again he emphasized the importance of works validating faith: "Though a man believes rightly on the Father, the Son and the Holy Ghost, yet if he leads not a right life, his faith will avail nothing towards his salvation." Or, "Faith is not sufficient to bring men to the Kingdom, nay, it even hath power in his way most to condemn those who exhibit an ill life." While he praises "right faith," he is convinced "unless we add also a life suitable to our faith we shall suffer the extremest punishment." Or in commenting on Ephesians 1:4, "That you may not then, when you hear that 'He hath chosen us,' imagine that faith alone is sufficient, he (Paul) proceeds to add life and conduct. To this end, saith he, that He (has) chosen us, and on this condition, 'that we should be holy and without blemish.'[20]

It is no surprise then that Chysostom's treatment of biblical texts perpetually seeks to determine the appropriate ethical lessons and the fitting ethical response of the Christian to the text. C. Marriot, one of the English editors of Chrysostom's works noted in discussing the *Commentaries on Matthew*:

> A modern reader must sometimes be struck with finding in St. Chrysostom a kind cf criticism, which we are apt to think belongs only to later times. His main object, however, is moral, and he searches out with diligence both the meaning and the applications of particular passages usually concluding with an eloquent exhortation to some special virtue.[21]

When we come to the ethical impact of the resurrection, Chrysostom repeatedly and in diverse ways connects the two. For example, in his second *Exhortation to the Fallen Theodore,* in which he strenuously seeks to dissuade the monk from renouncing his monastic calling, he holds that for the Christian, just the thought of the resurrection should be an encouragement for Christians to do good.

This passage acknowledges that unbelievers might not be readily impressed by the idea of the resurrection of Christ and consequently live dissolute lives. He was, however, taken aback by professed Christians who are not sufficiently impressed by the resurrection, not allowing it to influence their behavior. He saw it as a contradiction in terms. He wrote:

> but that we who are more firmly persuaded concerning the things of the other world than those of the present, should spend our life in this miserable and deplorable way and be no-wise affected by the memory of those things, but sink into a state of extreme insensibility—this is irrational in the highest degree. For when we who believe do the deeds of unbelievers, or rather are in a more miserable plight than they (for there are some among them who have been eminent for the virtue of their life), what consolation, what excuse will be left for us.[22]

Chrysostom sought to exhort Christians to renew their commitment to the life of Christian virtue. In the light of the resurrection he mounted a call to persistence and renewed effort. He used the example of traders whose ships have been shipwrecked, but who start again, plying the same sea lanes, "and this," he noted "when the loss which has befallen them was not owing to their own carelessness, but to the force of the winds." The implication is, of course, that by analogy, the Christian backslider has no such excuse. So he asked, of those "who have reason to be confident concerning the end," and who have the power to chose the right course, why they should "lie in idleness and keep our hands to ourselves." The passage concludes in a typical Chrysostomian way: "And would that we kept them (our hands) merely to ourselves and did not use them against ourselves which is a token of stark madness.[23]

Founded on a serious affirmation and belief in the reality of the resurrection, Chrysostom's appeal here is to show the incongruity between belief in the resurrection on the part of a believer and living a life destined to lead to eternal destruction. "Stark madness" is what his rhetoric calls it.

This scripture-based reasoning is seen also in several other places in Chrysostom's writings. A particular instance is found in his *Second Exhortation to Theodore*, where we find an argument seeking to show that in a just, moral universe, the rewards of virtue and the consequences of vice require recompense in this life and if not in this life, then in the resurrectional life after death. Chysostom's version of what Emmanuel Kant was to develop in his philosophy of the Practical Reason, however, remains Christian in that both divine judgment and resurrection are at the fore, not an impersonal moral universe and the postulate of an immortal soul. The passage, nevertheless, has an almost modern sound after sixteen centuries.

> If there is a God, as indeed there is, it follows that He is just, for if He is not just neither is He God, and if He is just He recompenses to each according to their desert. But we do not see all here receiving according to their desert. Therefore it is necessary to hope for some other requital awaiting us, in order that by each one receiving according to his desert, the justice of God may be made manifest. For this consideration does not only contribute to our wisdom about providence alone, but about the Resurrection.[24]

But even in this affirmation, the ever-practical Chrysostom immediately moved to normative or "ought" language, that is, to ethical prescription. Upon mention of the resurrection he exhorts:

> . . . and let us teach others, and let us do all diligence to shut the mouths of them who rave against the master, and let us ourselves glorify him in all things. For thus shall we win more of his care, and enjoy much of his influence, and thus shall we be able to escape from real evil, and obtain future good, through the grace and lovingkindness of our Lord Jesus Christ.[25]

Here, then, trust in the moral dimensions of the resurrection provoked Chrysostom to find ethical imperatives consisting of the requirement to "teach others," to defend faith in Jesus Christ, and to use all things in our lives as means for manifesting his glory. The rewards of such behavior for those who so act are more of his care, joy of life, receptivity to divine influence in our lives, the escape from real evil in this life, and the obtaining of future good in the next. It should also be noted that even as Chrysostom was encouraging particular forms of behavior appropriate to a believer in the resurrection, on the basis of their freedom to choose, he simultaneously indicated that all these consequences come "through the grace and lovingkindness of our Lord Jesus Christ," thus expressing in another context the perspective of "ethical synergy."[26]

In such argumentation Chysostom draws ethical implications from belief in the resurrection. That there is a resurrection forms a base for reasoning to moral imperatives. This was no invention of Chrysostom. He was following, rather, his beloved St. Paul in 1 Corinthians 15. In 1 Cor 15:12-19 the focus is on the truth or falsity of the doctrine itself. The argument is summarized in v. 17: "If Christ is not risen, then our preaching is empty and your faith is also empty." But the argument takes an ethical turn in vv. 32-34. "If the dead are not raised, 'Let us eat and drink, for tomorrow we die.' Do not be deceived: 'Bad company ruins good morals.' Come to your right mind, and sin no more" (1 Cor. 15:32b-34a). In the words of one commentator the Wisdom literature aphorism[27]"Let us eat and drink, for tomorrow we die," is a "motto (that) summarizes the selfish, unethical, purposeless existence of those without hope."[28]

A careful reading of the text shows that Paul did not fully enunciate his reasoning. There is, for instance, a logical jump between "tomorrow we die" and the second aphorism that comes from Greek antiquity "Bad company ruins good morals."[29]

The implication seems to be that unbelief in the resurrection implies the lack of a moral universe in which virtue has positive consequences and vice has negative consequences and that allowing oneself to live in the orbit of influence of those who disbelieve in the resurrection will also have corrupting moral implications.

Nevertheless, the course of Paul's argument is in all likelihood the source of Chrysostom's pattern of thought. In 1 Corinthians Paul's ethical argument from the resurrection seems to be a shorthand statement that Chrysostom has dealt with in an expanded paraphrase and development of the biblical text.

In the first *Homily of the Statues* Chrysostom deals with the question of theodicy, that is, the question that asks why a good God permits the righteous to suffer. He offered nine distinct responses to the question. The fifth response is based on the belief in the resurrection; it is a statement of what could be called a Christian "proto-Kantian" theodicy argument. According to Chrysostom, the fifth reason that God permits the just to suffer in this world is: "that our minds may be wise concerning the doctrine of a resurrection. For when thou seest a just man, and one abounding in virtue, suffering ten thousand evils, and thus departing the present life, thou art altogether compelled, though unwillingly, to think somewhat of the future judgment."[30]

As an aside, the theodicy arguments which Chrysostom presented seem to be based on reason, yet he was careful to note their biblical origin. He concluded his discussion by saying: "These then are the reasons; but it is necessary to establish them all from the scriptures, and to show with exactness that all that has been said on this subject is not an invention of human reasoning, but the very sentence of the Scriptures. For thus will what we say be at once more deserving of credit, and sink the deeper into your minds."[31]

Subsequently, in the same *Homily on the Statues,* he commented directly on the Pauline passage in question, developing a sustained theodicy argument, which, in part refers to the resurrection:

> . . . it is certain that (God) has prepared another, a better and brighter life, in which he will crown those who have wrestled in the cause of godliness,

> and proclaim their praises in the presence of the whole world. So that when you see a just man straitened and afflicted; and in sickness, and in poverty, as well as innumerable other woes, till he ends this present life; say to thyself, that if there were no resurrection and judgment, God would not have permitted one, who endured such great evils for His sake, to depart hence without enjoying any good thing; from whence it is evident, that for such He has prepared another life, and one which is sweeter and much more endurable. . . . (T)here is provided another life, in which he is about to recompense every man according to his deserts; one for his wickedness, another for his virtue. . . .[32]

There are numerous other dimensions of belief in the resurrection that Chrysostom points to in his biblical commentaries. It was his conviction that the resurrection is an element in encouraging moral endurance in periods of personal trial and difficulty. Thus, in his seventy-ninth *Homily on Matthew* he constructed a Job-like hypothetical case in which a virtuous man loses health, family, and possessions. In response to all of these, Chrysostom provided a repeated ethical refrain, "let him practice virtue." And in this case, virtue is to avoid experiencing sorrow for such losses, for what are such things for one "who learns to be wise touching the resurrection?" He concluded the passage with this exhortation: "Let us therefore be children in malice, and flee wickedness, and lay hold on virtue, that we may attain also to the good things eternal."[33]

In another of his *Homilies on Matthew*, the sixteenth, he described the resurrection as an antidote to moral laxity interpreting the Sermon on the Mount reference to the "least in the kingdom of Heaven," as having the resurrection as its reference point and requiring more than minimal behavior. Jesus, Chrysostom said,

> foreknew the laxity of the many, He foreknew that some would think these sayings were merely hyperbolical, and would argue about the laws, and say, What, if any one call another a fool, is he punished? If one merely look on a woman, doth he become an adulterer? For this very cause He, destroying such insolence beforehand, hath set down the strongest denunciation against either sort, as well them who transgress, as them who lead on others so to do. Knowing then His threat as we do, let us neither ourselves transgress, nor discourage such as are disposed to keep these things.[34]

Similarly, in the context of his discussion of the resurrection of Jesus in Matthew, he berated men for not responding to Jesus' needs as did the women at the tomb. These needs Chrysostom described as embodied in the hunger, thirst, nakedness, and homelessness of "the least of his brethren," thus combining the resurrection narratives with the end-time judgment as described in Matthew 25. So he exhorted, "Let us men imitate the women; let us not forsake Jesus in temptations. For they for Him even dead spent so much and exposed their lives, but we . . . neither feed Him when hungry, nor clothe Him when naked, but seeing Him begging, we pass Him by." Entrance into the Kingdom, Chrysostom said, is barred by such behavior. Speaking of rejecting Christ in the suffering neighbor, Chrysostom said to his listeners, "If thou hadst not turned away from Him (Christ), He would not have sent thee to hell, if thou hadst overlooked a chance person; but because it is He Himself that is despised, therefore great is the blame.[35]

Chrysostom summarized his own view on the ethical implications of the death and resurrection of Christ in his commentary on Romans 4:25 ("Who was delivered for our offences and was raised again for our justification"). He wrote "... the purpose of His dying was not that He might hold us liable to punishment and in condemnation, but that He might do good unto us. For for this cause He both died and rose again, that He might make us righteous."[36] The righteousness that Chrysostom spoke of here is synergistic. He affirmed the exclusive saving work of God as "His part." And he affirms the human being's response of faith as "our part." But, clearly, from all that has preceded, it is clear that conformity and harmony with the divine will as ongoing choice and actions serve to glorify God and realize God-likeness in human existence.[37] Thus, in his fourth *Homily on the Statues*, Chrysostom spoke in a quite ethical way when it comes to discoursing on the fear of death. Faith in the resurrection is expressed in actions and attitudes, here resorting to an approach more characteristic of the Epistle of James.

> If thou art a Christian, believe in Christ; if thou believest in Christ, shew me thy faith by thy works. But how mayest thou shew this? By thy contempt of death: for in this we differ from the unbelievers. They may well fear death; since they have no hope of a resurrection. But thou, who art travelling toward better things, and hast the opportunity of meditating on the hope of the future; what excuse hast thou, if whilst assured of a resurrection, thou are yet at the same time as fearful of death, as those who believe not the resurrection?[38]

## FOUR HOMILIES ON ROMANS—RESURRECTION AND ETHICS

The Chrysostomian references described above have come from various scattered exegetical passages. We can conclude this study on Chrysostom's approach to the ethics arising out of the resurrection of Jesus Christ by examining four homilies where the theme is dominant: Chrysostom's tenth, eleventh, thirteenth and twenty-fourth *Homilies on Romans*.

The tenth *Homily on Romans* is a treatment of Romans 5:12 through 6:4. It is the pericope that deals with the theme of death through Adam and life through Christ, a typological passage that sees in Christ the new Adam. According to St. Paul, death came through Adam, but life has come through Christ. The use of "death" and "life" terminology is worked out in themes such as "law," "sin," and "grace." This leads to a discussion of baptism, where St. Paul defined this Christian sacrament as participation in the death and resurrection of Jesus Christ. "Do you not know that all of us who have been baptized into Christ Jesus were baptized into his death? We were buried therefore with him by baptism into death, so that as Christ was raised from the dead by the glory of the Father, we too might walk in newness of life" (Rom 6:3-4). For Chrysostom, this reference to walking in newness of life leads inexorably to an ethical treatment of the resurrection and the moral dimensions of the resurrection faith in believers. The passage is striking:

> Here he hints, along with the duty of a careful walk, at the subject of the resurrection. In what way? Do you believe, he means, that Christ died, and that He was raised again? Believe then the same of thyself. For this is like to the other, since both Cross and Burial is thine. For if thou hast shared in Death and Burial, much more wilt thou in Resurrection and Life. For now since the greater is done away with, the sin I mean, it is not right to doubt any longer about the lesser, the doing away of death.

Following this affirming the participation of the baptized believer in the death and life of Jesus Christ, he moves to the ethical application.

> . . . after the resurrection to come had been set before us, (Christ) demands of us another, even the new conversation, which is brought about in the present life by a change of habits. When then the fornicator becomes chaste, the covetous man merciful, the harsh subdued, even here a resurrection has taken place, the prelude to the other. And how is it a resurrection? Why, because sin is mortified, and righteousness hath risen again, and the old life hath been made to vanish, and this new and angelic one is being lived in.

The ever realistic Chrysostom, however, could not help but note that Christian behavior does not consistently reflect the resurrection experience. He followed on the above with these practical observations at a time when there was a long catechumenate period before baptism in adulthood:

> But when you hear of a new life, look for a great alteration, a wide change. But tears come into my eyes, and I groan deeply to think how great religiousness Paul requires of us, and what listlessness we have yielded ourselves up to, going back after our baptism to the oldness we before had, and returning to Egypt, and remembering the garlic after the manna (Num 11:5.) For ten or twenty days at the very time of our Illumination, we undergo a change, but then take up our former doings again. But it's not for a set number of days, but for our whole life, that Paul requires of us such a conversation.[39]

The rest of the homily is an exhortation to a moral and spiritual battle against the forces that obviate the influence of the resurrectional life lived here on earth, an ongoing struggle against the wiles of the devil. The homily concludes with this exhortation:

> Do you see what his wiles are, what his varying warfare? Be then on thy guard, and arm thyself at all points with the weapons of the Spirit, get exactly acquainted with his plans, that thou mayest both keep from being caught, and easily catch him. . . . Let us then also be earnest in learning and avoiding his stratagems, that after obtaining a victory over him, we may, whether in this present life or in that which is to come, be proclaimed conquerors . . . .[40]

Chrysostom began his eleventh *Homily on Romans,* covering 6:5 through 7:18, by observing that Paul diverges from the pattern normally found in his other epistles where he divides his material between "doctrines" and "moral instruction." Rather, here, "he continually digresseth into exhortation." Resurrection and ethics continue to be a major theme for him in this homily.

While baptism and the death of the old man and the resurrection into the new life is a gift of grace, Chrysostom discerned here also another dimension to the new life in Christ. Synergy is once again discerned in the sacred text. Chrysostom wrote, "the remaining dead to sin after baptism must be the work of our own earnestness, however much we find God here also giving us large help." What is needed is a clear moral goal, a sharp focus on keeping the pure baptismal robe undefiled: "show thou forth the change in thine aims, that thou mayest not defile thyself again. For it is this and the like that he is counselling thee when he says, 'for if we have been planted together in the likeness of His Death, we shall be also in the likeness of His Resurrection.'"[41] Homily 11 proceeds to emphasize the integral incorporation of the Christian in the resurrection of Christ in both the moral and the eschatological senses. Thus baptism destroys "the body of sin" and dying with Christ is "not that ye should be destroyed and die, but so that ye sin not."[42]

In his commentary on v. 10 he argued that the passage "He died unto sin" points to a clear rejection of any ethical position supporting the maxim "the means justify the end." Chrysostom interpreted the verse to mean an opposition to those who would argue "Let us do evil that good may come." Commenting on verse 11 where Paul calls on his readers to be dead to sin and alive to God, Chrysostom interpreted ethically that "he that so liveth will lay hold of every virtue, as having Jesus Himself for his ally. For that is what, 'in Christ,' means."[43]

Commenting on verses 12 and 13, where Paul called upon his readers not to let sin reign in their bodies, nor to yield their members to be instruments of unrighteousness, Chrysostom reasserted the moral neutrality of the body and the self-determining decision-making of the moral agent as a part of the new life in Christ.

> The body then is indifferent between vice and virtue, as also instruments (or arms) are. But either effect is wrought by him that useth it. As if a soldier fighting in his country's behalf, and a robber who was arming against the inhabitants, had the same weapons for defence. For the fault is not laid to the suit of armor, but to those that use it to an ill end. And this one may say of the flesh too, which becomes this or that owing to the mind's decision, not owing to its own nature.[44]

St. Paul proceeded then on the positive tack, calling on the baptized who have been brought from death to life, to yield themselves to God as instruments of righteousness. Chrysostom was eager to avoid dualism that would see the members of the body or the body as a whole as the source of sinfulness and evil. Perhaps reacting to Gnostic attitudes, Chrysostom focused rather on the battle against sin and for righteousness which the Christian is called to wage. But he noted a difference between the soldier in military battle and the Christian's struggle. "In the case of wars, soldiers are often given up even against their will. But in this case, unless thou desertest of thyself, there is no one who will get the better of thee." That is a new appeal to the Christian's self-determining choice in the battle against evil and for virtue.

Yet even this is not accomplished without the grace of God. Commenting on verse 17, Chrysostom concluded: "Obedience from the heart shows the free will. But the being delivered, indicates the assistance from God. But what is the form of doctrine? It is living aright, and in conformity with the best conversation."[45]

In commenting on Romans 6:18 which speak of believers becoming servants of righteousness, Chrysostom discussed spiritual and moral death at great length, focusing on avarice which allows for no compassion and no almsgiving. He is vivid in his condemnation of greed and selfish attention to personal luxury as he exhorts his audience once again to minister to Christ in the person of the poor and dispossessed.

The thirteenth *Homily on Romans* covers 7:14 through 8:11 in which Paul contrasts law and life in the Spirit and treats at length the freedom that is given through the Spirit. In verse 9 St. Paul told the Romans that they are no longer "in the flesh" but "in the Spirit." Chrysostom was careful to give an ethical meaning to the term "flesh," once again combating a dualism that would see the body as evil. He said, "Here again, he does not mean flesh absolutely, but such sort of flesh, that which was in a whirl and thraldom of passions." Moral choice, is again at the center. Chrysostom explained.

> Some things are good, some bad, and some indifferent. Thus the soul and the flesh belong to things indifferent, since each may become either—the one or the other. But the Spirit belongs to things good, and at no time becometh any other thing. Again, the mind of the flesh, that is, ill-doing, belongs to things always bad. "For it is not subject to the law of God." If then thou yieldest thy soul and body to the better, thou wilt have become of its part. If on the other hand thou yield to the worse, then art thou made a partaker of the ruin therein, not owing to the nature of the soul and the flesh, but owing to that judgment which has the power of choosing either.[46]

Rom 8:10, which speaks of Christ residing in the believer, gives Chrysostom another opportunity to connect the resurrection to the moral life. Christ in us, he explained, means that we are dead to sin and that the Spirit gives true life "because of righteousness." The absence of the Holy Spirit results in "death, enmity against God, inability to satisfy His laws, and not being Christ's as we should be." These are the result of "the want of His indwelling." But the results of having the Spirit are "being Christ's, having Christ himself, vying with the angels (for this is what mortifying the flesh is), and living an immortal life, holding henceforward the earnest of the resurrection, running with ease the race of virtue." The rest of the homily is a moral discourse on the effects of the life that is characterized by the indwelling of the Holy Spirit, a resurrectional way of life in the present.[47]

The final *Homily on Romans* that deals almost exclusively with the resurrectional life is the twentyfourth, which comments on Rom 13:11-14. Looking forward to the resurrection has immediate ethical consequences. Paul's text provides a powerful sense of urgency with the words "for salvation is nearer to us now than when we first believed." The consequence of that urgency is ethical. "Let us then cast off the works of darkness and put on the armor of light; let us conduct ourselves becomingly as in the day, not in reveling and drunkenness, not in debauchery and licentiousness, not in quarreling and jealousy. But put on the Lord Jesus Christ, and make no provision for the flesh, to gratify its desires" (13:12b-14).

Chrysostom heightened the sense of urgency, not only in terms of the general judgment, but also in terms of the personal conclusion of each person's life on earth:

> You see how he puts the Resurrection now close by them. For as the time advances, he means, the season of our present life is wasting away and that of the life to come waxes nearer. If then thou be prepared, and hast done all whatsoever He hath commanded, the day is salvation to thee; but if the contrary, not so."

And he adds to heighten the pressure of the coming resurrection on the believers behavior, "the nearer the King may be at hand, the more ought they to get themselves in readiness; the nearer the prize is, the more wide awake ought they to be for the contest.[48]

Chrysostom then commented briefly on the kinds of behavior that are described by St. Paul as inappropriate in this urgent, preresurrectional state. He was careful to distinguish between drinking some wine and drunkenness and between marital intercourse and debauchery. "Putting on Christ" changes the focus, however.

> He no longer speaks of works, but he rouses them to greater things. For when he was speaking of vice, he mentioned the works of it: but when of virtue, he speaks not of works, but of arms, to show that virtue putteth him that is possessed of it into complete safety, and complete brightness. And even here he does not pause, but leading his discourse on to what was greater, a thing far more awe-striking; he gives us the Lord Himself for a garment, the King Himself: for he that is clad with Him, hath absolutely all virtue.[49]

The balance of Homily XXIV deals with specific moral issues, including lust, health, gluttony, luxury, worldliness, partying, filthy talk, unseemly behavior, bawdy songs, harlotry, family discord, fornication, abortion, superstition, and the like. One avoids all these by putting on Christ.

> That we may then escape from all these, let us put on Christ, and be with Him continually. For this is what putting Him on is; never being without Him, having Him evermore visible in us, through our sanctification, through our moderation. So we say of friends, such an one is wrapped up in such another, meaning their great love, and keeping together incessantly. For he that is wrapped up in anything, seems to be that which he is wrapped in. Let then Christ be seen in every part of us. And how is He to be seen? If thou doest His deeds.[50]

## CONCLUSION

This paper has sought to document St. John Chrysostom's understanding of the ethical implications of the resurrection of Jesus Christ and the resurrection of individual persons. The evidence seems clear enough that not only is there such a concept in the exegetical corpus of Chrysostom, but also that it is far from incidental in his thought.

The same, perhaps, can be said of the Eastern Orthodox liturgical tradition, since without question it is richly imbued with both the scriptural and patristic tradition, and in many ways, embodies the mainline Cappadocian and Chrysostomian mindset. I conclude this paper with three Eastern Orthodox liturgical expressions of this same ethos as a summary of Chrysostom's approach, This indicates a continuity between the golden-mouthed exegete and preacher of the fourth century and the contemporary worship of the Eastern Orthodox Church.

In June of 1982, I experienced the ethical power of belief in the resurrection of Christ when I participated in a World Council of Churches sponsored Orthodox Consultation on "Just Development for Fulness of Life" at Kiev in the then USSR. In our party were not only Orthodox theologians, but also ecumenical observers and staff. Also present was a Soviet economist. On the first Saturday of the Conference, we attended at St. Vladimir's Cathedral the evening vigil service which includes the Orthros or Matin Service. All of the hymnology of this worship focuses on the resurrection of Christ. A particularly strong affirmation of the resurrection is found in a hymn that comes immediately following the reading of one of eleven of a cycle of appointed biblical passages describing the resurrection of Christ. At that point in the service, the richly robed Deacon stepped out before the congregation gathered in that then officially atheistic land, raised his arms high, and began leading the whole in the singing of the hymn. All of us conferees, Orthodox and non-Orthodox alike were overwhelmed by the assertive power that came through to us as the people sang this affirmation of the resurrection. For days, we could not help but return to the impact that the hymn made on us as it was sung with such vigor and conviction and power by those oppressed Christians. I personally remember also the downcast eyes of our Communist economist participant. This remembrance came to me as I sought to summarize the emphasis of the resurrection as a source of moral and ethical experience in Chrysostom's exegesis of the New Testament witness. It might be read as a particular ecclesial expression of Chrysostom's resurrectional ethic in a concrete historical situation where moral and spiritual courage was demanded of believers. The text of the hymn is as follows:

> Having beheld the resurrection of Christ, let us worship the holy Lord Jesus, the only Sinless One. We venerate your cross, O Christ, and we praise and glorify your holy resurrection. You are our God. We know no other than you, and we call upon your name. Come all you faithful, let us venerate the holy resurrection of Christ. For behold, through the cross joy has come to all the world. Ever praising the Lord, let us praise his resurrection. For by enduring the cross for us, He has destroyed death by death.[51]

My second liturgical summary statement is the hymn known as the Fourth *Exaposteilarion* which reads as follows:

> Lightening bright with virtues, let us behold angels standing at the life-bearing tomb in brilliant garments, while the women bearing myrrh bow their faces to the earth. Let us learn of the rising of him who reigns over heaven and let us hasten with Peter to life in the tomb; marvelling at that which has happened, let us stay to behold Christ.[52]

I conclude with a Paschal Hymn, sung on the Feast of the Resurrection.

> It is the day of resurrection; be illumined for the feast; and embrace one another. Let us speak, brothers and sisters, even unto those who hate us and forgive all for the sake of the resurrection. And so together let us cry out: Christ is risen from the dead trampling down death by death and upon those in the tombs bestowing life.

## NOTES

1. Raymond E. Brown, *Biblical Exegesis & Church Doctrine.* New York: Paulist Press, 1985.
2. Ibid., 24-25.
3. *The Significance of the Message of the Resurrection for Faith in Jesus Christ* C. F. D. Moule, ed., *Studies in Biblical Theology*, Second Series, 8, (Naperville, IL: Alec R. Allenson, 1968), 7.
4. Ibid., 7.
5. Ibid., 39.

6. Stanley Samuel Harakas, "Tradition in Eastern Orthodox Thought," *Christian Scholar's Review* XX II:2 (December, 1992): 144-165.

7. Paul N. Tarazi, "Effective Preaching Today" *God's Living Word: Orthodox and Evangelical Essays on Preaching,* ed. Theodore G. Stylianopoulos, (Brookline, MA: Holy Cross Orthodox Press, 1983), 48.

8. Theodore G. Stylianopoulos, "The Living Sources for Preaching," Ibid., 77.

9. Ibid.

10. Oliver O'Donovan, *Resurrection and Moral Order; An Outline for Evangelical Ethics* (Grand Rapids: Eerdmans, 1986) 13.

11. Stanley Samuel Harakas, *Toward Transfigured Life: The Theoria of Eastern Orthodox Ethics* (Minneapolis: Light and Life Publishing Co., 1983), chapter 2.

12. All quotations and references to the writings of St. John Chrysostom in this paper are from *A Select Library of the Nicene and Post-Nicene Fathers of the Christian Church,* ed. Philip Schaff, First Series, (Grand Rapids: Eerdmans, subsequently identified as NPNF. *Against Marcionites* is found in NPNF IX), 202ff,

13. NPNF X, 524.

14. "But he answered them, 'An evil and adulterous generation seeks for a sign; but no sign shall be given to it except the sign of the prophet Jonah. For as Jonah was three days and three nights in the belly of the whale, so will the Son of man be three days and three nights in the heart of the earth.'"

15. *Commentary on Matthew,* Homily 43, NPNF X, 273.

16. *To Eutropius* II, 2 (NPNF IX), 253.

17. John S. Romanides, *To Propatorikon Harmartema* (Athens, 1957). See also, John Hick, *Evil and the God of Love* rev. ed. (New York: Harper and Row, 1978) especially in Part III, "The Irenaean Type of Theodicy."

18. See Stanley S. Harakas, "The Natural Law Teaching of the Eastern Orthodox Church," *The Greek Orthodox Theological Review* IX, 2 (1963-1964): 215-224. Reprinted In *New Theology* No.2, ed. Martin E. Marty and Dean G. Peerman; (New York: The Macmillan Co., 1965), 122-133; "Eastern Orthodox Perspectives on Natural Law," *Selected Papers: The AmericamnSociety of Christian Ethics,* ed. Max L. Stackhouse, (Newton Centre, MA), 41-56; "Eastern Orthodox Perspectives on Natural Law,"*American Journal of Jurisprudence* 24 (1979): 86-113; "The Natural Moral Law," *Toward Transfigured Life,* chap. 6.

19. See "Foundations for Christian Praxis," in Harakas, *Living the Faith: The Praxis of Eastern Orthodox Ethics* (Minneapolis, MN: Light and Life Publishing Co., 1992), 2, for a more extensive and detailed outline of the theologically based Eastern Christian approach to ethics.

20. George Wolfgang Forell, *History of Christian Ethics* (Minneapolis: Augsburg Publishing House, 1979), 1, 137-138.

21. "Preface to the Oxford Edition," (NPNF X), 1.

22. *Exhortation to Theodore* I (NPNF IX), 104.

23. *Exhortation to the Fallen Theodore* I (NPNF IX), 104.

24. *Exhortation to Theodore* II (NPNF IX), 115.

25. *To Theodore* II (NPNF IX), 115.

26. Ibid., 151.

27. See Wisdom of Solomon 2:6-9.

28. Mary Ann Getty, *First Corinthians, Second Corinthians* (Collegeville Bible Commentary, New Testament, 7 (Collegeville, MN: The Liturgical Press, 1983), 72.

29. Atrributed to Menander in his *Thaedra.*

30. *Homily on the Statues* I (NPNF IX), 336.

31. Ibid., The full text of Chrysostom's theodicy statement, which itself is of important ethical import, follows:

> The first reason then is, that God permits them to suffer evil, that they may not too easily be exalted into presumption, by the greatness of their good works and miracles.
>
> The second, that others may not have a greater opinion of them than be-

longs to human nature, and take them to be gods and not men.

The third, that the power of God may be made manifest, in prevailing, and overcoming, and advancing the word preached, through the efficacy of men who are infirm and in bonds.

The fourth, that the endurance of these themselves may become more striking, serving God, as they do, not for a reward; but showing even such right-mindedness as to give proof of their undiminished good will towards Him after so many evils.

The fifth, that our minds may be wise concerning the doctrine of a resurrection. For when thou seest a just man, and one abounding in virtue, suffering ten thousand evils, and thus departing the present life, thou art altogether compelled, though unwillingly, to think somewhat of the future judgment; for if men do not suffer those who have labored for themselves, to depart without wages and recompense; much more cannot God design, that those who have so greatly labored should be sent away uncrowned. But if He cannot intend to deprive those of the recompense of their labours eventually, there must needs be a time, after the end of the life here, in which they will receive the recompense of their present labours.

The sixth, that all who fall into adversity may have a sufficient consolation and alleviation, by looking at such persons, and remembering what sufferings have befallen them.

The seventh, that when we exhort you to the virtue of such persons, and we say to every one of you, "Imitate Paul, emulate Peter," ye may not, on account of the surpassing character of their good works, slothfully shrink from such an imitation of them, as deeming them to have been partakers of a different nature.

The eighth, that when it is necessary to call any blessed, or the reverse, we may learn whom we ought to account happy, and whom unhappy and wretched.

These then are the reasons; but it is necessary to establish them all from the scriptures, and to show with exactness that all that has been said on this subject is not an invention of human reasoning, but the very sentence of the scriptures. For thus will what we say be at once more deserving of credit, and sink the deeper into your minds.

32. Ibid., 339. See also p. 340, where Chrysostom added his ninth theodicy argument based on Rom 5:3-5: "For tribulation worketh patience; and patience, probation; and probation, hope; and hope maketh not ashamed."

33. *Homily on Matthew* LXXIX ( NPNF X), 479f.

34. *On Matthew* 16 (NPNF X), 107.

35. *On Matthew* 88, (NPNF X), 522-523.

36. *Homily on Romans* IX (NPNF) 395.

37. Ibid., 396.

38. *Homily on the Statues* IV (NPNF IX), 373.

39. *Homily on Romans* X (NPNF,X), 405-406.

40. Ibid., 408.

41. *Homily on Romans* XI (NPNF, XI), 408-409.

42. Ibid., 409.

43. Ibid., 410.

44. Ibid., 410-411.

45. Ibid., 412.

46. *Homily on Romans* XIII (NPNF XI), 435.

47. Ibid., 436.

48. *Homily on Romans* XXIV (NPNF XI), 517.

49. Ibid., 518.

50. Ibid., 520-521.

51. *The Service of the Sunday Orthros*, ed. N. Michael Vaporis (Brookline, MA: Holy Cross Orthodox Press), 74.

52. Ibid., 83-84.

# THE WOMEN AT THE TOMB: WHAT ARE THEY DOING THERE?

CAROLYN OSIEK

This article will explore the role and function of the women in the empty tomb narratives of the gospel tradition. What purpose do they play in the resurrection kerygma of the early church? Why is the story of their first arrival at the tomb so persistent that it continues into the later apocryphal gospels? It has become an exegetical commonplace that women could not be legal witnesses in ancient Judaism, and thus these tomb narratives were not counted among official appearance stories. But if this is so, why were these narratives preserved at all? It is thought by some biblical scholars that the empty tomb stories are secondary to the appearance stories, and even perhaps invented by Mark. If this is so, why women? It would seem to have fit the kerygmatic purposes of early Christian preaching eminently better to have the male disciples come first to the tomb—or, if it be argued that, having fled at the arrest, according to the narrative they would not have known where the tomb was, then even Joseph of Arimathea, who surely could have come to check on his handiwork!

The discussion of this question will be in three parts. Part one will summarize the work on these passages done by scholars using redaction criticism. Part two will examine surrounding issues from the perspective of social history and social construction of meaning, especially with regard to women's subcultures, roles in burial customs, and public testimony. Part three will apply to these findings a feminist analysis using both a hermeneutic of suspicion and of remembrance.

## REDACTIONAL EMPHASES

All four gospels contain accounts of the women as first arrivals to the tomb on Easter morning, but they differ greatly in detail. The common thread to all four accounts is that at least one woman disciple of Jesus, namely Mary Magdalene, came first to the tomb after the sabbath, found it empty, and went away again. Also common to the Synoptics is that they (Mary Magdalene and at least one other) received a message from someone(s) to interpret the meaning as the resurrection of Jesus. The number and names of the women are different in each case, as shown below.

| | |
|---|---|
| Mark 16:1 | Mary Magdalene, Mary mother of James, Salome |
| Matt 28:1 | Mary Magdalene and the other Mary |
| Luke 24:10 | Mary Magdalene, Joanna, Mary mother of James, and the others with them. |

John 20:1 Mary Magdalene

In addition:

Gospel of Peter 12:50 Mary Magdalene and her women friends
Epistula Apostolorum
Ethiopic 9 Sarah, Martha, Mary Magdalene
Coptic 9 Mary, the daughter of Martha, Mary Magdalene
Only the Epistula Apostolorum does not place the name of Mary Magdalene first.

## *MARK 16:1-8*

One can now speak of a scholarly consensus that the original ending of Mark is at the end of v. 8. The same cannot be said for the questions surrounding the composition of those last eight verses. Some detect the presence of literary sources in the text itself. For others, 16:1-8 is an integral literary unit composed by Mark. For still others, this literary unity is sufficient indication that Mark not only composed the narrative, but invented it.[1] If one wants to discount all stories of angelophany and search for the historical "bare bones," the result is, not surprisingly, exactly what was given above as the line common to all four canonical gospels: some women disciples arrived first at the tomb, found it empty, went away confused.

The women who came at sunrise were the same three who were present and witnessed the crucifixion along with other women disciples (15:40-41), and the two Marys saw the burial (v. 47), even though one of the sons of the second Mary is omitted alternately in 15:47 and 16:1. (To add to the confusion, Codex Vaticanus tries to make her into two people at 15:40: the wife of little James and the mother of Joses. See the conundrum posed by 6:3, where James and Joses are the brothers of Jesus, which would make this Mary the same as the mother of Jesus.) In spite of some confusion about the male relatives of the second Mary, there is a continuity in the women's experience. It is explicitly stated that they saw *(θεωρουσαι)*, even though at a distance (15:40), the crucifixion of Jesus and where he was buried (v. 47; Salome has disappeared for the burial, but has rejoined the two Marys at the tomb on Sunday morning). The usual interpretation of their distance from the scene is avoidance of the political danger that closer association would bring (also in Matt 27:55 and Luke 23:49, but contrast John 19:25).

The reason given for their return, the unfinished anointing of the body, is highly suspect. It occurs only in Mark and Luke. In Mark, the end of the passion narrative offers no explanation why they could not finish the task on Friday, so that their reason for returning seems artificial. Moreover, reopening the tomb to anoint the body nearly two days later has been seen by most commentators as incredible. It has been objected that what is envisioned is not complete anointing, but rather a general honorific sprinkling with aromatics around the corpse, as in 2 Chron 16:14 or Josephus *Antiquities* 15.61, prophetically anticipated in Mark 14:8.[2] But when this anointing is to be done more than thirty-six hours after burial, it still strains credibility.

Those who would see an original, straightforward narrative behind the present text would see it composed of something like vv. 1, 2, 4, 8. V. 3, the women's question to each other about how they will gain access to the tomb, is literary embellishment to heighten the sense of amazement in v. 4 when they find the stone already rolled back. The rather subdued angelophany (vv. 5-7), if indeed the modest account of a young man in a white robe can even be called that, introduces the kerygmatic message of Jesus' resurrection, and is therefore secondary. V. 7 introduces yet another motif, return to Galilee in keeping with Jesus' own prediction in 14:28, and is perhaps inserted at an even later point.

The complex question of Mark's puzzling ending cannot be discussed here and is not relevant for this investigation, except inasmuch as the silence of the women affects their credibility as witnesses. This will be taken up in part three.

## *MATT 28:1-10*

Matthew's empty tomb narrative elaborates considerably the simple account of Mark. Two of Mark's three women remain, but they have company: the guards that have been stationed at the tomb (Matt 27:62-66). The women came, not to finish anointing, but simply to "see" (θεωρῆσαι) the tomb, to continue the faithful vigil they had been keeping at the time of burial (27:61). And there was plenty to see once they got there: an earthquake, and an angel who descended, rolled away the stone, and sat on it (28:2-3). Women and guards were witnesses to the shattering events immediately surrounding the actual resurrection. The contrasting reaction reveals the difference of response. While the guards accepted bribes to falsify what they witnessed (vv. 11-15), meanwhile back at the tomb, the women received the angelic message in approximately the same terms as in Mark, including the promise of seeing Jesus himself in Galilee (vv. 5-7). As contrasted with Mark, they fled the tomb not in fear and panic, but in fear and great joy to tell the other disciples (v. 8).

The subsequent appearance of Jesus cutting them off at the pass as they ran (vv. 9-10) is the most difficult part of the narrative and may be an addition. It adds nothing to the angel's message, but only repeats the message to go to Galilee. Moreover, it seemingly contradicts the angel, who had just told them to deliver the message that "you will see him in Galilee." Two verses later, they saw him at Jerusalem—and with nothing new to say. The Synoptic pattern of an angel(s) who sent women to male disciples who, in Matthew and Luke, are then sent to the world, is disrupted. This sudden and strange appearance of Jesus, however, serves to reinforce the essential message: he is risen. Other aspects of its significance include the following: it forges the first link between the empty tomb and appearance traditions; it is the first evidence of the tendency, to be developed in Luke 24 and John 21, to relocate appearances in Jerusalem; and the women's response of worshipful grasping of Jesus' feet (v. 9) is evidence of the inevitable tendency to materialize the appearances.[3] In addition, for Matthew, the first appearance of the risen Jesus was to women disciples.

## *LUKE 24:1-11*

Only in Luke are the women disciples mentioned and partially named early on in Jesus' ministry (8:2-3). There with him in Galilee, in addition to the twelve, were women who had been healed and exorcised: Mary Magadalen, Joanna, and Susanna, who is never mentioned again. With them were "many others," all of whom practiced διακονια with the twelve. Only here and in Mark 16:9 is Mary Magdalene a former demoniac—and nowhere in the New Testament is she a prostitute! Joanna may have been a woman of some status on the Herodian ladder, and inexplicably, traveled without her husband among a group of whom Herod did not approve.[4] The women reappear in 23:49-55 as part of the group of those who had followed Jesus (the language of discipleship) from Galilee to Jerusalem. According to Acts 13:31, they therefore form part of the group of witnesses to the events of Jesus' death and resurrection.

Luke is the first evangelist to imply that the male disciples were present at the crucifixion along with the women (23:49), even if at a distance. Only the women, however, witnessed, the burial (v. 55), so that the textually uncertain visit of Peter to the tomb (24:12) must still presuppose the communication of its location by the women. They will remain nameless until 24:10. Here, in contrast to Mark, they have a reason to return Sunday morning to finish their anointing: the first sundown of sabbath was already beginning while Jesus was being buried (v. 54), and the women were observant of sabbath regulations (v. 56).

Though there is no mention in Luke's burial account of the stone being rolled over the tomb entrance, it is presupposed in 24:2, for there, it has already been rolled back. Luke, in common with Mark and against Matthew, does not narrate the actual movement of the stone. Only in Luke, the women first saw for themselves that Jesus' body was not there—before they were informed as to the meaning of its absence. Then they were instructed by the two men in dazzling robes, not by means of kerygmatic statements, but two familiar Lukan devices. The first is a rhetorical question: "Why do you look for the living one among the dead?" (v. 5; compare Acts 1:11). The second is a memory help: "Remember how he told you about this in Galilee" (vv. 6-7), followed by their remembrance of his words, leading to understanding and proclamation. Even though, only in Luke, the women were not given a specific command to tell what they have seen, they did it anyway—but in vain, for they were not believed until Peter verified for himself (vv. 8-9,11-12) and appearances of Jesus later in the day confirmed what had happened.

At 24:10, three of the women are finally named: Mary Magdalene, Joanna (see 8:2), and Mary mother of James (or wife, if Mark 15:40 is not to be presumed), but there were unnamed others with them. Joanna, the political question mark, has persisted from 8:2 along with Mary Magdalene.

For Luke, the women were certainly counted among the disciples. The angelic message to them at the tomb is not one of direct address, a statement to be repeated to the men. Rather, the message is directed to the women themselves. It is they who are to remember how Jesus, while still in Galilee, predicted his passion and resurrection. Only once in Luke's Gospel, at 9:22, are both passion and resurrection made part of a prediction that is not directed specifically to a closed group, but to the disciples in general. The women disciples, already mentioned in 8:2-3, are therefore part of the group of disciples who received the prediction in chapter 9,[5] as well as the disciple-witnesses from Galilee in Acts 13:31. In Luke's narrative, they form part of an inclusive pattern of women figures beginning with the prophets Mary and Anna in the infancy stories, through, among others, Martha and Mary (10:38-42), Mary and the women in the upper room at Pentecost (Acts 1:14), and the women prophets of Joel (Acts 2:18).

## *JOHN 20:1-2, 11-18*

With the first two verses of John, we may be once again very close to an original form of the story: a woman disciple goes early Sunday morning to the tomb; finds the stone rolled back; and runs to tell other disciples. The beloved disciple is of course a Johannine insertion, as is Mary's immediate assumption that the body has been stolen. John does not say explicitly that she noticed the body was not there (compare only Luke 24:3), yet her message presupposes it. Mourning and preparation of a body for burial are social activities for women; the group of women is no doubt the earlier version. It has been reduced by John to Mary Magdalene alone for two reasons. First, the ensuing dialogue between her and Jesus in vv. 11-18 was composed as a private encounter, and it is possible that the original narrative continued from v. 1 to v. 11 without the intervening episode. Second, the focus on her prefigures her centrality in later apocryphal Easter stories as a major authority on communication from the risen Jesus. Some think that the plural "we" in v. 2 is a remnant of the earlier version and implies other companions, who are not otherwise mentioned for the reasons just given.

In vv. 11-18, Mary Magdalene is mourner, lover, and momentarily uncomprehending foil for Jesus' revelation. Only in John is the mourning of the women at the tomb, women's special role at a funeral, made explicit: she stood outside the tomb weeping (v. 11). But looking in, she "sees" (*θεωρεῖ* cf. Matt 28:1, etc.) two angels in white garments, one at the head and one at the foot of the place where the body of Jesus had been (v. 12).

> Ask an audience of ordinary Christians what Old Testament scene comes to mind as they picture two angels in a small dark space stationed one at the head and one at the foot of a shelf or slab, and almost immediately someone will respond, "The ark of the covenant in the Holy of Holies." That response is naive, uncomplicated, and correct.[6]

Mary's assumption of body snatchers in vv. 2, 13, 15 is portrayed as the raving of a distraught person, for who would steal the body except the disciples, to whom she first reported the loss? Yet it is a strange echo of the false explanation of the empty tomb in Matt 27:62-66. The motif also prepares for the scene of teasing encounter and recognition that is a perennial favorite for those who ponder the scriptures. Jesus' gentle rebuke about her clinging to him in v. 17 recalls the women's grabbing hold of his feet in Matt 28:9, the only other canonical account in which the risen Jesus appears to women at the tomb (with perhaps Mark 16:9, where the location of his appearance to Mary Magdalene is not specified). Like the women in the accounts of Mark and Matthew, she is given an explicit commission to tell the male disciples, not this time about a coming appearance in Galilee, but about Jesus' ascension/exaltation. The words of her message to the disciples are the foundation text for later portrayals of Mary Magdalene as privileged recipient of revelation from the risen Jesus and "apostle of the apostles": "I have seen the Lord, and this is what he said to me" (v. 18; compare 1 Cor 9:1).

## *GOSPEL OF PETER*

The persistence of the story of women at the tomb is demonstrated by the second-century redactor of this text, who found it necessary to include them, even though they arrive at the tomb after a plethora of witnesses—soldiers, scribes, and elders—have already seen the stone rolled back, two men of transcendent height enter the sepulcher and emerge with Jesus in the middle, with the talking cross behind them, and yet another angelic figure enters the tomb to guard it from the inside and wait for the women! (10:38-11:44).

After all these nocturnal events, Mary Magdalene, a woman disciple *(μαθήτρια)* of the Lord, set off for the tomb early in the morning with her women friends *(τὰς φίλας)*. As in Mark and Luke, they had unfinished business there, but as in John, it is mourning, not anointing. Their reason for not doing it earlier was fear of the Jews. As in

Mark, they wondered who will roll back the stone for them, but found the task already done and a young man who gave them the message of the resurrection. Why they had less fear of the Jews now, especially given the crowd that spent the night at the sepulcher, and why they needed the stone rolled back in order to mourn, are questions not entertained. Also as in Mark, they fled afraid, and it is not said that they told anyone (12:50-13:57). Here, however, they do not have to: half the world already knows! It is interesting to note, however, that the narrative does not provide a line of direct communication about the resurrection events to the male disciples.[7]

Here the story of women at the tomb is still thought important enough to keep in the narrative, even though it seems to serve no purpose, neither first witness nor medium of communication to the other disciples. It can only have been included because it was so much a part of the Easter story that the redactor could not leave it out.

A look at all five of these narratives leads to the conclusion that behind them lies a core version in which Mary Magdalene is the key figure who arrived first at the tomb, found it empty, and went away confused. If this story is secondary to the appearance narratives and late in coming, then the question must again be asked, What purpose does it serve? Does the proclamation of the resurrection necessitate an empty tomb? It would seem not: as is well known, Paul does not allude to the empty tomb tradition—a fact usually put forth in support of the secondary character of the story—nor does the preaching in Acts, though Acts 2:29-31 and 13:34-37 perhaps presuppose it, both in reinterpretation of Ps 16:10 (15:10 LXX).

An analysis of the relationship between resurrection beliefs and resuscitated body in the first-century Mediterranean world cannot be done here.[8] Most texts are ambiguous, but some, e.g., 2 Macc 7:11, 23, seem to suggest a close connection, as does one Greco-Roman apotheosis story, that of Hercules by the first-century BCE historian, Diodorus Siculus *Bibliotheca historica* 38.3-5). Hercules mounts the funeral pyre, which is consumed by a bolt of lightning. Those who come afterwards to gather up the remains find no bones, and conclude that Hercules has been translated to the realm of the gods. Paul's analogies to seed sown and astral bodies in 1 Cor 15:35-44 are open to a variety of interpretations, but it does seem as if some continuity with the physical is supposed in the pneumatic transformation.

However, a close examination of the resurrection teaching of both Paul and Acts reveals that the core event is the appearances of the risen Christ. The allusions to Ps 16:10 in Acts 2:29-31 and 13:34-37 are not offered as proofs, but as supporting scriptural arguments. Beyond these passages, the silence of Paul and of Acts about the empty tomb tradition cannot be taken as proof of its secondary nature, for the author of Acts of course knows that tradition. Rather, their silence is indication that the empty tomb tradition is not foundational to the kerygma of the resurrection. For the earliest Christian community, it served "not as the origin and cause of their Easter faith, but as a vehicle for the proclamation of the Easter faith which they already held as a result of the appearances. It is as such that the Christian historian and the community of faith can accept the report of the empty tomb today."[9]

If this is so, the question remains with even greater persistence: what purpose does the tradition of the women at the empty tomb serve? Why was it kept in this form at all?

## SOCIOLOGICAL ISSUES

In this section, we will consider several aspects of women's cultural behavior in traditional Mediterranean societies and particularly in Judaism, as these considerations bear on the empty tomb narratives: the role played by women in funerals, women's subcultural narrative traditions, and the question of women as witnesses in rabbinic Judaism.

In many traditional societies including those of the eastern Mediterranean, it is women who prepare a body for burial, while men actually convey the body into the tomb. This fits well the gospel accounts: the women prepared the aromatic spices that were wrapped into the shroud and deposited around it, while Joseph of Arimathea (assisted by Nicodemus in John) made the public contact with the authorities, placed the body in the tomb, and secured it. Both men and women lament, often publicly (e.g., 2 Sam 13:31; 18:33-19:8; Job 1:20; 2:12-13; Ezek 29:30-366; Mark 5:38; John 11:33), but it is especially women who carry the tradition with their own particular and culture-specific customs.

The special role of women in mourning is often threatening to male familial and religious authorities, for it is perceived as giving them a power of contact with the dead. Thus woman, who is perceived by male society as having closer connection with birth, is also perceived as having closer contact with death, and that connection with the unclean and the unknown is terrifying and contaminating.[10] Perhaps the suspect motive of unfinished anointing attributed by Mark and Luke to the gospel women for returning to the tomb is further from the actual situation than that provided by the other accounts. For Matthew, they returned simply to see the tomb (28:1); for the Gospel of Peter, to do what women do for their loved ones who die (12:50); and perhaps John is the most forthright and least threatened by women's presence, for Mary Magdalene is simply there, weeping (20:11).

The suggestion has been made that the empty tomb story was preserved (or originated) in women's groups, and finally made its way into the male "mainstream" canonical tradition. Certainly many traditional cultures segregate male and female company in everyday social interaction, and many eastern Mediterranean cultures yet today belong in this category. One need only be present in a village of Greece, Turkey, or an Arab country for the cycle of work and recreation in an ordinary day to be aware of this. In such a society, women have their own oral traditions and storytelling practices, passed on from generation to generation, that portray life and events from the women's point of view.[11] It has been frequently noticed that the apocryphal gospels and acts feature stories about women disciples and especially women leaders in unprecedented numbers when compared to their canonical counterparts. Indeed, the question is regularly asked whether this is one of the reasons for their noncanonical status.[12]

Cycles of stories that originate in women's storytelling circles presumably tell the women's side of an event. This is precisely what the empty tomb stories do, with appearances of the risen Jesus added to Matthew's and John's versions. A different light is shed on the original function of the empty tomb narrative if it can be seen as a "private" version from the world of women, over against the "public" version of appearances to the male disciples, like the very early list in 1 Cor 15:5-7. This list includes no appearances to women. Could it be that the reason for Paul's silence about appearances to women, let alone the empty tomb, is not because the story is secondary, but because it has not yet made its way from the "private" female kerygmatic tradition to the "public" male kerygmatic tradition?

This brings us to the question of the ability or inability of women to be public witnesses according to Jewish law. It has become an unexamined scholarly commonplace in Christian exegesis that women's incapacity to serve as public witnesses is a major reason for the exclusion of appearances of the risen Jesus to women in the official testimonies of Acts and 1 Corinthians 15. This judgment relies heavily on a statement by Josephus (*Antiquities* 4.219) to the effect that Moses' legislation included a prohibition of women serving as legal witnesses because of their "lightness and presumption" *(διὰ κουφότητα καὶ θράσος, τοῦ γένους αὐτῶν)*, a prescription not included in the biblical law codes, but quite congruous with Josephus' valuation of women.

In fact, the inability of a woman to serve as witness in ancient Judaism is not so clear in Mishnaic law. Use of these sources to shed light on first-century Judaism must always be done with caution, since the compilations were done several centuries later. Nevertheless, several points may be relevant. First, women were disqualified from serving as witnesses in a case that necessitated bringing an accusation against another. This is an exemption, not an exclusion, since those not exempted are required to bear witness when necessary. Women were therefore exempted from being compelled to initiate public testimony of a crime committed. This situation does not apply to our case. Second, a woman could testify in matters of credibility: especially on questions that pertain particularly to women (e. g., virginity—including her own); when she was the only one present; in order to free herself or another from a legal obligation (e.g., the death of a husband); and in certain cases when men were not present or it would not be appropriate for them to be there. In business matters, a woman could take an oath of deposit and swear to her own honesty. Women's testimony was valued and drawn upon in the sphere of private affairs, but not in public, reaffirming a traditional distinction often made by modern scholars. That is, in domestic, family, and private law (including business contracts), women functioned as legal persons. But the general reluctance in ancient Mediterranean society to see women as public spokespersons or officeholders applies here as well.[13]

But how does all of this apply to the gospel empty tomb narratives? In all four gospels, Mary Magdalene and others are credibility witnesses, a credibility that is patently rejected by the male disciples in Luke 24:11. In Mark, Matthew, and Luke, the women were the continuous witnesses to Jesus' death, burial, and empty tomb. In Matthew and John, as well as Mark 16:9, they were the first to have an appearance of the risen Christ. In John 20:18, Mary Magdalene gives testimony in formulaic language: "I have seen the Lord, and these are the things he said to me" (cf. 1 Cor 9:1). Credibility is exactly what is at stake in their witness, a witness that is variously received by the male disciples until it is corroborated by their own experience. The silence of later preaching about the women's witness is not so surprising in the public speeches of Acts, located for the most part in public situations with unbelievers. Any respectable ancient eastern Mediterranean male would try to shield the women of his group from such public scrutiny and the risk of scorn. Paul's silence about the women in his enumeration of appearances in 1 Cor 15:5-7, however, in the in-house environment of a group of Christian house churches, is more difficult to explain and will be discussed further below.[14]

## A FEMINIST ANALYSIS

We turn now to an analysis of our findings from the perspective of feminist hermeneutics. First, a hermeneutic of suspicion presupposes that a critical approach to the narratives is necessary in order to expose the androcentric bias operative in the selective transmission of the tradition.

Mark's silencing of the women in 16:8 is subject to many diverse interpretations. One effect, however, is to eliminate the women as witnesses and discredit their reliability. One way of reading the verse is that they did just the opposite of what they were commanded, creating the ultimate failure of discipleship and apostleship in Mark. While those earlier in the Gospel who were told not to proclaim what they had seen did so anyway (1:44-45; 7:36), now when proclamation is finally mandated, the women fail to do it.

What is far more serious, the denial of any historicity to the empty tomb stories completely dismisses the women's role in the original resurrection experience, for without the empty tomb, they play no part. Only the second ending of Mark, recognized by scholarly consensus as secondary and as late as the second century, does not explicitly locate the appearance of the risen Jesus to Mary Magdalene at the tomb (Mark 16:9).

Why did Paul and Acts pass over the empty tomb narratives, and therefore the role of the women, in complete silence? One of two alternative answers is usually given. First, the whole motif of the empty tomb is secondary and late, and Paul did not mention it because he did not know of it. Since it is not an apologetic story and offers no new proof on its own, it makes no difference whether there were men or women at the tomb. This reason, of course, does not explain Luke's silence in Acts, for Luke surely knew the story and has already told it. Though the empty tomb seems presupposed twice in Acts (2:25-31; 13:34-37), it is never made an explicit part of the resurrection witness. The second reason offered, therefore, is that resurrection faith from the very beginning was based not on the empty tomb but on testimony to the appearances of the risen Christ, and it is to this that the earliest kerygma appealed. With this explanation the role of the empty tomb stories is moot; the empty tomb can stay, but it is simply not necessary. It enhances the meaning of the resurrection, but does not add further proof, for the simple reason that the explanation, without supernatural intervention, could just as well be that the body was stolen.

Still a third explanation offered is that Paul represents the combination of Luke's Jewish-Christian Jerusalem tradition with Paul's Hellenistic tradition that does not include the empty tomb, at the expense of others like the Johannine.[15] In this case, Mark and Matthew would represent a Galilean tradition that features the women who came from Galilee. Again, this is a possible explanation for Paul, but does not explain the silence regarding the empty tomb in the preaching of Acts. A fourth explanation, suggested above in part two, is that the empty tomb stories originated in women's circles, and had not yet made their way into the male kerygmatic tradition at the time of the writing of 1 Corinthians. Again, this does not explain the absence of the empty tomb motif in Acts.

However possible or probable some of the above explanations may be, none of them take into account the effect of the elimination of the women's witness. Given the assumed androcentric bias of the accounts (which could have operated almost unconsciously and need not presume active misogyny), it is possible that the empty tomb stories are very old, but are passed over in silence by Paul and Acts precisely *because* they involve the testimony of women. That is, they are not considered as proof of the resurrection, not because faith is based on appearances, but rather the other way around: faith is based on appearances, not the empty tomb, because the empty tomb necessitates reliance on the credibility of women, whereas the abundant male experiences of appearances do not. It is significant for this argument that the appearances to women (Matt 28:9-10; John 20:11-18) do not feature in 1 Cor 15:5-7 either. Once the empty tomb is eliminated, it is not difficult to eliminate also the appearances to the women, which are tied to the tomb narratives and setting except in Mark 16:9.

Yet the empty tomb and the appearances to the women could not be completely eliminated, despite the evidence from Paul and Acts that this was tried. The authority of Mary Magdalene's testimony could not be so easily repressed in the memory of the early church, even if it did not develop until much later in orthodox circles. In other traditions, the tension between the developing authority of the twelve with Peter as their spokesman and that of Mary Magdalene as primary witness can be seen in such documents as Gospel of Thomas 114 and the fragmentary Gospel of Mary. In the former, a Coptic collection of Jesus' sayings from the gnostic Nag Hammadi library, Peter tried to dismiss Mary from the disciples as unworthy of eternal life. Jesus rebuked him by assuring that by becoming spiritual, that is, male, Mary too—and every female who makes herself male—will enter the kingdom of heaven. Whatever the symbolic meanings of female and male in this account, it is clear that the authority of Peter and that of Mary face off against each other, and Mary is included rather than rejected—but only at the expense of what modern interpreters would consider her integral feminine self.

The Gospel of Mary, preserved partially in Coptic from Nag Hammadi and partially in Greek from the early third century, includes Mary's communication to the disciples of the special revelation given her by the risen Christ, a frequent motif in gnostic gospels. But unlike most, here her testimony is followed by Peter's refusal to accept it, since he refused to believe that the Savior spoke to Mary rather than to him and the male disciples. He asked rather petulantly if Jesus preferred her to them. Peter was rebuked by Levi, who declared that the Savior knew her well and loved her more than them (Gospel of Mary 2-31). This time Mary is fully vindicated. These glimpses from the early church of traditions in competition, probably based on John 20:11-18, show how strong was the enduring memory of Mary Magdalene, and how much of a threat her memory was to those who would reject her authority.[16]

The stories of the events at the tomb from the experience and the memory of women erupt into the "public" world and the public testimony of the written gospel accounts, prompting the celebration of a hermeneutic of remembrance. The empty tomb narratives mean that the least significant members of the community were entrusted with the first Easter encounter and the first mandate to proclaim it, reaffirming once more that the last shall be first and the poor shall be blessed. The women disciples who followed Jesus from Galilee to Jerusalem, even to his death on a cross, faithfully performed their *diakonia* of service, witness, and representation (Mark 15:40-41; Matt 27:55-56; Luke 8:1-3; 24:10). The empty tomb narrative is an epiphany story. It is the women's story, and they are the protagonists, for the story is about how they are changed, just as surely as Acts 9:1-19 is about how Paul is changed.[17]

The purpose of the empty tomb stories has less to do with proof than with meaning. The empty tomb indicates not the presence of Jesus (except in the two instances of appearances), but his absence: "He is risen, he is not here." Yet if the entire story is secondary, it surely would have disappeared, or at least the women would have vanished from it, for they and the story came to serve no kerygmatic purpose in the canonical tradition. But they remained because the memory of their role was so persistent that it could not be removed. Its very persistence must indicate that something actually happened that Sunday morning at the tomb.

## NOTES

1. Examples of these three positions, in the same order, are: Reginald H. Fuller, *The Formation of the Resurrection Narratives* (New York: Macmillan, 1971), 50-70; Frans Neirynck, "Marc

16, 1-8 tradition et rédaction," *Ephemerides theologicae lovanienses* 56 (1980): 56-88; Adela Yarbro Collins, "The Empty Tomb and Resurrection according to Mark," The *Beginning of the Gospel: Probings of Mark in Context* (Minneapolis: Fortress, 1992), 119-48. A summary of opinions on the historicity of the empty tomb to 1970 can be found in Edward Lynn Bode, *The First Easter Morning: The Gospel Accounts of the Women's Visit to the Tomb of Jesus* (Analecta Biblica 45; Rome: Pontifical Biblical Institute, 1970), 151-59. See also Pheme Perkins, *Resurrection: New Testament Witness and Contemporary Reflection* (Garden City: Doubleday, 1984).

2. Luise Schottroff, "Mary Magdalene and the Women at Jesus' Tomb," in *Let the Oppressed Go Free: Feminist Perspectives on the New Testament* (Louisville: Westminster/John Knox, 1991), 168-203 [181 and 200 n. 42].

3. Fuller, *Formation of the Resurrection Narratives*, 79.

4. Compelling portraits of Mary Magdalene as one healed of mental illness and of Joanna as a well-to-do and independent lady are given by Elizabeth Moltmann-Wendel, *The Women around Jesus* (New York: Crossroad, 1982), 61-90, 131-44.

5. Maria-Luisa Rigato, "'Remember" . . . Then They Remembered': Luke 24:6-8," in *Luke and Acts*, ed. Gerald O'Collins and Gilberto Marconi (New York/Mahwah, NJ: Paulist Press, 1993), 93-101, 232-35.

6. Robert H. Smith, *Easter Gospels: The Resurrection of Jesus According to the Four Evangelists* (Minneapolis: Augsburg, 1983), 161.

7. While the Gospel of Peter contains invaluable information about the development of gospel traditions, I am not persuaded by the argument that its earliest core predated and influenced the canonical tradition; cf. John Dominic Crossan, *The Cross That Spoke: The Origins of the Passion Narrative* (San Francisco: Harper and Row, 1988).

8. See especially George W. E. Nickelsburg, *Resurrection, Immortality, and Eternal Life in Intertestamental Judaism* (Cambridge, MA: Harvard University Press, 1972).

9. Fuller, *The Formation of the Resurrection Narratives*, 70.

10, The tradition of women's lament as a form of alternate social power still survives in rural Greece, but is rapidly disappearing. See especially Gail Holst-Warhaft, *Dangerous Voices: Women's Laments and Greek Literature* (London/New York: Routledge, 1992); Anna Caraveli, "The Bitter Wounding: The Lament as Social Protest in Rural Greece," in *Gender and Power in Rural Greece*,, ed. Jill Dubisch, (Princeton: Princeton University, 1986), 169-94.

11. See, e.g., Dubisch, *Gender and Power in Rural Greece;* Lila Abu-Lughod, *Veiled Sentiments: Honor and Poetry in a Bedouin Society* (Berkeley: University of California, 1986).

12. See, for example, Stevan L. Davies, *The Revolt of the Widows: The Social World of the Apocryphal Acts* (Carbondale/Edwardsville, IL: Southern Illinois University, 1980); Dennis R. MacDonald, *The Legend and the Apostle: The Battle for Paul in Story and Canon* (Philadelphia: Westminster, 1983); Virginia Burrus, *Chastity as Autonomy: Women in the Stories of the Apocryphal Acts* (Studies in Women and Religion 23; Lewiston/Queenston: Edwin Mellen, 1987).

13. Moshe Meiselman, *Jewish Woman in Jewish Law* (New York: KTAV Press, 1978),73-80; Judith Romney Wegner, *Chattel or Person? The Status of Women in the Mishnah* (New York: Oxford University Press, 1988), 120-26, 188-89. Wegner's conclusion is that in matters of sexuality and reproduction, women are treated legally as men's property, while in all other aspects, they are legal persons in their own right.

14. At issue here is the symbolic location of the house church: a public gathering, as suggested by Paul's selection of the word εκκλησια, or a private, semi-household gathering, as suggested by its location in a private house.

15. Francois Bovon, "Le Privilège Pascal de Marie-Madeleine," *NTS* 30 (1984): 50-62 [52].

16. See Gerald O'Collins and Daniel Kendall, "Mary Magdalene as Major Witness to Jesus' Resurrection," *Theological Studies* 48 (1987), 631-46; Martin Hengel, "Maria Magdalena und die Frauen als Zeugen," *Abraham unser Vater, Festschrift für Otto Michel zum 60. Geburtstag* (Leiden: Brill, 1963), 243-56

17. L. Schottroff, *Let the Oppressed Go Free*, 183.

# FACING TOWARD THE MILLENNIAL YEAR 2000 UNDER BIBLICAL GUIDANCE WITH A FOCUS ON THE RESURRECTION

JOHN P. NEWPORT

Fred Polak, the prominent futurologist, in his study, *Image of the Future,* contends that the most urgent problem facing humankind in this time of change as we approach the millennial year 2000 is to find or develop a worthy central focus or model to guide and empower us and give positive shape to our future.[1] We need a balanced worldview which will provide the stories through which human beings can view reality. We need a worldview which answers the basic questions of who we are, where we are, what is wrong, and what the solution is.

In the context of this symposium, our presupposition is that the worldview which meets this urgent need is found in the concept of the Kingdom of God or the epic biblical drama focused on the resurrection. N. T. Wright sees the biblical drama as consisting of five acts. The first four acts are Creation, the Fall, Israel, and Jesus. Jesus, particularly in his death and resurrection, is climactic and conclusive. Act five consists of several scenes. The first scene involved the writing of the New Testament including the writing of the gospels. This formulation was begun in the earliest post-Easter church. It included the task of reflecting on, drawing out, and implementing the significance of the first four acts, more specifically of act four, in the light of acts one to three.[2]

It is important to note that the resurrection story about Jesus could only make sense in the context of telling Israel's story in the form of Jesus' story. The gospel of the early church, of Paul, and of the evangelists is that the promises of the Jewish scriptures have come true in the resurrection of Jesus. That is why Paul and others kept insisting that Jesus' death and resurrection happened "according to the scriptures" or in fulfillment of them.

Thus we see that the gospels and the epistles were written to invite the readers to enter a worldview. In this worldview there is one God, the Creator of the world who is involved in a redemptive program in his world through his chosen people Israel. Israel's purpose, say the evangelists, is now complete and her own long bondage ended in Jesus, especially in His death, resurrection, ascension, and the coming of the Spirit. The Apostle Paul in his own unique way, particularly in Romans and Galatians, repeats this story. He retells the Jesus story believing the climactic moment has already arrived, and the time to implement the achievement is already present. Paul, like Luke, believed both that the end had come and that the end was yet to come. 1 Cor 15 is the fullest version we have of his retelling of the still future part of the Jewish story. The exodus of Israel was a model of the death and resurrection of Jesus, and both of these events point forward to a greater exodus to come when the whole cosmos will be liberated from Egypt, its present state of futility.

Paul's own vocation as apostle to the Gentiles makes sense in such a narrative. Paul rethought the fundamental Jewish story in the light of Jesus' life, death, and resurrection. Paul at one fixed point in the early years of Christianity retold the story in substantially the same shape as the story told by Luke, Matthew, and Mark. It is the Israel story, fulfilled and transformed by the Jesus story.

For John, Jesus' disciples will go out from the microcosmic world of Israel into the larger world of the Gentiles to announce to the non-Jewish world that its Creator God, the God of Israel, has redeemed it. John's gospel shares the same large story-world which characterizes the synoptics and Paul. For John the logos became a human being.

According to Oliver O'Donovan, the Christian kerygma or drama has as its focal point or starting point the resurrection. The meaning of the resurrection, as the Apostle Paul presents it in 1 Cor 15, is that it is God's final and decisive word concerning the life of his creature, Adam. It is in the first place God's reversal of Adam's choice of sin and death: "As in Adam all die, so also in Christ shall all be made alive" (1 Cor 15:22). In the second place, and precisely because it is a reversal of Adam's decision to die, the resurrection of Christ is a new affirmation of God's first decision that Adam should live. However, this affirmation goes beyond and transforms the initial gift of life: "The first man Adam became a living being; the last Adam became a life-giving spirit" (1 Cor 15:45).[3]

The work of the Creator who made Adam, who brought into being an order of things in which humanity has a place, is affirmed once and for all by the resurrection. It might have been possible before Christ rose from the dead for someone to wonder whether creation was a lost cause. If the creature consistently acted to uncreate itself and with itself to uncreate the rest of creation, did this not mean that God's handiwork was flawed beyond hope of repair? It might have been possible before Christ rose from the dead to answer, yes. Before God raised Jesus from the dead, the hope that we call "gnostic," the hope for redemption *from* creation rather than *for* the redemption of creation, might have appeared to be the only possible hope. "But in fact Christ has been raised from the dead . . . " (1 Cor 15:20). That fact rules out those other possibilities, for in the second Adam the first is rescued. The rebellion of Adam's will, his fateful leaning towards death, has not been allowed to uncreate what God created.

O'Donovan makes it clear that in making the resurrection our starting-point we do not intend to isolate it from the other saving events which the gospel narrative proclaims, least of all from the death of Christ which preceded it and from the ascension and the coming of the Spirit which followed it. These three events are bound up with the resurrection in a mutual relationship.

Richard Tarnas describes in dramatic terms the power of the resurrection in the early church. The early Christians lived in a state of continuous astonishment at the miraculous historical redemption they believed had just taken place. They eagerly anticipated Christ's second coming, the parousia ("presence"), when he would return from the heavens in full glory before the entire world. However, their awareness was centered on the liberating fact that Christ had already initiated the redemptive process—a triumphant process in which they could directly participate.[4]

If the Judaic religion was a great yearning, Christianity was its glorious fulfillment. The life, death, and resurrection of Christ had attained the miracle of the ages, and the resulting emotion was therefore one of ecstatic joy and gratitude. The meaning of Jesus' life was not just that he had brought new teachings and spiritual insight to the world. Rather, by sacrificing his divine transcendence to a full immersion in the agonies of human life and death, within the definite historical conditions of a specific time and place—"suffered under Pontius Pilate"—Christ had forged a fundamentally new reality.

For the Christian, after the resurrection, the world was not an evil imprisonment, not a dispensable illusion, but the bearer of God's glory. History was not an endless cycle of deteriorating stages, but the matrix of humanity's redemption. The gates of paradise, implacably closed at the Fall, had been reopened by Christ.

Ted Peters asks the important question. If what happened on that first Easter was not a historical event, then how do we account for its subsequent cultural, social, political, and eccesiastical influence? How could a nonhistorical nonevent have such an influence? There must be a historical dimension to Jesus' resurrection. The eschatological new reality has entered the flow of historical events in the person of Jesus. Even though the fullness of its transforming power remains outstanding, it has come to authentic expression in the person of Jesus as one event among others within finite history.[5]

The implications of the Kingdom of God, of the epic biblical drama and Christian kerygma focused on the resurrection, can be developed and amplified in terms of three biblical principles: 1) a transforming personal power is made available in the Kingdom; 2) the Kingdom of God (the redemptive activity and rule of God) is designed to work through Christian churches or spiritual Israel in the present stage; 3) the final stage of the Kingdom will be inaugurated by the parousia, the second coming of Christ.

## THE KINGDOM'S TRANSFORMING PERSONAL POWER

An elderly deacon of a Kentucky church used to pray:"O Lord, save us and at *last* when we get to heaven, Give us eternal life." I would respond, "Brother Anderson, you don't have to wait until you die to get at least the down payment on eternal life." In other words, this "age to come" has already intruded into and is now being established in this "age" through the incarnation, atonement, and resurrection of Christ and the extension of his work by the Spirit.

In Luke 17:20-21 the Pharisees asked Jesus to give them a timetable for the approach of the eschatological Kingdom. Jesus replied that the Kingdom of God was already in their midst, but in an unexpected form. It was not accompanied by the signs and outward display that the Pharisees expected and without which they would not have been satisfied. They were blind to the fact that the inbreaking of God's rule, expected at the end of the age, was already occuring in the person and mission of Jesus.

One of the disconcerting facts of our time is the chasm that exists between academic study of religion and the reality of religious experience manifested in transformed lives. A return from a sabbatical leave underscsored this chasm for me. I had been engaged in an abstract, intellectual approach to religion at a prestigious university, but as fascinating and important as this academic work is, I encountered something much more fundamental among ordinary Christians in one of the leading mission minded churches of our time. More or less spontaneous prayer sessions on Saturday evening demonstrated the power of faith as people prayed for mission programs in California and Korea, talked of their opportunities for witness, and told of the ongoing transformations Christ was effecting in their own lives.

The New Age movement now offers an alternative approach to radical personal and social transformation. But it offers a different frame of orientation than does the biblical drama. It is seeking to replace both secular humanism and traditional biblical religion. It says that it is reviving forgotten traditions and promising hope for a new personal and social transformation. Humans are not depraved or dependent on any outside source for deliverance or strength. A person's blindness, which is the root of all his or her problems, can be eliminated by a change or transformation of consciousness. With New Age transformation people realize their own godhood. The limitations of a supposedly finite and imperfect being yield to the limitless potential of the truly enlightened being. Jesus, and other significant religious teachers like Buddha or Krishna, were particularly transparent as bearers of the Divine, or Christ Principle. Such teachers appear regularly throughout history to illustrate the realized life and to train people in particular techniques that facilitate self-awareness of one's inherent divinity. Christ is separate from Jesus. The "Christ" is the perfect god idea—the awareness of the divinity within. Jesus had "Christconsciousness" or the "Christ Spirit" as much or more than anyone, but everyone can have the Christ Spirit. To use popular New Age phrases: we, too, may share the "Christ consciousness" or "the cosmic Christ Spirit."

Christianity faced challenges similar to the New Age movement in the first century. Basic to the Christian response then and now is to focus on the fundamental problem of the human condition. Humans have an essential warping within their nature, and the list of human evils is seen as the product of that warping. This warping separates humans from God, binds the will, and perpetually leads to the re-emergence of idolatry and self-centeredness. This condition defeats or distorts all attempts at reform. Human history demonstrates that as one manifestation of evil is overcome, a new one arises to take its place.

Christians, with their understanding of the human condition, affirm that the problem requires outside intervention to correct the warping and to re-establish contact with the Ultimate Reality in the universe, the Living God. That intervention occurred in Jesus Christ, who alone, as the instrument of the grace of God, can correct the human situation.

As a corollary, Christians also assert the uniqueness of Jesus. He is not one avatar among many. He is God present, and definitively so. He did not manifest a Christ Principle, a modern abstraction of New Age values, rather, he fully incarnated God. He is not primarily a moral example (though he is certainly that as well), but the connecting link by which humanity, warped and unable to fulfill the Divine intention, is brought back into touch and fellowship with God and finds salvation.

In the writings of Paul, the Spirit makes real, in an immediate personal sense, the objective event of Christ's death and resurrection. Saving faith comes only when the outward fact of Christ penetrates to the inner heart of a person and takes possession there. This is the work of the Spirit for "no one can say that Jesus is Lord except by the Holy Spirit" (1 Cor 12:3). The Christian can also know the fellowship and power of the Holy Spirit in the continuing Christian life.

In summary, in New Age spirituality, the truth of human worth is exalted without the balancing idea of human sinfulness. In contrast, the biblical gospel preserves both the worth and the sinfulness of the human person in a delicate balance. Humans are of great worth to God. But humans are sinful and unworthy of God's favor. Nevertheless, God chooses to help humans in and through his incarnate Son, his life, death, resurrection, and the work of the Holy Spirit.

## THE KINGDOM AT WORK THROUGH THE CHURCHES

According to the biblical revelation, God began his redemptive work through Abraham. Out of Abraham's loins came a family, then a tribe, then a nation. Christians need a sense of (re)living the life of this remarkable redemptive movement. One of the most moving of such experiences for me was participation in a Passover celebration at Jewish Theological Seminary arranged by Abraham Heschel. There I saw reenacted the events that helped to constitute the Hebrew nation as a redemptive factor in history.

According to everything that we know of the early Christians, both within and outside the canonical New Testament, they asserted that Israel's purpose had come to its head in Jesus' work, which itself had led up to its appropriate, though highly paradoxical, culmination in His death and resurrection. Those who now belonged to Jesus' people were not identical with ethnic Israel, since Israel's history had reached its intended fulfillment.

These new people claimed to be the continuation of Israel in a new situation, able to draw freely on Israel's images to express their self-identity. They were also able to read Israel's scriptures through the lens of the Messiah and the Spirit and apply them to their own lives. James 1:1 speaks of the Christian people as the twelve tribes in the dispersion. Paul in Gal 6:16 speaks of the Christians as constituting the Israel of God (at least according to many interpreters). I Pet 2:9-10 refers to Christians as the chosen race, as a royal priesthood, as a holy nation.

We should note that the church as God's new creation in Christ is not to be equated with the Kingdom of God. The Kingdom is the rule of God, whereas the church is the human community under that rule. George Ladd stated that the church is created by the Kingdom and is a witness to the Kingdom, an instrument of the Kingdom, and the custodian of the Kingdom.[6]

In a basic sense the church is the presence of the future in the midst of the old. Although the old creation is dying and will be destroyed (at the second coming), a new creation has been born and is growing up in the midst of the old. A new thrust was released in the death and resurrection of Christ. It is here now, present in this life, and will be fully realized in the new heavens and the new earth. Attention will be given to three purposes of the church: 1) to create and exhibit authentic Christian community; 2) to exhibit moral and ethical responsibility; and 3) to evangelize.

First, a basic purpose of the church is *to create and exhibit authentic Christian community* (John 13:34; Matt 22:37-39; Acts 2:44-47; 1 Cor 13:14).

The initial statement of the importance of worship in forming community is found in Acts 2:41-42, 46-47. No detailed prescriptions for worship are given by Paul. In the epistles that have been preserved he wrote of worship incidentally. However, in the epistles to the church at Corinth, which was apparently inclined to spiritual excesses and licentiousness, Paul gave some guidelines. Worship should involve at least proclamation of the Word, baptism, and Lord's Supper.

The church has not only to thank the preaching of the gospel for its origin, but its continued existence is dependent on the inviolate preservation of this preaching. The narration of the story of the deeds of God is a sign of the presence of the Spirit and a tool the Spirit uses to build the Church.

According to Geoffrey Wainwright, worship is crucial and must be built around the epic narrative drama that centers upon its chief character, the risen exalted Lord Jesus Christ. Wainwright points to the Book of Revelation as an example of this emphasis.[7]

This centrality of Christ in worship is the reason for the praise and festive banquet emphases in the early church. Today it is expressed in both a more ordered way in some churches and in a more spontaneous way in other more charismatic churches.

For Wainwright, it is important to maintain this epic drama emphasis because it enables modern day Christians to avoid both pragmatism and psychological manipulation. In pragmatism, worship practices are selected for the immediate visible results which they produce. Such an approach involves the use of psychological tools to manipulate the emotional responses of persons. It is the incorporation into worship of the rationale that "the end justifies the means" and, therefore must be rejected.

Following the epic drama of the Bible in worship should help to establish a foundation which is objective and God-oriented rather than just subjective and human-oriented. The insights of aesthetics and pragmatics are not to be disregarded, but they must not be permitted to be determinative.

Baptism plays an integral role in this drama of worship. The New Testament portrays baptism as a symbolic death to sin and spiritual resurrection which is grounded in the death and resurrection of Jesus. According to Wainwright, baptism should follow the sermon.[8] Others suggest that baptism is appropriate at the first of a service to remind the people of the call of Christ to death to the old way and the resurrection to a new life. In either case, the importance of baptism ought continually to be displayed to congregations. As the classic treatment of this theme in Romans 6 shows, human transformation is found in living out the dying and rising of Christ. Not only is the moral impact of the resurrection important here, but the hope of future resurrection for humans is expressed by their identification through baptism with the resurrection of Jesus.

The role of the Lord's Supper is equally important in worship. The Lord's Supper points back to both the crucifixion and the resurrection. It is a "memorial of the blessed sacrifice of his Son." The participant remembers the formative events of the community's history and of his or her personal pilgrimage. It is the ordinance of mourning and joy, memory and hope (1 Cor 24-26).

The Supper is also a communion now with Christian people in anticipation of life together in the New Heaven and the New Earth. Baptism and the Lord's Supper both draw the eye up to the most striking feature of the life of the early community: the worship of the crucified and resurrected Jesus.

Second, another basic purpose of the church is*to exhibit moral and ethical responsibility* (James 2:14-17; Rom 2:6, 13-16; Gal 5:22; Rev 20:12). In addition to the obvious necessity of personal morality motivated by the resurrection, two issues require comment: 1) the Christian response to the danger of false religions; 2) the obligation of Christians to society.

The Christian response to false religion is treated in various texts, notably Rev. 13:11-14; Matt 7:15; 1 Tim 4:3-4; and 1 John 4:1. According to Rev 13:11-14, next to the antichrist himself, the most evil thing in the world is false religion. Religion can be used to put a veil of sanctity around every kind of evil and prejudice and hate and personal power drive. We saw this in Guyana and Jonestown. We grimace when we read about the Bakkers, the Swaggarts, the Tiltons, and Koreshes and other Christian leaders closer to our own Christian ministries. There is reason for society's cynicism. Religious people can use the Bible to justify personal causes and the status quo. It is no wonder that God judges churches and denominations as well as evil nations.

In contrast, the early church maintained a strong and clear ethical code. We can trace this from Paul's appeals to his converts, through the *Didache*'s description of the true way of life, to Justin's invitation to Antoninus Pius that he make impartial investigation of the Christians and discover for himself just how upright their behavior was. This suggests, remarkably enough, that the appeals of the first generation or two of Christians had been sufficiently successful for subsequent generations to say, "See how differently we behave from you pagans!" The Christians did not expose their children, nor did they indulge in sexual immorality. What is more, they did not commit suicide; and in particular—astonishing in a world where trust and affection were normally confined to family and friends—they cared for one another across the barriers formed by normal culture.

That there was a striking difference in general praxis between pagans and Christians is without doubt. That there was even a viable *expectation* of a striking difference is remarkable in itself.

Early Christians took it for granted that in the details of their behaviour they should be significantly different, in clearly defined ways, from their pagan neighbors. According to O'Donovan, Christian ethics "springs from" God's gift in Jesus Christ.[9] The life and teaching of Christ, his death, resurrection and ascension, his sending of the Spirit, and his expected return to judge, all these can and do incite believers to ethical seriousness.

The other issue requiring comment, the Christian's obligation in society, is treated throughout the New Testament, but one should note at least Rom 13:8f.; Matt 25:31-46; and Luke 4:8-19. The church has both a spiritual mission and a cultural mandate. Its primary goal is to bring the glad tidings of reconciliation and redemption to all races and nations, but it is also responsible for teaching people to be disciples of Christ in the very midst of the world's plight and dereliction. M. Erickson agrees that the crucial issue in scripture is our bondage in sin, and the separation and estrangement from God which sin has produced.[10] Political freedom, economic sufficiency, and physical health, important as they are, are secondary to spiritual destiny. Not nearly enough is said in liberation theology about what the New Testament clearly indicates to be the primary dimension of salvation.

Since we have indicated that the context for the purpose of the church is provided by the eschatological "already-not yet" theme, it should be noted that this theme provides a strong motivation and dynamic context for Christian ethics. Jesus asserted that his followers would remain *in* the world. He also declared that all authority had been given to him and that the god of this world was being ousted. It therefore follows that while Christian ethics has a personal and interior dimension, it must also have a public and exterior proclamation arising from Jesus' authority and based upon his conquest. This proclamation is the gospel of Christ whose rule is not postponed to the chronological end of the ages, but has even now begun. The chief purpose of New Testament eschatology is not to encourage speculative fascination with world politics but, rather, to compel a deep and unremitting commitment to both evangelistic and ethical action in the world.

G. Fackre contends that as the eschatological expectations of the early Church lengthened, the sense of responsibility for the secular systems and processes increased.[11] That expanded perspective, at worst, has led to the captivity of the Church by the authorities and powers. At best, the Church has issued a prophetic challenge to these secular structures in obedience to the Lordship of Christ.

We must steer clear of both a theocracy, where the church actively wields political power, and a rationalistic, egalitarian democracy, where the voice of the people is equated with the voice of God. Democracy in the Christian context is based on the axiom that all people are equal before God—all are created in his image and all have sinned and fallen short of his glory. We need today a democracy anchored in theonomy, in which ultimate authority is assigned to the living God rather than to the nation or religious institution.

Third, a crucial and dominant part of the function of God's people and the churches is *direct missionary and evangelistic endeavor* (Matt 28:18-20; Acts 1:7-8; 15:13-17; Rom 10:13-15). The evangelistic task is part of the Christian fulfillment of Judaism. I remember well Professor Abraham Heschel emphasizing that Israel's purpose was to be a universal spiritual light to the Gentiles. He then lamented the fact that the Jewish people were not fulfilling this dominant universal mission spoken of by the prophet Isaiah. Following Rosenzwieg, Heschel adopted the double covenant view. He contended that through Christianity, God's covenant with Israel was opened to the Gentiles. As I was leaving New York City to go to the Far East on a mission under the auspices of the Southern Baptist Foreign Mission Board, Heschel put his arms around me and prayed that many Gentiles would come into the covenant through my witness to Jesus Christ.

The New Testament goes beyond Heschel and affirms that all people (Jews and Gentiles) must hear and receive the Good News of Christ to come into the covenant. Early Christians believed that what they had found to be true was true for the whole world. The impetus to mission sprang from the very heart of early Christian conviction. If we know anything about early Christian praxis, at a non- or sub-literary level, it is that the early Christians engaged in mission, both to Jews and to Gentiles. The irresistible expansion of the Christian faith in the Mediterranean world during the first 150 years is the scarlet thread running through any history of primitive Christianity. This missionary activity was not an addendum to a faith that was basically "about" something else (e.g., a new existential self-awareness). World mission is the first and most obvious feature of early Christian praxis.

The New Testament writers claimed that, though there is only one god, all human beings of themselves cherish wrong ideas about this one god. In worshipping god thus wrongly conceived, they worship an idol. Pagans worship gods of wood and stone, distorting the creator by worshipping the creature. Jews, Paul argued in parallel with this, have made an idol of their own national identity and security, and so have failed to see what the covenant faithfulness of their God, the God of Abraham, has done in Jesus Christ.

The New Testament writers also saw a relation between the Christian witness and the fulfillment and end of history (1 Cor 9:16; Rom 1:14; Eph 3:1; Rom 10:14ff.; Matt 24:14). As we have seen, the Church stands between the dawning of the Kingdom with power in the cross and resurrection and the coming of the Holy Spirit and its full consummation in the *parousia.* Further, the Church's preaching is not just a demonstration that the Kingdom has come with power. This preaching and witness is a precondition for the final glorious unveiling of the Kingdom. The Gentiles must be gathered in before the Lord comes in glory. The full consummation cannot be made manifest until all nations have heard the good news. Oscar Cullmann brings this out very forcibly.[12] The Kingdom is already being realized in history. However, the full realization waits on the accomplishment of the world mission.

This is the theme of Paul in Romans 9-11, which in many ways is a commentary on Mark 13:10: "The gospel must first be preached to all nations." In Romans 10, Paul contends that God is following an exact plan. There must be offered to all an opportunity to hear the gospel (Rom 10:14). The Jews have already heard it, but not all have received it. Therefore the call now goes to the Gentiles. The full plan is surrounded with mystery, but within that mystery he clearly saw his own calling as apostle to the Gentiles (Rom 11:13). This understanding of Paul is supported by Johannes Munck in his study of the apostle.[13]

Yet, with the focus on evangelism, there is an emphasis on religious freedom in relation to Christian mission. The religious freedom emphasis teaches that while religious convictions in communities are of crucial importance, human sin and finiteness make it impossible for any one group to claim that they represent the absolute truth. Therefore, religious communities are to share their vision by persuasion and incarnation rather than by utilizing civil powers or brainwashing to enforce their basic ideas and worldviews. In such an atmosphere the biblical faith can freely proclaim and share its highest insights. Biblical people should hold and witness to their ultimate religious convictions with a sufficient degree of humility to allow them to live peacefully with those who have other convictions.

Such an approach is actually in keeping with the biblical interpretation of sin. According to this teaching, pride and self-centeredness constitute the essence of sin. Authentic biblical faith, therefore, should encourage humility and moderate pride.

In fact, George Lindbeck affirms that the biblical doctrine of sin shows forth when organized denominations or church groups seek to use political force to dominate culture.[14] Ambitions of this kind are forbidden to the servants of a crucified Messiah. It was the forgetting of this prohibition which was the great sin of the Church during the age of medieval dominance. Not only did the church acquire influence; that in a sense was inescapable, but it sought to promote and maintain that influence by worldly means.

It should be noted that the attempt to commandeer the state on behalf of the church confuses the roles of both state and church. To make Christianity the religion of the state is to rob it of its universal character and to reduce the Almighty to a national icon. The missionary witness is thereby greatly impaired, if not nullified.

To impose Christianity on society or seek to make it the legal basis of a social order generates undue hostility in a pluralistic context. More importantly, it undermines the uniqueness of the Church. It also fails to recall that it is the Church, not America or any other nation, that is a "chosen people, a royal priesthood, a holy nation, a people belonging to God, that you may declare the praises of him who called you out of darkness into his wonderful light" (1 Pet 2:9).

Undergirding the threefold purpose of the church to create community, to live ethically, and to evangelize are two biblical emphases, apocalyptic and prophetic.

The apocalyptic concept recognizes the reality and continuing power of evil and Satan in history and anticipates their defeat. In the New Testament, especially in the first three Gospels, Satan and the demonic appear openly and in an extensive way. It is the contention of C. K. Barrett, James Kallas, George Ladd, and others that the demonology-eschatology motif is a dominant theme in the first three gospels and Paul.[15] The New Testament teaches that satanic forces have a measure of real control in the world.

Although the satanic and demonic emphasis is central in the New Testament, after Christ won the victory over Satan with the cross and the resurrection, there is less in the New Testament about exorcism (driving demons out) and more about the great commission with its emphasis on preaching, teaching, and baptizing. George Ladd feels that a more satisfactory translation of Col 2:15 is that of the RSV which understands the verse to mean that Christ has disarmed the spiritual powers, stripping them of their insignia of rank or of their arms.[16] Thus the verse states that by his death and resurrection Christ triumphed over his spiritual enemies, winning a divine victory over the cosmic powers. The fallen angels are ultimately helpless before the power of God and his angels. Furthermore, in the New Testament, all such spiritual powers are creatures of God and therefore ultimately subject to his power.

We need to remember, however, that though Christ's triumph is a decisive triumph, a once-for-all victory, it does not immediately issue in the abolition of rebellion at the human or cosmic level. As John saw, the powers of this world are passing away (1 John 2:17), but they still constitute a power with which one must deal.

How one deals with the demonic and expectation of God's victory affects how one relates to other Christians. Many see rigid dispensationalism as overstating the demonic influence. With the rise of dispensationalism there was a strong tendency to give up on this world and look forward to the world to come. Some advocates of dispensationalism even went so far as to suggest that efforts at social amelioration were actually counterproductive. This is true in the logic of dispensationalism because things had to get worse before they would get better through thc pretribulation rapture and the return of Christ.

The dispensational vision also illumines the anti-dialogue or anti-fellowship attitudes of some parts of evangelical Protestantism. The mainstream Christian church (especially Catholic but also the majority of Protestants) which did not accept the dispensational doctrine came more and more under the accusation of being nominal or "lukewarm" and finally was even identified with the forces of the antichrist which would arise in the last days to persecute the true Christians. This led to demands for ecclesiastical "separation." G. Marsden suggests that they often maintained a steadfast refusal to cooperate with apostates and even sometimes with friends of apostates.[17] This pessimism of some Christians is the opposite of some other extremes such as recent attempts by the religious right to control politics or the postmillenial assumptions of reconstructionists who would seek to set up a theocracy.

A biblical balance on how Christians relate to government can be observed from texts like Rom 13:1-7 and Rev 18:1-3 and 9-10. The apocalyptic, or negative viewpoint, which is developed especially in times of radical change and persecution, does not dominate the Old Testament or New Testament. More characteristic is the prophetic emphasis of the Old Testament, the prophets and Jesus and Paul. So, for the Christian a pessimism regarding the world which releases the Christian community from responsibility in order to withdraw is not possible. God has not withdrawn himself, but is able and will do signs and wonders for which we must diligently look and expectantly wait. Our responsibility is here in this life now, and there must be no evasion of it.

Evil and good continue to exist side by side. Conflict between the two continues during the present age. However since Christ has won the victory the ultimate outcome of the conflict is never in doubt. The enemy is fighting a losing battle.

The prophetic (or sovereignty) idea emphasizes that Almighty God continues his activity in history despite the power and work of the evil one. God ploughs up the soil of humanity making it ready for the seed of authentic Christianity and an appreciation of God's revealed creational, ethical way of life. We should not be surprised that a Christless or even anti-Christian autonomy and ideology threatens to disintegrate life. However, these forces are repeatedly limited, held back, turned back, or converted by the positive signs of Christ's reign in the world. This fact should fill us constantly with gratitude and amazement, giving us power to enter the future without fear and with the expectation of seeing new signs.

For example, the Bible states that God used Assyria, Babylon, and Persia to discipline the Hebrew people to bring them back to his redemptive purposes. Later he used Rome and Greece to prepare for the ministry of Jesus and for the mission of Paul at the "kairotic" time in history.

In our era, which is surely one of the most dramatic periods in human history, God is plowing up the soil of humankind in Asia, Africa, the former Soviet Union, Eastern Europe, and South America, and *even* in our own country, making it ready for the seed of the gospel.

In the United States we see the human soil being plowed up in readiness for the gospel and creation ethics. For example, the AIDS crisis and the family crisis are opening up doors for a presentation and appreciation of the Christian view of sexuality and the family. Christian counseling, youth ministry, and children's work have taken on new relevancy.

The crisis related to male dominance and sexual abuse has plowed up new openings for the study and incarnation of the biblical model of the relation of the male and the female. We are finding afresh in this remarkable Christian model, reciprocity, respect, diversity, and the union of male and female in love and obedience in Jesus Christ. We are to submit to one another in Christ and in love.

The hunger and housing crisis is opening doors for contextual evangelism and compassion. The racial crisis is opening doors for the biblical teachings on the worth of all humans made in the image of God. In Christ, there is no East nor West nor slave nor free.

The economic crisis has opened the door for the biblical teachings on justice and compassion and a critique of unbridled consumerism. The environmental crisis calls for a critique of consumerism and an emphasis on the biblical doctrine of creation and environmental responsibility. The breakup of the hierarchical model is giving opportunity for us to emphasize servant leadership in pastoral ministry.

There is a crisis related to the negative power of television, music, and the popular media. This opens the door for new opportunities to use the arts in a more constructive manner.

Widespread concern about aging, death, and dying has opened the door for geriatric programs and interest in Christian teachings on the life beyond.

The popularity and growth of charismatic groups emphasizing emotion calls for a restudy of balanced spiritual formation and music programs and Christian apologetics based on faith and reason.

We would agree with Max Stackhouse when he contends that these cultural changes and crises are opening up new doors for the right kind of sharing and witness in the context of prayer, religious liberty, and love.[18] William Martin's new biography of Billy Graham shows how unparalleled doors have opened for the mature Graham.[19] What a day for every facet of the work of the churches!

## THE FINAL STAGE OF THE KINGDOM INAUGURATED BY THE PAROUSIA

A Hindu student once told me. "I just don't understand you. In the first place you don't look like a religious leader. You are too fat. I think of a religious leader as a thin, emaciated sort of person who spends his time contemplating the other world. In the second place, I can't understand this emphasis on attempting to get people involved in history and mission. I think of a religious leader as someone who teaches me a yoga technique to restore my atman or soul to Brahman, or to reach a nirvana stage."

My response could only be a contrast between the biblical idea of history with that of much of the Hindu world. Instead of the myth of eternal return or reincarnation or the cyclical view of history, the biblical idea has a strong sense of the historical and the future. History has a purpose, a beginning, and an end. It is moving towards its climax. People who are a part of the redemptive community have a tremendous sense of urgency and involvement.

The life of the Christian does indeed have a constant tie with the contemporary Lord and Head of the church, but it has a time framework in two other quite notable respects. The Christian view of history has a constant backward look. It has its basis and justification in God's central and decisive act in Jesus of Nazareth—his life, ministry, death and resurrection. But the Christian perspective faces not so much backward as forward. With the risen Lord, the Christian faces forward and moves forward to the full realization at the end of the age. This means that Christians live with tension. The time of the church is the time in which God has begun his decisive redemption but has not yet fully completed it. This redemptive time must move forward under the Lordship of Christ until the day when Christ comes to complete his work. Thus the New Testament never floats off into the stratosphere of timelessness to seek there a perfect bliss.

In fact, the Christian understanding of the movement of history towards its climax helps to explain the dynamic of the early Church. The Apostle Paul would write, "We should redeem the time." We should have a sense of spiritual responsibility. We should have moral courage that does not worry about pragmatic results. We should have incentive.

The "not-yet" emphasis in the New Testament puts us in touch by the Spirit with the future. Our anchor is lodged in the "not-yet" and our life is given direction and firmness. In the New Testament, the eschatological hope remains as an undergirding emphasis. Christ will be manifested, and we shall be manifested with him in glory (Col 1:27; 3:4). Christians still await a Savior from heaven (Phil 3:20-21). The church is, however, a colony of heaven, and the heavenly life may be enjoyed here and now. The New Testament is concerned with the present life in Christ in the church and in the world.

An authentic Christian attitude is characterized by differences *with,* not withdrawal *from* the world. It is also marked by radiation. Christians are not only to be a light in the world (Phil 2:1; Eph 5:8) but also the light of the world (Matt 5:14).

Justin Martyr in the middle of the second century is as emphatic as anyone that the second coming will happen. He did not know when; but then the key passages in the New Testament always said that it would be a surprise. Tertullian, at the end of the second century, looked forward to Jesus' return as the greatest show on earth, outstripping anything one might see at the stadium or theater.

As far as the early Christians were concerned, the most important event—the resurrection of Jesus—had already happened. One did not need to worry about the timing of that which was still to come. Back in the first generation, Paul could quite easily see the whole complex of events, including the Lord's return, as being likely to happen at any time. 1 Thess 4 and 5 bear witness to that. But there is no suggestion that the Lord's return itself must happen within a generation, or that its failure to do so would precipitate any sort of crisis.

In short, the eschatological expectation of the first Christians bestowed a unique vantage point from which to view every dimension of reality. It also gave them a unique impulsion to act in light of this hope. Their eschatology was not merely a set of beliefs concerning future events but also the attitude or atmosphere aroused by these events.

The "already-not-yet" eschatological vision is the glow that suffuses everything here and now in the dawn of an expected new day. The early Christians symbolized this unique eschatological view of life and history by repeating an untranslated Aramaic word when they met each other on the streets—Maranatha, Maranatha (Our Lord Comes). They had learned to live with the biblical paradox—the Kingdom is already here but it has not yet come in its fullness. Christ has come, he is coming, and he will come.

We cannot resolve this paradox, but while it is still day, we must redeem the time and buy up the opportunity.

## CONCLUSION

I know that for many people this is a time of anxiety and even perplexity in the midst of the chaos, crises, sin, and difficulties of our time. But if we have the larger biblical vision, we can see that in another sense this is one of history's greatest times for authentic Christianity.

The central biblical image of the Kingdom of God has great importance and relevance for our time. Christians can and need to face the Millenial Year 2000 with the central biblical vision of the Kingdom focused on the resurrection as dominant in our lives. I hope that we can incarnate this model in its delicate, biblical balance. I hope that we will continue to pray with authenticity the two biblical prayers. "Thy kingdom come, on earth as it is in heaven," and the last prayer of the Bible, "Even so, come, Lord Jesus."

## NOTES

1. Fred Polak, *Image of the Future* (San Francisco: Jossey-Bass, 1973).

2. N. T. Wright, *The New Testament and the People of God* (Minneapolis: Fortress Press, 1992), 132, 141ff.

3. Oliver O'Donovan, *Resurrection and Moral Order* (Grand Rapids: Eerdmans, 1986, 13f.

4. Richard Tarnas, *The Passion of the Western Mind* (New York: Ballantine Books, 1991), 121f., 127f.

5. Ted Peters, *God—the World's Future* (Minneapolis: Fortress Press, 1992), 194f.

6. George Eldon Ladd, *A Theology of the New Testament* (Grand Rapids: Eerdmans, 1974), 111-119.

7. Geoffrey Wainwright, *Doxology* (New York: Oxford University Press, 1980), 166f. and 242.

8. Ibid.

9. Oliver O'Donovan, *Resurrection and Moral Order* (Grand Rapids: Eerdmans, 1986), 12.

10. Millard Erickson, *Christian Theology*, 3 vols. (Grand Rapids: Baker, 1984), II, 562f.

11. Gabriel Fackre, *The Christian Story*, 2 vols. (Grand Rapids: Eerdmans, 1987) II, 232.

12. Oscar Cullmann, *Christ and Time* (Philadelphia: Westminster, 1964) and *Salvation in History* (New York: Harper and Row), 1965.

13. Johannes Munck, *Paul and the Salvation of Mankind* (Atlanta: John Knox Press, 1959).

14. George A. Lindbeck, "The Church's Mission to a Postmodern Culture," *Postmodern Theology*, ed., Frederick B. Burnham, (San Francisco: Harper and Row, 1989), 54-56.

15. C. K. Barrett, *The Holy Spirit and the Gospel Tradition* (London: SPCK, 1958), 46-68; James Kallas, *Jesus and the Power of Satan* (Philadelphia: Westminster, 1968), 202-215; and Ladd, *Theology*, 400-403 and 434-436.

16. Ladd, *Theology*, 435.

17. George Marsden, *Reforming Fundamentalism* (Grand Rapids: Eerdmans, 1987), 135-138, 148, 162-165, 190-192.

18. Lectures given at Southwestern Baptist Theological Seminary, 1992.

19. William Martin, *A Prophet with Honor* (New York: William Morrow, 1991).

# RESURRECTION, COSMIC LIBERATION, AND CHRISTIAN EARTH KEEPING

ROGER E. OLSON

> For the creation waits with eager longing for the revealing of the sons of God; for the creation was subjected to futility, not of its own will but by the will of him who subjected it in hope; because the creation itself will be set free from its bondage to decay and obtain the glorious liberty of the children of God. We know that the whole creation has been groaning in travail together until now; and not only the creation, but we ourselves, who have the first fruits of the Spirit, groan inwardly as we wait for adoption as sons, the redemption of our bodies. For in this hope we were saved.
>
> (Romans 8:19-24a, RSV)

One might very well wonder what this famous statement of Paul's regarding the future has to do with the resurrection of Jesus. I believe that the Easter event lay not in the background, but in the foreground of the apostle's mind as he wrote this. Thus, this passage as no other provides the linkage between several issues crucial for a holistic theology for today: liberation, resurrection, eschatology, and ecology. I will argue that the linchpin in this systematic theology is the resurrection of Jesus' *corporeal* body.

The central questions with which I deal are "Is hope for the renewing of the cosmos a part of Christian eschatology assured by the resurrection of Jesus' body?" and "If so, what does this say for a Christian doctrine of nature and a Christian praxis of earth keeping?" I agree with Karl Heim, one of this century's greatest and most neglected Christian thinkers, that "The new and fundamental conception that Paul brought us, and the only thing which delivers us from nihilism, is the conviction that the resurrection of Christ is not merely a miracle which happened to a particular individual, but the beginning of a total transformation of the whole cosmos."[1]

I also agree with Lee Daniel Snyder that the resurrection of Jesus is "the key concept for a Christian understanding of nature."[2] If we see nature from the perspective of the *new creation* promised and proleptically presented in the Easter event, we are better prepared to understand, value, protect, and enhance it. Only when we know of its fulfillment can we truly "groan together with it" and become partners with God in overcoming its infirmity.

The earliest Christians understood the resurrection of Jesus Christ as the prolepsis of the final and complete liberation of all creation from its bondage to decay and of the perfect transformation of the cosmos into God's kingdom of glory in which God will be "all in all." A recovery of this dimension of the resurrection can, I believe, contribute to an enriching of evangelical concern for and involvement in stewardship of nature.

Unfortunately, themes which belong together in contemporary Christian theology have been pulled apart so that there is an appalling lack of systematic reflection to undergird sound pastoral teaching and exhortation. This is nowhere more evident that in the doctrine of nature—which receives little attention from theologians or pastors. The interdependence of certain biblical and theological themes needs to be rediscovered for the sake of a renaissance of evangelical concern for and involvement with the redemption of the natural environment. These themes which are intrinsically interrelated are: Jesus' resurrection, liberation, eschatology, and ecology.

The resurrection has received a great deal of attention in the last few decades of Christian theology. No one has done more to place it at the center of theology than Wolfhart Pannenberg, who almost single handedly recovered the event from the debilitating effects of demythologization and dehistoricization in the theologies of R. Bultmann and K. Barth. However, Pannenberg's reflections were limited to the *historicity* of the Easter event and its significance for christology, eschatology, and anthropology. This led to a certain *anthropocentrism* in his doctrine of the resurrection which neglected its significance for a Christian view of the nonhuman natural world. For Pannenberg, the Kingdom of God proleptically realized in Jesus' resurrection is *the unity of humanity,* but what of the *unity with the nonhuman natural world?* What does the resurrection say about the future and present of the natural cosmos? On this subject Pannenberg has had little to say.

Few theologians have attempted to relate the resurrection to *ethics.* The most notable exception is British theologian Oliver O'Donovan whose book *Resurrection and Moral Order* (Eerdmans, 1986) placed the Easter event at the heart of Christian ethics. Like Pannenberg, however, there is a severe anthropocentric constriction of the doctrine of the resurrection in this otherwise very helpful work. O'Donovan restricts his ethical reflections almost entirely to the significance of Jesus' resurrection for the *human* world order with little about its import for an ethic of nature.

Two German theologians, both now deceased, pointed the way toward a more holistic and systematic use of the resurrection. Erlangen scholar Walter Künneth and Tübingen professor Karl Heim contributed independently what might be called a "resurrection ontology"—a Christian view of the entire universe, including both human and nonhuman natures, centered around and based upon the resurrection of Jesus. To this we will return.

Liberation theology has been the focus of much attention by both theologians and pastors in recent decades. Unfortunately, the concept of "liberation" has been limited almost exclusively to the human world as the "full humanization of man [sic]." Once again, especially in light of the present ecological crisis, one cannot help but notice a severe anthropocentric constriction in most liberation theology. For many liberationists, the *exodus event* rather than the *Easter event* is the centerpiece of reflection on the nature of God's liberating activity. To date no major work on the liberation of the entire cosmos has appeared, and no liberation theology has utilized the resurrection of Jesus as the central theme for explicating what liberation means.

In a similar way, eschatological theology has become a major influence in contemporary theology without significant reflection on the interdependence of its central theme with resurrection, liberation, or ecology. Jürgen Moltmann launched the so-called "Theology of Hope" with his book of that title in 1964. Since then numerous theologians have utilized this future-orientation in developing their views of God, Christ, salvation, and ethics. In spite of promising beginnings, however, this school of thought has underutilized the resurrection of Christ and its anticipation of the new creation for developing a Christian view of nature. Two of Moltmann's recent books, *God in Creation* (Fortress Press, 1992), and *The Spirit of Life* (Fortress Press,1993), have pointed toward a new Christian emphasis on ecology, but rather than basing this on the Easter event, they have drawn more on a panentheistic doctrine of the Holy Spirit.

Finally, a spate of theological works has appeared recently on Christian ecology, and more are sure to be offered in the near future. Unfortunately, most of these ignore a strong biblical foundation, borrowing for instance on pagan images such as the "Mother Goddess" myth, or seeking their biblical-theological foundation in the doctrine of creation rather than the model of new creation anticipated in Jesus' bodily resurrection.

Rosemary Ruether's recent *Gaia and God* (Harper, 1992) represents the first failing—an ecofeminist theology of earth healing which totally ignores the resurrection and practically deifies nature. It is of little help to evangelical pastors or lay people who wish to develop a sound biblical view of ecology.

Better is Douglas John Hall's *Imaging God: Dominion as Stewardship* (Eerdmans, 1986) which bases a Christian theology of the natural environment and ethic of environmentalism on the doctrine of the *imago dei*. Once again, however, the contribution of the resurrection is virtually ignored.

A recent entire issue of *Evangelical Review of Theology* (April, 1993) was devoted to "Evangelicals and the Environment: Theological Foundations for Christian Environmental Stewardship." As creative and helpful as these articles are, they do not include any serious or sustained reflection on the significance of the Easter event for an evangelical witness in relation to the natural world.

What is needed is a biblically informed systematic theology of nature aimed at a Christian ecological stewardship which brings together in intimate interdependence the themes of resurrection, liberation, eschatology, and ecology. To date this has hardly been attempted and cannot be fulfilled within the confines of this brief essay. However, I will attempt to sketch out the direction such reflection might take, beginning with an investigation of Paul's theology of cosmic liberation, moving on to its basis and guarantee in Jesus' bodily resurrection, and ending with some reflections on the ethical implications for contemporary Christian environmental life and witness.

What is the New Testament's view of *nature*? In contrast to all forms of *gnosticism*, Paul and other New Testament writers emphasize both its *goodness* and its *materiality*. In contrast to modern *naturalism*, they emphasize its *openness* and *potential for redemption*. Perhaps the most fascinating aspect of Paul's theology of nature lies in the passage from Romans 8 with which I began. It is a vision of God's future act of absolute and total redemption of the entire natural universe.

For Paul, the natural universe is "creation" and therefore God's. God is its author and sustainer. However, something has gone terribly wrong with God's creation. It has been subjected to futility by coming into bondage to decay. Paul's theology of the "fall" is not limited to the human story, but widens to encompass all of natural created reality. (I will leave aside questions such as how the "fall" affected angels or whether they are part of the "natural universe.") In this theology of fallen creation Paul compares the universe to a prisoner serving a life sentence yearning with every fiber of his being for deliverance and to a woman in birth pangs looking forward to the new life to come forth from the struggle.

Nature, then, is not *meant* to be subject to corruption, bound to decay. This state of futility in which life is gained and kept only through a struggle for survival, which is cut short or slowly dies out, is not the natural state of affairs in the universe. It is the "fallen" condition and somehow nature itself knows this. It yearns to be free and groans for liberation.

Karl Heim described this fallen state of nature beautifully:

> Everywhere there reigns an unremitting warfare. Creatures, which need each other for their life, obstruct and destroy each other. The whole of nature is pervaded by an unsatisfied need. Paul can therefore speak in ch. VIII of his Epistle to the Romans of a groaning of the whole creation crying out for deliverance from the bondage of corruption.[3]

Paul is describing more than just the concept of "nature red in tooth and claw" in his theology of cosmic bondage. Not only animal and plant life, but the realities of time and space may be involved in the brokenness of "futility." Can liberation from bondage to decay be conceived without a healing of time itself?

Karl Heim described the fallenness of the natural world in terms of a fall into "polarity." The subjection to futility and bondage to corruption and decay which are part and parcel of Paul's theology of cosmic liberation are undergirded by the condition of *polarity* within space and time. The opposition of past and future and fleeting transitoriness of time in which it is impossible to grasp the present are not part of God's original design and will be overcome in the consummation. The spatial limitation of materiality is also part of this "principle of polarity" which grips nature in an unfulfilled and even fallen state.[4]

How did this bondage to corruption occur? Paul points to a mystery and all we can say is that the world of nature in which we now live is no longer as it came from the hand of God or is not yet as God intends it to be. Whether one regards the "fall" as in some sense historical and involving nature itself or as the "not-yetness" of the creation is not crucial. The point is that for Paul the natural, physical world, including time and space, are not fulfilled as God intends them to be. It is safest to conclude with Heim that "The insoluble nature of this ultimate riddle of our whole world existence belongs, like everything else, to the fallen state of this world."[5] In any case, the sovereign God who creates the world of nature is not uninvolved in its subjection to futility, but "subjected it in hope" with the aim and intention of a redemption greater than original creation.

Heim and others who have investigated the fallenness of nature and all that that means have generally overlooked the newest and perhaps most pressing aspect of nature's bondage to decay—the destruction of nature by human technology. On the one hand, nature has fallen into corruption, which at the very least means the biological principle of life only by death. This is what modern naturalists consider purely natural and what Paul believed to be a sign of nature's bondage. But on the other hand, nature is also in the grip of a bondage Paul did not foresee. We are all becoming aware today of the devastating effects of human exploitation of nature and disregard for its limited resources. I believe it is perfectly appropriate for us to*read this new situation back into* the meaning of Paul's description of nature's plight in Romans 8. Part of the fallenness of nature is its *openness* to being raped by humans. The actual rape of nature by humans is another shackle added to its imprisonment and another cause for its groaning.

Paul is less interested in the exact *cause* of this situation of cosmic bondage than in its eschatological liberation, and so we should focus more on the latter than the former *except*, insofar as understanding our own role in nature's groaning can help us begin to groan together with it and help liberate. What does Paul see ahead for the natural order? What will this liberation for which it cries out be like?

Here I cannot avoid indulging in some speculation since the apostle gives little by way of specific information. However, I am not speculating alone but following clues left before me by such great thinkers as Karl Heim and Walter Künneth.

First of all, the liberation will be a *transformation of this cosmos* and not its obliteration or substitution with something entirely different. In the consummation toward which Paul looks in hope and for which nature groans *this* same universe will be liberated, renewed, and united with heaven. Again, Paul is thinking of a comparison between the new creation and the bodily resurrection of Jesus Christ in terms of *continuity and discontinuity.* Just as with his discussion of the resurrection in 1 Corinthians 15, here the apostle allows no spiritualistic dilutions of the faith. Just as his theology of life after death might be called a resurrection realism, so his view of the future can be called a "realism of the world to come."[6] Karl Heim emphasized this realism in his eschatological-resurrectional ontology against all modern forms of gnosticism which would reduce world redemption to an existential myth or, on the other hand, to a spiritualized state of affairs. "If God is to have the final say in world events," Heim declared, "then his will must materialize."[7] Surely Heim has caught the spirit of Paul's antignostic message with his statement that "The battle [to master reality] is fought in the narrow space of corporality" and not in some supra-material, spiritual realm.[8] Karl Barth's friend and partner in the formation of "dialectical theology," Edward Thurneysen, stated this Pauline realism of cosmic redemption more brilliantly and beautifully than anyone else:

> The world into which we come in the future of Jesus Christ is thus not another world, it is this world, this heaven, this earth, but both of them having passed away and been made new. It will be these woods, these fields, these cities, these streets, these men, who will be the scene of redemption. Now they are battlefields . . . one day they will be fields of victory."[9]

The other side of Paul's realism of the world to come is hinted at in Thurneysen's description of the consummation: " both of them [heaven and earth] having passed away and been made new." Just as Paul's realism of the resurrection contains both continuity and discontinuity [between the body buried and that raised] so there is *discontinuity* between nature as we know it at present (even apart from pollution) and nature as it will be in its redeemed state. The "passing away" Thurneysen expects should not be interpreted as total destruction. Rather, it is the first moment of a process of *transformation* to a new condition.

What is the liberated form of nature toward which Paul stands on tiptoe, as it were, gazing forward together with the whole of creation? Karl Heim stresses the change just as radically as the identity with the old world. The liberation will not involve merely an "improvement of some things" in this present world so that only the gravest abuses will be abolished. It will not be a mere turning over of a new leaf any more than Jesus' resurrection was merely a resuscitation of his crucified body! Rather, as with Jesus' bodily resurrection, Paul envisions a new form of nature with a new principle of life not subject to corruption and decay:

> The abolition of the present world form will show itself negatively in that the rigid, fundamental law, to which all life in the present world order is subject, and without which we cannot imagine any life in the present age, will be cancelled—the biological principle that life can only be increased

> and multiply by a process in which other life is suffocated and destroyed with pain and deadly torture.[10]

Of course this radical transformation must necessarily imply a new form of material existence which we can hardly imagine. Once again, the analogy with resurrection is inescapable. Walter Künneth labels this new reality of both resurrection body and new creation of nature "ein verklärtes leibhaftes Sein"—a transfigured corporeal (or physical-bodily) being.[11] This "new corporeality" will not be a purely spiritual being such as God has, but will be beyond even the gross materiality with which creation began. Transformed by the Spirit of God—like Jesus' body—nature itself will be loosed from its bondage to material limitations within space and time. As we will see, the only way to imagine this is to look to Jesus' bodily form of existence during the period between Easter and the ascension. This is the new form of creaturely existence Paul struggles to describe in chapter 15 of 1 Corinthians, and here in Romans 8 he applies it to the entire cosmos. Here theological words fail and the theologian is forced to turn to doxological language to describe this new form of corporeal existence which is the precondition to God being "all in all." Hendrikus Berkhof sums up this future liberation of creation foretold by Paul in words that slide from the theological into the doxological:

> Everything will share in that glorification. This includes whatever we may then call "nature": the earth, this minute planet on which God started this grand experiment; and time and space, without which human existence is unthinkable. Space does not become the unbounded free space of God, but it will border on it, be open toward it, and thereby be unimaginably enlarged. And time is not turned into the eternity of God, yet past-present-future will not be dissociated and ebb away, but constitute an unimaginable togetherness as a paradigm of eternity.[12]

All this is to say that part and parcel of the New Testament "blessed hope" of believers is the redemption of creation and that this new creation is a *liberation* of something beloved by God which presently groans in a state of bondage to death and decay. This future liberation will *not* be a release from material existence, as gnosticism in all its forms hopes for, however, but a transformation to a hardly imaginable new corporeal existence analagous to Jesus' bodily existence after his resurrection.

I now turn to the main point of this essay: the centrality of the resurrection of Jesus to this entire eschatological promise and hope of cosmic liberation. Although Paul does not specifically mention Jesus' bodily resurrection in Romans 8 he clearly has that event in mind as he struggles to describe the redemption hope of the cosmos. That nature will be liberated in the ways described earlier is for Paul grounded entirely in the reality of the Easter event just as our hope for personal bodily resurrection is so grounded (1 Corinthians 15). Walter Künneth is correct that "It is certain that Pauline eschatology makes the perfecting of our earthly corporeality definitely dependent on the bodily resurrection of Jesus. . . . "[19]

The connection between Jesus' resurrection and the consummation and all that that includes is more than simply an *anticipatory* connection. That is, Jesus' resurrection does *more* than merely *foreshadow* or *prefigure* the new creation of our bodies and nature itself. Rather, "The reality of the resurrection is already the eschaton and does not merely have a relation to it."[14] In Paul's mind is the idea that just as Jesus' death cancelled the bond of guilt which stood against sinful humanity creating reconciliation between God and the human race, so Jesus' resurrection cancelled the curse which sin and the fall have brought upon nature creating a new kind of nature free of the law of sin and death. The full effect of the atonement in complete reconciliation between God and the new humanity is yet future—the world, the flesh and the devil still have their say. Yet, on the cross the cause and proleptic realization of God-human reconciliation objectively happened. So the full effect of the resurrection upon physical nature is yet future—in the meantime it remains in bondage to decay. Yet, in the resurrection the cause and proleptic realization of cosmic liberation objectively happened.

So, in a way similar to Irenaeus' recapitulation theology of Jesus' atoning life and death, Paul's theology is one of cosmic *precapitulation.* By his resurrection in a new bodily form Christ Jesus provides a new head (*kephale*—understood as ontological source) for nature ahead of time. Now nature itself is summed up in and lives from its future renewal in hope because of Jesus' bodily resurrection.

This is what Künneth and Heim mean by "resurrection ontology." For Paul and hopefully for us, the resurrection becomes a liberation from the misery which sin and the fall bring to the temporal order. Thus, it is the answer to the question of meaning raised by our existence threatened by decay and death.[15] Because of it, we Christians see nature in a new and different way. Because we know of its future liberation we "hear" its groaning *as* a cry for freedom and cry along with it "Maranatha!"—"Lord Jesus, come quickly!"

So, the resurrection of Jesus is for Paul a *cosmic event* —in fact, *the cosmic event!* It is identical with the inauguration of the total transformation of the natural world including our bodies. "The resurrection of Jesus as cosmic event signifies the change of the entire universe from its death-destiny to a destiny of life.[16] Künneth and Heim both rightly interpret the new mode of existence Paul looks forward to for nature as strictly analogous to Jesus' new mode of existence after his resurrection. In fact, the two modes are one new mode of existence separated only by earthly time. Künneth calls it a "new corporeal-ontological reality.[17] Heim calls Jesus' new body the *prototype* of the new, perfected physical world.[18] At the very least it involves a materiality not subject to the law of death: an imperishable and incorruptible corporeality.

Beyond liberation from the law of death, however, Jesus' resurrection also established a new ontological reality not subject to the "mortal law of mutual displacement." In other words, the new nature will exist like Jesus' resurrection body in a new dimension which transcends ordinary physics. There will be a "transformation of time and space" by the abolition of the "law of polarity."[19] Jesus' body, though truly corporeal and existing in relation to other bodies, had (or "has") properties not known in nature. It could appear and disappear and pass through matter. Karl Heim looks forward to a similar state for all of nature in the liberated creation. He draws on the parable of the "Flatlanders" who lived in a four-dimensional reality which remained totally inscrutable to those living in two or three dimensional realms.[20] Exactly how to picture this is, of course, beyond our ability since we live in that lower state of fewer dimensions under the law of polarity. We do have the forty days of Jesus' earthly existence between Easter and Ascension, however, with which to imagine what the future condition of the entire cosmos might be like.

The question with which I began was whether the redemption of the entire cosmos—of nature itself—is assured by the resurrection of Jesus Christ. I believe it is. While we can say little about the exact nature of the future mode of existence of the liberated creation, I believe *that* part of the proclamation of the Easter message is that all creation will be liberated from bondage to decay. The resurrection of the dead to a new and incorruptible *bodily* existence applies to *both* individual person *and* the universe itself because of Jesus' incarnate intersection with nature.

The practical and ethical implications of this holistic understanding of resurrection as cosmic liberation are fairly clear. Just as the resurrection of Jesus forms the *ontological* ground and basis of the future liberation of nature, so it also forms the *ethical* ground and basis for a future-oriented ethic of environmental stewardship or "earth-keeping." It is to this connection between resurrection and Christian ecological ethics that I now turn.

I propose two theses regarding this connection. First, Carl Braaten was quite right when he declared that our present ecocrisis is a *spiritual crisis* beyond the scope of technological salvation.[21] Second, in light of this, the resurrection of Jesus Christ can and should provide the critical principle and driving force for Christian stewardship toward healing nature.

First, how can Christians see the ecocrisis as anything *less* than a spiritual crisis in light of the theology of nature outlined by Paul in Romans 8? There Paul makes clear that creation (nature) is *suffering* and in need of *liberation*. Certainly this is not to say that technological answers based on scientific theories and innovations are to be eschewed. Of course not. However, it is to say that for a Christian such approaches and answers cannot be the final word anymore than ideological and social engineering solutions can be seen as panaceas for human social problems. The latter point is better understood by many Christians today than is the point about nature. In light of Paul's theology of promised cosmic liberation in Romans 8, nature must be recognized by Christians as part of God's redemptive plan and action, and proclamation and social action must extend in that direction under correct spiritual and theological principles.

Once one sees the spiritual dimension of the ecocrisis, the temptation of romanticism creeps in. That is, just as some have fallen to the mistaken notion that the answer to problems of oppression and exploitation of the poor, or of ethnic minorities or women, is to romanticize them to the point almost of worshipping them, so some have concluded that the spiritual solution to the ecocrisis is to worship Mother Nature. Of course, in both cases, the "worship" is not blatant, but hidden in half-true cliches such as "preferential option" and "Gaia."

The proper direction, provided I believe by the resurrection, is Christian realistic identification with nature in its suffering. Peter Stuhlmacher pointed in this direction in his 1987 essay on the ecological crisis and biblical theology:

> In the midst of the ecological crisis, it is our task to prevent God's creation from being completely victimized by civilization or from being deified by the apostles of nature who are hostile to civilization. In view of the ecological crisis, we must try first to empathize with creation, consciously and repentantly groaning with it—to use the words of Paul—as it lies in travail.[22]

How can the resurrection of Jesus provide help to Christians and the church in the spiritual ecocrisis? I propose that it provides help in two ways: first, as a driving motive in liberating activity; and second, as a critical principle for involvement in ecopraxis.

The resurrection of Jesus Christ is the event which drove the earliest Christians out into the then known world evangelism and mission. The *ethical* significance of the resurrection has not been as widely or deeply explored among Christians until recent times, but today it is becoming more apparent that it relates not only to evangelism, but also to the world of social structures. Oliver O'Donovan, Regius professor of moral and pastoral theology at Oxford University, has recently provided a full-scale treatment of that relevance in *Resurrection and Moral Order: An Outline for Evangelical Ethics* (Eerdmans, 1986). However, few interpreters have sought to apply the resurrection to the ethics of environmental stewardship. Once again, Karl Heim pointed the way forward years ago:

> If we do not transpose the power of the risen Christ into action then we live in an illusion. . . .Genuine and undivided love and devotion for this earth and the physical existence of the individual and the community can arise only from faith in the risen Christ. . . .Our confession of the Risen One is not genuine if it does not immediately and naturally place us in an attitude of responsibility for the terrestrial reality in which we find ourselves according to God's ordinance.[23]

The resurrection body of Jesus Christ connects body, and therefore nature, with spiritual and moral reality. It is an extension of and new dimension to the incarnation. It clearly declares that God loves and cares for nature and intends its redemption. If God loves and intends to redeem something, how can we be indifferent to it now? The only possible escape would be to claim that the resurrection body of Jesus was *not* part of nature, but transcends it in some ethereal, spiritual way. However, that contradicts the inner logic of Paul's theology of cosmic liberation in Romans 8 and brings us to a consideration of the second point—the resurrection of Jesus as the critical principle for a Christian theology of cosmic liberation.

A "critical principle" is an absolute touchstone of moral and ethical truth which can be applied to a specific area of moral existence. Karl Heim articulated the critical principle provided by the resurrection for a Christian attitude toward nature: "The Resurrection of Christ is in the first place God's great 'yes' to life as contrasted to any autumnal hankering after Nirvana."[24] In other words, no Christian can hold or condone an attitude toward nature which demeans it or ignores its plight because in the resurrection God has affirmed the earth and life on it. The resurrection was no escape from planet earth. Rather, it was God's announcement and prolepsis of earth's final and total liberation from everything anti-earthly, including death and decay.

There is another side to this critical principle, however. Not only does the resurrection affirm life on earth (nature), but it also forbids any shallow optimism. The earth and nature must be *transformed*. "Turning over a new leaf" will not do. In the ultimate and final end, God must redeem nature supernaturally. Just as the kingdom of God among men and women cannot happen merely by social engineering, so the new earth cannot appear merely through ecological activism. However, the resurrection does provide the hope that sustains fervent effort to approximate the new, liberated creation which lies in the future.

Liberation is God's activity and its approximation in anticipation is delegated to us. That leads Christians into ecopraxis under the rule of the resurrection as critical principle. What shape might this resurrection-based ecopraxis take? First, the church must begin raising Christian consciousness about the groaning of creation and its need for liberation. This task corresponds to one of liberation theology's forms of mission with something that might be called a "pedagogy of ecoppression." Christians need to be made more aware of God's concern for nature and his intent to redeem us and it together. I believe the majority of Christians who think about the future of the earth tend to imagine it as a total destruction and not as a renewal. They need to be taught from pulpit and lectern that the resurrection of Jesus Christ calls for Christian action on nature's behalf.

Second, the church must become a "community of light" in the midst of a darkening of nature. From recycling on church property to demonstrations against the most egregious examples of corporate pollution, the church needs to hold up a prophetic example and show society that the body of Christ cares about the future of nature.

Third, the church must make concrete and specific proposals for a better future for nature. Every church of any size, and entire Christian denominations, should appoint committees similar to missions committees with the specific task of "imagineering the future" in environmentally sensitive ways based on the critical principle of the resurrection.

## NOTES

1. Karl Heim,*The World: Its Creation and Consummation. The End of the Present Age and the Future of the World in the Light of the Resurrection* (Philadelphia: Muhlenberg Press, 1962), 137.
2. Lee Daniel Snyder, "Some Thoughts on a Theology of Resurrection," *Encounter* 36 (Winter, 1975), :67.
3. Heim, *The World*, 109.
4. Heim, *The World*, 112ff.
5. Heim, *The World*, 129.
6. Walter Künneth, *The Theology of the Resurrection* (London: SCM, Press, 1965), 288.
7. Heim, *Jesus the World's Perfecter: The Atonement and the Renewal of the World* (Edinburgh and London: Oliver Boyd, 1959), 170.
8. Heim, *Jesus*, 168.
9. Edward Thurneysen, "Christus und seine Zukunft," *Zwischen den Zeiten* 1931, part 3, 209.
10. Heim, *The World*, 117.
11. Walter Künneth, *Entscheidung heute: Jesu Auferstehung—Brennpunkt der theologischen Diskussion* (Hamburg: Friedrich Wittig Verlag, 1966) 84.
12. Handrikus Berkhof, *Christian Faith: An Introduction to the Study of the Faith*,, rev. ed. (Grand Rapids: Eerdmans, 1986), 541.
13. Künneth, *The Theology of the Resurrection*, 237.
14. Künneth, *The Theology of the Resurrection*, 242.
15. Künneth, *The Theology of the Resurrection*, 217ff.
16. Künneth, *Entscheidung heute*, 196.
17. Künneth, *Entscheidung heute*, 205.
18. Heim, *Jesus*, 173.
19. Heim, The *World*, 137ff.
20. Heim, *The World*, 138-139.
21. Carl Braaten, *Eschatology and Ethics: Essays on the Theology and Ethics of the Kingdom of God* (Minneapolis: Augsburg Publishing House, 1974), 184.
22. Peter Stuhlmacher, "The Ecological Crisis as a Challenge for Biblical Theology," *Ex Auditu* III (1987), 14-15.
23. Heim, *Jesus*, 179-180.
24. Heim, *Jesus*, 174.

# RESPONSE TO ROGER OLSON'S PAPER

STEVEN BOUMA-PREDIGER

## RESURRECTION, COSMIC LIBERATION, AND CHRISTIAN EARTH KEEPING

Was famous nineteenth century atheist Ludwig Feuerbach right when he claimed that "nature, the world, has no value, no interest for Christians" since "the Christian thinks only of himself and the salvation of his soul?"[1] Was James Watt, former Reagan era Secretary of the Interior and devout Christian, correct when he asserted that we should not care too much for the natural world, e. g., national parks and wilderness areas, since Jesus is coming back soon? Was renowned medieval historian Lynn White Jr. accurate in his claim that "Christianity bears a huge burden of guilt" for the ecological crisis?"[2]

These questions raise important and timely concerns about the relationship between Christian theology and the current plight of the earth. As indicated by the above, many people believe that Christianity, and especially Christian theology, sanctions the plundering of the earth. Many claim that one of the primary causes of contemporary ecological degradation is the world-negating beliefs and practices of the Christian church.

In sharp contrast to the above perspective, Roger Olson argues that Christian theology, especially certain claims about the resurrection of Jesus, not only does *not* sanction the exploitation of the earth, but that *properly* understood such theology provides good grounds for an ethic of earthkeeping—of care for the earth and its many creatures. He asserts that texts like Rom 8:19-24 provide "the linkage between several issues crucial for a holistic theology today: liberation, resurrection, eschatology, and ecology" (123). More exactly, his thesis is that "the linchpin in this systematic theology is the resurrection of Jesus' corporeal body" (123).

Olson's thesis is in my view, both right-headed and much needed. In other words, his claim that the resurrection of Jesus' corporeal body is crucial for understanding the cosmic scope of redemption and the flourishing of all of God's magnificent creatures is as biblically sound and theologically warranted as it is all too often ignored and overlooked. Such a claim, and the more earth-affirming theology that it generates, is a necessary corrective to the creation-denying theology and *de facto* worldflight practices of the Christian church. In short, I heartily endorse his major argument.

Olson explicates his thesis in a number of very helpful ways. For example, he is quite correct to criticize much of contemporary theology for being too anthropocentric (124). Nonhuman creation is noticeable by its absence in many such writings. In addition to Künneth and Heim I would add American Lutheran ecumenical theologian Joseph Sittler to the list of exceptions to this claim. As early as 1954 Sittler was doing Christian theology informed by ecological concerns and with great sensitivity to the cosmic scope of divine grace.[3]

In addition, Olson rightly emphasizes that the redemption and liberation of creation "will be a *transformation of this cosmos* and not its obliteration or substitution with something entirely different" (127). Contrary to the ever popular James Watt eschatology, which claims that there is *only dis*continuity between this world and the next, Olson forcefully maintains that there is *continuity* as well as discontinuity between this mode of existence and the mode of existence of the eschatological consummation. An important biblical text in this regard is the often mistranslated 2 Peter 3:10. Rightly understood, in my view, this text speaks of basic *continuity*—the earth will be *found*—not discontinuity between this world and the next.[4]

Olson rightly draws out an important implication of the previous claim, namely, that redemption does *not* mean an *escape* from materiality, but rather a *new mode* of *corporeal* existence. In keeping with the penultimate confession of the Apostle's Creed, he maintains that the "radical transformation" of the eschaton "must necessarily imply a new form of material existence which we can hardly imagine" (128) and thus "this future liberation will *not* be a release from material existence" (128). He thus argues that since Jesus' resurrection is the ground for all resurrection, and since his resurrection was corporeal, "the eschatological promise and hope of cosmic liberation" must involve a (transformed) corporeal creation (128). Olson makes it clear that, pace James Watt, for God matter matters.

In addition to making these important claims about the *nature* of redemption, Olson also makes claims about the scope of redemption. In other words, he not only rightly argues that the consummation will be a transformation rather than obliteration of creation, but also that the resurrection of Jesus is "the inauguration of the total transformation of the natural world including our bodies" (129). Redemption is an event *cosmic* in scope and thus inclusive of all of nonhuman creation. As the often misunderstood or overlooked covenant with creation found in Gen 9 indicates, God does not save or redeem only humans. In verses 8-17, six times the text refers to a covenant which God makes with *non*human creatures. *All* creatures are beneficiaries of God's grace.

Finally, Olson is quite right to assert that "our present ecocrisis is a *spiritual crisis*" (130). As the authors of a recently published volume claim, "the global environmental crisis . . . is fundamentally a moral and religious problem."[5] If, as Olson states, "nature must be recognized by Christians as part of God's redemptive plan and action," then the exploitation of our nonhuman siblings is a matter of central theological importance. As Sittler eloquently and passionately puts it:

> When we turn the attention of the church to a definition of the Christian relationship with the natural world, we are not stepping away from grave and proper theological ideas; we are stepping right into the middle of them. There is a deeply rooted, genuinely Christian motivation for attention to God's creation, despite the fact that many church people consider ecology to be a secular concern. "What does environmental preservation have to do with Jesus Christ and his church?" they ask. They could not be more shallow or more wrong.[6]

Let me turn now to some of my questions. These questions fall into *two main* categories. First, I am unclear as to the meaning of certain key terms or expressions. For example, it is unclear to me what is meant by "openness" (125, 126). Creation, it is stated, is open. Does this mean nothing more than that it is *possible* for creation to be redeemed and exploited? Or does it mean that we live in a *nondeterministic* universe? Or does it mean that we live in an *unfinished*, developing cosmos? To take another example, what is meant by the expressions "the spatial limitation of materiality" (126) and "the gross materiality with which creation began?" (128) How is gross materiality different from nongross materiality?

To press the point further, with what are we dealing here? If one speaks of the "nonhuman natural world" (124), then what is the human natural world? What precisely is the meaning of the "natural physical world" (126, 129) or "physical nature" (126, 129)? Is there nonnatural or nonphysical nature? If "for Paul the natural universe is creation" (125) and if creation is synonomous with nature (130), then why use the secularized term nature at all—a term that usually implies that nonhuman creation is autonomous and unrelated to God? As many rightly argue, it makes a difference whether the nonhuman world is spoken of as creation or as nature.[7] As Sittler reminds us:

> The term "creation" contains and requires a God-postulation. Until we get this through our heads, and admit nature as *creation* into our reflective nexus, and permit nature there to retain its intransigent reality, we shall neither theologize soberly nor be theologically guided to act constructively.[8]

In short, there is a need to clarify crucial terms—terms which bear directly on important claims regarding the nature of redemption and resurrection existence.

Second, I want to ask a question which was asked many times during the symposium: from what exactly are we and our non human neighbors delivered? In Olson's paper I find two distinct concepts of the fall. First, fallen creation is subject to decay (125, 126) and corruption (126) and exists in a state of futility (126). This concretely means that creatures are locked in a "struggle for survival" and "unremitting warfare" (125). Creatures are bound to the "biological principle of life only by death" (126). This "law of death" (129) will be overcome in the consummation. But is this the most adequate reing of Paul in Romans 8? What do ματαιότης and φθορά mean here? Furthermore, does this mean that in the eschaton there will be no death of any kind at all? Is creaturely existence possible without death of some sort?

But fallenness is also understood as bondage to time and space itself (126)—as "bondage to material limitations within space and time" (128) But is bondage to time and space, whatever that exactly means, really a result of the fall? Are humans *qua* creatures not *essentially* temporal and spatial? Will the new nature mean that we as humans somehow cease to be temporal at all i.e., eternal, or non-spatial? My concern is that resurrected human existence not be conceived of as noncreaturely existence, for the denial of creatureliness is the primary sin. These last questions point to a related question: given that the creation will be transformed rather than obliterated, what is the precise nature of the transformation? What does it mean to say that resurrection existence is "a total transformation" (123) or "new form of creaturely existence" (128 )?

These questions should not detract from the aforementioned positive comments regarding this paper. Olson has creatively put before us an extremely important question, namely, whether Christian theology can any longer remain on the sidelines with respect to the issue of ecological degradation. He has argued on grounds internal to the Christian faith itself that Christians have every reason to be better keepers of the earth. The bodily resurrection of Jesus the Christ implies that *all* creation will be *transformed*, not destroyed. Redemption is the restoration of creation rather than the obliteration of creation. Given both the crisis of our age and the demands of biblical faith, Christians must vigorously act in ways consonant with that belief. Once again, Joseph Sittler puts the point most forcibly:

> If in *piety* the church says, "The earth is the Lord's and the fullness thereof" (Ps. 24:1), and *in fact* is no different in thought and action from the general community, who will be drawn by her word and worship to "come and see" that her work or salvation has any meaning? Witness in saying is irony and bitterness if there be no witness in doing.[9]

## NOTES

1. Ludwig Feuerbach, *The essence of Christianity* (New York: Harper and Row, 1957), 287.

2. Lynn White, "The Historical Roots of our Ecologic Crisis," *Science* 155 (1967): 1207.

3. For a defense of this claim see, e. g., Peter Bakken's fine University of Chicago dissertation, "The Ecology of Grace: Ultimacy and Environmental Ethics in Aldo Leopold and Joseph Sittler;" and my University of Chicago dissertation "Toward a New Christian Theology of Nature: A Critical Comparison of Rosemary Radford Ruether, Joseph Sittler, and Jürgen Moltmann."

4. For corroboration of this reading, see, e..g., Richard Bauckham, *Word Biblical Commentary 50: Jude and 2 Peter* (Waco: Word, 1983).

5. Steven Rockefeller and John Elder, ed., *Spirit and Nature: Why the Environment is a Religious Issue—An Interfaith Dialogue* (Boston: Beacon, 1992), 1.

6. Joseph Sittler, *Gravity and Grace* (Minneapolis: Augsburg, 1986) 15.

7. Robert Quam, "Creation or Nature? A Manner of Speaking," *Word and World* 11 (Spring 1991): 134-136. See also Loren Wilkinson et al., *Earthkeeping in the 90's* (Grand Rapids: Eerdmans, 1991), 347ff.

8. Sittler, *Essays on Nature and Grace* (Philadelphia: Fortress, 1972), 99

9. Sittler, "Evangelism and the Care of the Earth," in *Preaching in the Witnessing Community*, ed. Herman Stuempfle (Philadelphia: Fortress, 1973), 104.

# THE FAMINE OF THE WORD *

Sermon preached during the Sunday Morning Service
October 10, 1993

Elizabeth Achtemeier

*Scripture Readings:* Amos 8:11-14; 1 Cor 15:12-28

> Behold, the days are coming, says the Lord God,
> When I will send a famine on the land:
> not a famine of bread, nor a thirst for water,
> but of hearing the words of the Lord.
> They shall wander from sea to sea,
> and from north to east;
> They shall run to and fro, to seek the word of the Lord,
> but they shall not find it.
>
> (Amos 8:11-12)

We live in a culture in which a lot of frantic searching is taking place. *The Washington Post* used to publish a weekly guide of things to do, and one of the sections in that guide was entitled simply "Coping." Under that heading were listed all sorts of groups to whom readers could go for help—a mental health clinic, a women's rap group, a coffee for Parents without Partners, a Crisis Intervention Counseling service—all places where people who were searching might find some satisfaction.

There is a hunger abroad in the land, and an uneasiness—an uneasiness that perhaps we have lost the key to life, or maybe even our souls. And so people are searching, searching frantically for something to feed their inner selves. Books on how to find inner peace or outer confidence, or on how to get one's head together, crowd the bookstores and their best seller lists every year. And of course, spiritual groups and gurus of every kind claim millions of adherents. In short, we have a modern American duplicate of the picture Amos gives us in our text—of people wandering from sea to sea, running to and fro, sometimes aimlessly, sometimes desperately seeking a word from God.

The difficulty is that so few seem to be finding that word, and the question that therefore naturally arises is, Just what have we church leaders been doing? We are the

---

* An earlier version of this sermon was printed in *Faith and Mission* 2 (1985): 64-69. Permission granted to reprint the sermon.

stewards of the Word of God, are we not? At least that is the way Paul describes us—as stewards of the mysteries of God, required to be faithful, sent by our master to hand on the word and to make disciples of all nations. Why is it, then, that it takes a Dr. Kevorkian's helping terminally ill patients to end their lives to start our church people discussing the issues of death and dying? Is it because we church leaders have failed to grapple with the deepest enigmas of human life and have not communicated a gospel at whose center is an empty tomb?

I am haunted by this text from Amos—haunted because it seems to picture so well what is happening in our churches: the vast, milling corporate throng of people coming to us Sunday after Sunday and are failing to find in our words and actions the Word of God to feed their lives.

We church leaders are always ready to blame someone else for the famine of the Word of God, of course. It is our materialistic culture which keeps our people from hearing, we say. It is the heedless pursuit of pleasure, the scramble after a buck, the abandonment of all values and morals that have turned the masses away from our message.

But Amos lived in the same sort of society, where the sabbath was but an irritating interruption in the commerce of buying and selling, where wealth and status were the goals and "never mind the poor," where the worship experience was abundantly enjoyed, but rarely applied to life, where the Word of God was turned into a sanction of the status quo. Amos too served a people of heedlessness and hedonism, of violence and vulgarity, who had lost the truth of God in their lives and so had become like sheep without a shepherd.

But strange as it may seem, it was precisely institutional religion which Amos blamed for that faithless situation. We should never forget that it was Amaziah, the priest of God, who himself forbad the prophet to preach, and who drove him away from the king's sanctuary at Bethel. It was the religious leaders who brought on the judgment of the famine of the Word of God. And thus it was within the temple, the prophet said, that God would begin his judgment. In Amos' words: "I saw the Lord standing beside the *altar,* and he said, 'Smite the capitals until the thresholds shake, and shatter them on the heads of all the people' " (9:1). It was upon the heads of the worshipping community that the wrath of God would fall, because the populace was searching for the Word of God, and they had not found it in organized religion.

Could it be that Amos' indictment is also against us and that there is a famine of the Word of God in our land precisely because we church leaders have failed to proclaim the message? Could it be that people come to us week after week, searching for the Word of God, and go away unfed and hungry, because instead of giving them the bread of heaven and the water of eternal life, we try to feed them with the fruits of our own sinful desires instead?

What is it that we argue about in the Christian Church these days? Our main arguments are about sex, aren't they? Most of the national assemblies of our mainline denominations have been spending their time trying to decide if they can possibly summon up the courage to say that, according to the scriptures, sexual intercourse should be limited to marriage, and single people should be celibate—and that in a nation simply devastated by adultery and AIDS, by rape on college campuses and teenagers having children, or single-parent homes sunk into poverty, by homosexuality grown increasingly strident, and by an abortion rate that slaughters 1 1/2 million children every year. No, we have not fed our people with the Word of God, and they are dying from the famine.

But then the theory in the halls of many of our academic institutions is that there really is no Word of God to preach and teach anyway—no objective speaking through the scriptures by the Holy Spirit. No, goes the theory, the Bible means only what its interpreters bring to it. It has no real truth behind it. And so it can mean whatever we want it to mean, and finally everyone can do whatever he or she wants to do. Right and wrong are relative. There is no such thing as Truth. And God? Well, we can make him or her into any sort of deity we desire, with no authority of a biblical text hanging over our manufactured idol.

I sometimes wonder, friends, if you and I have slipped into that position, or maybe just have decided to remain silent about the truth of the scriptures. Or worst of all, are we starving people for the Word of God because somewhere along the line, we have stopped believing it ourselves? And so now, rather than proclaiming the gospel, we are using our positions in the church and classroom simply to feed our own pride? There can be something terribly demonic about being a leader in the religious field—to see ourselves as professional holy men and women, with built in authority and status. That position can end up as nothing but an ego-trip, in which, almost unbelievably, we use the terrible need of others for our self-gratification. When a person tells us that a lecture or a sermon was helpful, we feed on the glory it brings us, and we forget that the disciple is never above his or her master. And our master emptied himself of every glory and became obedient, even unto death on a cross. "Why do you call me good?" Jesus asked. "No one is good but God alone." But we have forgotten that Word of our Lord in our churches and classrooms, and use the scriptures to our own advantage.

But into our hands, good Christians, into our hands—unworthy empty vessels though we be—God has entrusted his gospel. Think of the power—the terrible, terrible power—he has thereby entrusted to us: the power to change people's lives, the power to speak the Word of the cross and thereby to prompt the return of some lost son to the house of his heavenly Father, the power to proclaim the resurrection to a grieving mother and thereby to give her hope that her child is not dead, but alive in Christ and shall embrace her once again.

Is it any wonder that Jesus commands us, Take the good news into all the world? Or is it any wonder that the prophets, the bearers of the Word of God, were warned: "If you do not speak my Word to the people, their blood is on your hands?" You and I are entrusted with a gospel that can make all things new. Is it any wonder then that if we withhold that gospel and cause one child of God to stumble, it would be better for us to have a great stone placed round our necks and to be drowned in the depths of the sea?

You see, the very heart of the gospel which is entrusted to us is the announcement of the resurrection of our Lord, the proclamation that Christ is alive, and that therefore we can find eternal life and purpose for living in him. And I want you to imagine for a moment just what it means to some soul if we do not let him know that, if we just keep silent in our world and never share our faith that Jesus Christ is risen. Paul put the consequences of such silence very clearly in our New Testament lesson: "If Christ has not been raised, " he wrote, "your faith is futile and you are still in your sins. Then those also who have fallen asleep in Christ have perished. If for this life only we have hope in Christ, we are of all people most to be pitied." Can you imagine what it means for someone to be in that siuation—to experience the famine of *that* Word of God? Never to have the gladness of Easter's triumph so shared with them that they can clutch it to their heart with joy and live day by day with its assurance?

That is indeed a pitiful fate, as Paul said it is, because for a person without the gospel, there really is nothing more to this world than the jungle out there in our city street. For a person without the gospel, evil and violence and vulgarity are just going to have their way until they slowly destroy all that is lovely and pure and innocent, and society comes crashing down around the heads of our children and our grandchildren. If Christ be not risen from the dead, and if we do not feed people with that Word, then there remains in their hearts the conviction that the Pilates and Herods of this world have won, and that they had better get busy therefore looking out for number one. If life is to the ruthless and strong, then never mind who gets hurt in the scramble. It is the person who is shrewd and knows how to take care of himself who is going to survive the battle. Jesus loved people, someone could reason, but he got nailed to a cross for his compassion; let's not make the same mistake and end up poor and dead. And that is the life-style we can leave people with if we do not lead them to trust that Jesus Christ overcame the grave and now reigns with the Father in glory.

If Christ has not been raised, if we do not let that be known in our world, if we do not end the famine of the Word of God, then it is precisely as Paul said it is—all faith is futile. There is no meaning to our history; there is no guiding hand, no loving purpose being accomplished, no divine plan being worked out. You and I and all folk are just living out our seventy or eighty years, pouring out our work, our care, our love and suffering for a world going nowhere at all, for an evil joke called human life, perpetrated by chance.

Do you realize what that would mean if it were true? How many gentle, gracious lives would have been faithfully lived in vain? How many Christian martyrs would have given their blood for no cause at all? How many sufferers would have borne their pain patiently for naught? How many common prayers would have echoed futilely through the reaches of an empty heaven?

For you see, if Christ be not risen from the dead, then there is no goal to it all. We shall all simply fall off the edge of time into the black hole of void, There will be no face of a loving Master waiting for us there, no countenance shining with the radiance of the knowledge of God's glory. There will be no voice to say to a Dietrich Bonhoeffer or to a Martin Luther King, Jr. or ever to you and me, "Well done, thou good and faithful servant. Inherit the kingdom prepared for you." If Christ be not raised from the dead, the face at the end is the mask of death, and it is that dark, dumb, monstrous thing that turns the handle of this evil show.

Worse still, if we do not end the famine of the Word of God and let men and women believe that Christ is risen, we can leave them thinking there is no forgiveness from the Father. Christ's compassionate prayer for us on the cross—"Father, forgive them for they know not what they do"—that prayer has been heard by no one, and it reflects no heart of divine love, for if Christ be not raised there is no God of triumphant goodness and we are still in our sins. And can you imagine what it means not to know any forgiveness in a world such as ours? Never to know any pardon for those multitudinous evils of society in which we are daily implicated? Never to experience any grace toward our own personal failures? Never to have the chance of starting over, in a new beginning? Never to be able to escape the guilty burden of a past which can only be done away by God?

Some years ago, when we lived in Pennsylvania, the newspaper one day carried the story of a farm woman who had walked out with her little daughter to collect the mail at the rural mailbox. The box was on the other side of the road, and the mother sent the little girl across to it. There was a good deal of traffic on the road, and the daughter waited for the mother's signal before coming back. Finally the mother called out, "O.K., come on, there is no one coming," and the daughter started back across the road. At midpoint she was struck and killed by a car which the mother had simply failed to see. Can you imagine what it would be like to be without God and live as a parent with that guilty burden? Not only to lose one's child—but never to know any final forgiveness, never to have a heavenly Father, who knows what a child's death is like, to bend over one to wipe away the tears and to ease the aching heart, never to have any day whenthe past is pardoned and a new beginning is given? That is where we leave people, if we do not lead them into the faith that Christ is risen from the grave, and that therefore there is indeed a Father who has forgiven us all our evil—all our sin, all our shortcomings, all our terribly human mistakes.

Not to know and trust Christ risen from the dead means finally not to be human, for it means really that there is nothing and no one beyond us in whose image we are made and to whom we owe our being. Think of it! Not to stand under the stars at night and to marvel at the love of him who made them! Not ever to sense that there is Mystery beyond what we can see and feel and hear, and that somehow we were made to respond to that Mystery with all our hearts and souls and minds.

But it is in fact as Paul put it in our New Testament lesson, isn't it? In fact, Christ has been raised from the dead, the first fruits of those who have fallen asleep. In fact, Jesus Christ lives and now dwells in our midst as Lord. You and I know those things—despite all our failures in the church. We know them to the depths of our being. And we know them precisely because God has fed us with his Word. He has spread out his table before us. He has nourished our lives with his merciful message. He has filled our cup to running over with his incarnate Word of love. We now know from whence we came and to whom it is we are going. We now experience his forgiveness, without measure, as our daily sustenance. We now live in hope by his promise of a final kingdom, where he will be all in all, and where injustice and pain, and sorrow and sighing will be done away forever. We now experience, like meat and drink, his meaning and purpose, his comfort and guidance, and our souls are fed and our lives are sustained in joy, through our daily round.

And now, this morning, you and I are called to share the life-giving Word with which God has fed us. Now all of us are asked to go out into the world that is striving under a famine of the Word, and we are commanded by our Lord, as he commanded Peter, "Feed my sheep! Oh, feed my sheep!" Share the glad news of the gospel, Christians. Live it! Teach it! Proclaim it! Christ our Lord now lives and reigns! Jesus Christ is risen!

Amen.

# BIBLIOGRAPHY*


Anderson, Ray S. *Theology, Death and Dying.* New York: Basil Blackwell, 1986.
Anderson examines death from within the circle of faith in Jesus Christ who overcame death in the resurrection. His mindset is faith seeking understanding.

Barth, Karl. *The Resurrection of the Dead.* Translated by H. J. Stenning. New York: Fleming H. Revell Company, 1933.
An analysis of 1 Corinthians 15. Barth addresses the importance of 1 Corinthians in understanding the testimony of the New Testament. He argues that a misunderstanding of the resurrection underlies all the problems at Corinth.

Barth, Markus, and Verne H. Fletcher. *Acquittal by Resurrection.* New York: Holt, Rinehart and Winston, 1964.
This work focuses on the resurrection of Jesus Christ understood as the foundation of righteousness, justice, and salvation.

Benoit, Pierce, and Roland Murphy, ed. *Immortality and Resurrection.* New York: Herder and Herder, 1970.
This collection contains articles on the resurrection of Christ as it relates to the meaning of life, Jesus' resurrection the ground for human resurrection, questions of details of the resurrection and the relevance of New Testament data to ascertain answers. There is tension between the opinions of the various authors.

Boliek, Lynn. *The Resurrection of the Flesh.* Grand Rapids: Eerdmans, 1962.
A study disclosing what the early church actually meant in its confession of the resurrection of the flesh and how this creedal phrase functioned.

Bowen, Clayton R. *The Resurrection in the New Testament.* New York: The Knickerbocker Press, 1911.
Bowen exegetes the texts dealing with the resurrection of Jesus and the future resurrection of Christians from the dead. This work is intended to provide readers with a thorough discussion of passages on the resurrection in the gospels and epistles.

Braaten, Carl. *Eschatology and Ethics.* Minneapolis: Augsburg Publishing House, 1974.
Influenced by Pannenberg, Braaten enlarges the project of eschatological interpretation in theology to show that ethics are eschatologically based.

Braaten, Carl E. *The Future of God: The Revolutionary Dynamics of Hope.* New York: Harper & Row, 1969.
A constructive, systematic outline of the theology of the future derived from the Christian vision of the Kingdom of God. Braaten shows how the Christian hope is grounded in the resurrection of Jesus understood as the power of the future beyond the finality of death.

Brown, Raymond E. *A Risen Christ at Eastertime.* Collegeville: Liturgical Press, 1991.
Brown does a basic yet solid coverage of the gospel accounts.



* Gratitude is expressed to two of my assistants, James Smollon and Michelle Clifton, for their effort in compiling and editing this bibliography.

Candlish, Robert S. *Studies in First Corinthians 15.* Grand Rapids: Kregel, 1989.
This is a reprint of a work originally published in 1863 as *Life in a Risen Saviour*. Candlish's purpose is not so much to expound 1 Corinthians 15 exegetically, but to illustrate the line of argument pursued in it, which is the bearing of the resurrection on the believer's spiritual and eternal life.

Carnley, Peter. *The Structure of Resurrection Belief.* Oxford: Clarendon Press, 1987.
A critical assessment of modern hermeneutics from a theological perspective.

Clark, Neville. *Interpreting the Resurrection.* London: SCM Press, 1967.
Neville probes the foundation of the New Testament and is concerned with setting forth the faith in a way that will aid preaching, hearing, and understanding.

Clark, Theodore R. *Saved by His Life: A Study of the New Doctrine of Reconciliation and Salvation.* New York: Macmillan, 1959.
Clark is a Southern Baptist who identifies problems in the standard account of soteriology which does not give adequate attention to the resurrection.

Cooper, John W. *Body, Soul & Life Everlasting.* Grand Rapids: Eerdmans, 1989.
This book provides a discussion of the body and soul and how they bear on our personal beliefs and hopes in light of Old Testament anthropology, anthropology of intertestamental eschatology, New Testament eschatology, and philosophical anthropology.

Craig, William Lane. *Assessing the New Testament Evidence for the Historicity of the Resurrection of Jesus.* Lewiston: The Edwin Mellen Press, 1989.
Craig's work focuses on the historicity of the resurrection by looking at New Testament witnesses and evidence in the gospels. He seeks to provide an apologetic defense of the belief in the resurrection.

__________*The Historical Argument for the Resurrection of Jesus during the Deist Controversy.* Lewiston: The Edwin Mellen Press, 1985.
Craig addresses the importance of the historicity of the resurrection of Jesus for the Christian faith which in the past has been obscured by dialectical and existential modes of thinking in theology.

Cullmann, Oscar. *Immortality of the Soul or Resurrection of the Dead. The Witness of the New Testament.* London: The Epworth Press, 1958.
Cullmann contrasts the New Testament witness to the primitive Christian hope of the resurrection with the serene philosophical expectation of the survival of the immortal soul.

Davis, Stephen T. *Risen Indeed: Making Sense of the Resurrection.* Grand Rapids: Eerdmans, 1993.
A Christian philosopher's unique examination of the ontology of resurrection.

De Boer, Martinus C. *The Defeat of Death: Apocalyptic Eschatology in 1 Corinthians 1 and Romans 5.* Sheffield: JSOT, 1988.
Using the work of E. Käsemann and J. C. Beker as a point of departure, this work examines death, resurrection, and apocalyptic eschatology in ancient Hebrew texts and Paul's writings. Soteriological tensions such as "already" and "not yet" are examined in light of the findings.

Derrett, J. Duncan M. *The Anastasis: The Resurrection of Jesus as an Historical Event.* Warwickshire: P. Drinkwater, 1982.
Derrett looks at the experience of Jesus by focusing on the term "anastasis" in light of the ancient Western world, the Jewish world, and the modern world. He also discusses the theology of the message of the disciples.

Durrwell, F. X. *The Resurrection.* Translated by Rosemary Sheed. New York: Sheed and Ward, 1960.
A biblical study of the theology of the resurrection that also emphasizes the redemptive value of Christ's suffering.

Evans, C. F. *Resurrection and the New Testament.* Naperville: A. K. Allenson Inc., 1970.
Approaching the resurrection from a biblical theology perspective, Evans looks at the resurrection tradition in Corinthians and the gospels. He includes discussion of the resurrection faith.

Evans, Ernest, ed. *Tertullian's Treatise on the Resurrection.* London: S.P.C.K., 1960.
Evans' work discusses what Tertullian and his contemporaries thought about the resurrection and what argument they used to support their conviction. Evans restates the doctrine of the resurrection and of the final judgment which he sees as more acceptable to modern thought.

Fackre, Gabriel. *The Christian Story: A Narrative Interpretation of Basic Christian Doctrine.* Grand Rapids: Eerdmans, 1978.
An investigation of basic doctrines in the Christian story by a systematic theologian.

Finger, Thomas N. *Christian Theology: An Eschatological Approach.* Vol. 1. Nashville: Thomas Nelson, 1985.
A systematic theology based on eschatology that examines fundamental themes and wrestles with major issues including the resurrection.

Fuller, Daniel P. *Easter Faith and History.* Grand Rapids: Eerdmans, 1965.
Fuller starts with the problems of historical method and studies the question of whether the event of the resurrection can be accepted and verified as history or whether it must simply be accepted as an object of faith. His book studies the manner in which this question has been discussed from the Age of Enlightenment through Campenhausen, Pannenberg, and the Dialectical Theology of today.

Fuller, Reginald H. *The Formation of the Resurrrection Narratives.* New York: Macmillan, 1971.
Fuller gives a fundamental redaction-critical study of Paul and the gospel accounts with some coverage of later material.

Gaffin, Richard B. *The Centrality of the Resurrection: A Study in Paul's Soteriology.* Grand Rapids: Baker Book House, 1978.
Gaffin is a Reformed New Testament scholar who has become a systematic theologian. Discussing the change that has taken place in Reformed theology's interpretation of Paul's thought, Gaffin works at uncovering the basic structure of Paul's resurrection theology, showing that the central theme of Christ's resurrection governs the whole of Paul's theology.

Goppelt, Leonhard, Helmut Thielicke, and Hans-Rudolph Müller-Schwefe. *The Easter Message Today.* Translated by Salvator Attanasio and Darrell Likens Guder. New York: Thomas Nelson & Sons, 1964.
Three essays written to help the pastor illumine the meaning of the resurrection in teaching, preaching, and counseling. Historical research, and reflective, systematic, and theological thought are used to address issues of contemporary life.

Habermas, Gary R. and Antony G. N. Flew. *Did Jesus Rise from the Dead*? San Francisco: Harper & Row, Publishers, 1987.
A debate between Habermas and Flew on the central issue of Christian doctrine and the question of whether the physical resurrection of Jesus must be accepted as a historical fact.

Harris, Murray J. *From Grave to Glory.* Grand Rapids: Zondervan, 1990.
A review of New Testament evidence for the resurrection, historical evidences for the resurrection, and the theological implications of the event.

__________*Raised Immortal: Resurrection and Immortality in the New Testament.* Grand Rapids: Eerdmans, 1983.
A conservative New Testament exegete who has suffered the misfortunes of being targeted by conservative apologists for his explanations of the New Testament teaching about the nature of Christ's risen body.

Heim, Karl. *Jesus the Lord: The Sovereign Authority of Jesus and God's Revelation in Christ.* Translated by D. H. Van Daalen. London: Oliver and Boyd, 1959.
Heim, writing in post World War II Tübingen, confronts his reader with the "either-or" decision that those who hear the gospel must face.

__________*Jesus the World's Perfector: The Atonement and the Renewal of the World.* Translated by D. H. Van Daalen. London: Oliver and Boyd, 1959.
In light of the question of our destiny, Heim draws attention to the fact that God may have rea-

sons for restraining power until judgment day and that the question of guilt must be solved first. He addresses the atonement, the place of the resurrection of Christ in the plan for perfecting the world, its meaning in our present lives, and the resurrection as distinguished from all events on our level.

__________*The World: Its Creation and Consummation: The End of the Present Age and the Future of the World in the Light of the Resurrection.* Translated by Robert Smith. London: Oliver and Boyd, 1962.

Heim looks at the end of the present age and the future of the world in light of the resurrection.

Hick, John H. *Death and Eternal Life.* San Francisco: Harper & Row, 1976.

Hick traces the belief in an afterlife from its beginnings to current rejections by humanists. This vast study surveys various religious traditions. It has a major section on Christian approaches to the after-life, exploring both New Testament views as well as important Christian thinkers.

Hoekema, Anthony A. *The Bible and the Future.* Grand Rapids: Eerdmans, 1979.

Hoekema provides a thorough treatment of the biblical teaching on the future. The resurrection is dealt with in light of its centrality to the Bible's eschatological message. He tries to show that the incarnation and the bodily resurrection prove that the body is not evil but good.

Hooke, S. H. *The Resurrection of Christ as History and Experience.* London: Darton, Longman & Todd, 1967.

Hooke attempts to arrive at the meaning of the resurrection of Christ for Christians today by looking at the wider background of religious ideas and speculations against which the belief in resurrection developed in Israel. He examines the accounts of the resurrection in the gospels as well as Paul's understanding.

Hughes-Games, J. *On the Nature of the Resurrection Body.* London: James Nisbet & Co., 1898.

In this literal interpretation of scripture, Hughes-Games contemplates the world to come and the eternal future.

Jansen, John F. *The Resurrection of Jesus Christ in New Testament Theology.* Philadelphia: Westminster, 1980.

Jansen is a New Testament scholar who proposes a theology of the resurrection which unifies the focus of the New Testament as a whole.

Kaiser, Otto and Eduard Lohse. *Death and Life.* Translated by John E. Steely. Nashville: Abingdon, 1981.

Kaiser and Lohse examine the biblical texts on the grounds of expectation of the resurrection of the dead and the victory over death in Christ's resurrection. They consider death, resurrection, and immortality in the Old Testament and in early Judaism in a religio-historical context.

Kelsey, Morton. *Resurrection: Release from Oppression.* New York: Paulist Press, 1985.

Kelsey presents a picture of the events of Easter Sunday and of the days following as the risen Christ met his disciples and friends. He intersperses the narrative with reflections and reactions to the events.

Kennedy, H. A. A. *St. Paul's Conception of Last Things.* London: Hodder & Stoughton, 1904.

Kennedy investigates Paul's eschatology in light of the religious concepts of the Old Testament. He sees Christ's resurrection as the basis for the inspiring prospect the apostle reached.

Kesich, Veselin. *The First Day of the New Creation.* Crestwood: St. Vladimir's Seminary Press, 1982.

Kesich analyzes primitive Christian preaching about the resurrection. He deals with the works of modern exegetes as well as problems of a historical and exegetical character.

Küng, Hans. *Eternal Life?* Translated by Edward Quinn. London: Fount Paperbacks, 1985.

Küng addresses death as an entry into light and surveys models of belief in eternity in various religions. He deals with the resurrection of the dead as a question that has tormented humanity from the beginning as well as with the difficulties of the resurrection.

Künneth, Walter. *The Theology of the Resurrection.* St. Louis: Concordia, 1956.

Künneth writes of the redemptive significance of the resurrection from a Lutheran point of view. This is one of the most significant theologies of the resurrection.

Ladd, George Eldon. *I Believe in the Resurrection of Jesus.* Grand Rapids: Eerdmans, 1975.
Ladd looks at the Old Testament, contemporary Judaism, and the New Testament to find the ideas which account for the rise of the resurrection faith. He surveys modern historical explanations and the nature of the resurrection in the New Testament and evaluates its importance for the totality of biblical revelation.

Lampe, G. W. H. and D. M. Mackinnon. *The Resurrection.* Philadelphia: The Westminster Press, 1966.
A dialogue about the resurrection which seeks to provide understanding of the Easter gospel.

Lapide, Pinchas. *The Resurrection of Jesus: A Jewish Perspective.* Translated by Wilhelm Linss. Minneapolis: Augsburg, 1983.
A Jewish scholar situates the Christian belief in the resurrection within the Jewish understanding of apocalyptic messianism.

León-Dufour, Xavier. *Life and Death in the New Testament.* Translated by Terrence Prendergast. San Francisco: Harper & Row, 1986.
León-Dufour addresses how Jesus and Paul approached the fact of their own deaths and the deaths of others. He discusses the mystery of death through faith in the resurrection.

__________*Resurrection and the Message of Easter.* Translated by R. N. Wilson. New York: Holt, Rinehart and Winston, 1971.
A faith reply to a question of fact—did Christ rise? He faces the problem of language and the way in which we may express the significance of the resurrection event in the present day.

Martin-Achard, Robert. *From Death to Life.* Translated by John Penney Smith. Edinburgh: Oliver and Boyd, 1960.
A study of the development of the doctrine of the resurrection in the Old Testament. Martin-Achard looks at passages which illustrate the emergence of the doctrine in ancient Israel and early Judaism.

Marxsen, Willi. *The Resurrection of Jesus of Nazareth.* Translated by Margaret Kohl. Philadelphia: Fortress, 1970.
This is an influential essay that attempts to interpret the resurrection in modern terms.

__________*Jesus and Easter: Did God Raise the Historical Jesus from the Dead?* Translated by Victor Paul Furnish. Nashville: Abingdon Press, 1990.
Marxen takes readers step by step through the important and intricate issues involved in the title. He articulately discusses the consequences of historical and exegetical studies for theology, the church, and lives of individual Christians.

Milligan, William. *The Resurrection of Our Lord.* New York: The Macmillan Co., 1917.
Milligan emphasizes the full importance of the truth of the resurrection as a miracle of a new creation within God's overall plan for the world.

Minear, Paul S. *To Die and to Live: Christ's Resurrection and Christian Vocation.* New York: The Seabury Press, 1977.
Minear asserts that all Christian vocation is derived from the "twin event". He uses five main texts to illumine this idea: Acts 3:15, Gal. 6:14-15, Eph. 3:8-10, John 17:20-24, Mark 13:24-27.

Moltmann, Jürgen. *The Theology of Hope.* New York: Harper & Row, 1967.
This is a reinterpretation of the doctrine of eschatology as a doctrine of hope. He shows the cross and the resurrection as the New Testament expression of revelation.

Moltmann-Wendel, Elisabeth. The Women around Jesus. Translated by John Bowden. London: SCM Press, 1982.
Simple but profound reflections on the events from the women's perspectives.

Morison, Frank. *Who Moved the Stone?* London: The Century Co., 1930.
Morison, a lawyer wrestling with his own skepticism, wrote a very different book than he set out to write. The facts have not changed, but his interpretation of them did after an intensive examination.

Moule, C. F. D. *The Significance of the Message of the Resurrection for Faith in Jesus Christ.* Translated by Dorthea M. Barton and R. A. Wilson. Naperville: Alec R. Allenson, Inc., 1968.
Four essays by German scholars which lead the reader through closely reasoned investigations of the scope and limits of the New Testament evidence for the Easter faith.
Murray, G. R. Beasley. *Christ is Alive!* London: Lutterworth Press, 1947.
A critical estimate of historical evidence and an exposition of lessons drawn from the New Testament.

Niebuhr, Richard R. *Resurrection and Historical Reason.* New York: Charles Schribner's Sons, 1957.
An attempt to understand the connection between the biblical proclamation of the resurrection of Christ and the order of theological thought. Niebuhr examines historical consciousness in light of the Church's history.

O'Collins, Gerald. *Interpreting the Resurrection: Examining the Major Problems in the Stories of Jesus' Resurrection.* New York: Paulist Press, 1988.
This brief work examines major problems that arise from the testimony of Paul and the gospel writers. He approaches these questions "through the head, the hands and the heart".
__________*Jesus Risen: An Historical, Fundamental and Systematic examination of Christ's Resurrection.* New York: Paulist Press, 1987.
This major work is an exercise of "Easter faith seeking understanding" written from a scholar's perspective. O'Collins provides a comprehensive survey of the questions dealing with the resurrection, including the thought of 20th century European theologians. He discusses the meaning of the resurrection for Christian life.
__________*The Resurrection of Jesus Christ.* Valley Forge: Judson Press, 1973.
A critical survey of recent scholarship on the resurrection as examined under history, faith, and theology. It includes critiques of Bultmann, Marxsen, Lampe, and Geering.
__________*What are they Saying about the Resurrection?* New York: Paulist Press, 1978.
O'Collins provides a concise overview of the current interpretations of the resurrection and evaluates their strengths and weaknesses.
O'Donovan, Oliver. *Resurrection and Moral Order: An Outline for Evangelical Ethics.* Grand Rapids: Eerdmans, 1986.
This is one of the most significant recent works on the resurrection, especially because of the way it bases ethical thinking and living on the resurrection.
Orr, James. *The Resurrection of Jesus.* New York: Hodder and Stoughton, n.d.
A capable theologian of the last century who was well aware of exegetical and doctrinal issues and who sought historical truth and the implications for the believer and the unbeliever.

Osborne, Grant R. *The Resurrection Narratives.* Grand Rapids: Baker Book House, 1984.
A redactional study of the accounts of the resurrection through the eyes of each evangelist. Osborne brings out the distinctive theological emphasis of each.

Perkins, Pheme. *Resurrection: New Testament Witness and Contemporary Reflection.* Garden City: Doubleday, 1984.
Perkins provides a thoughtful investigation of belief in the resurrection in the Old Testament and Judaism and in the New Testament documents. She deals with the centrality of the proclamation of Jesus' resurrection in the earliest preaching of the gospel.
Perrin, Norman. *The Resurrection According to Matthew, Mark, and Luke.* Philadelphia: Fortress Press, 1977.
Perrin examines the resurrection of Jesus in the gospels of Matthew, Mark, and Luke to explore what each evangelist is attempting to communicate to the reader.

Peters, Ted. *God—the World's Future: Systematic Theology for a Postmodern Era.* Minneapolis: Fortress Press, 1992.
This major work explicates a coherent scheme for organizing Christian doctrine and theology. In an ecumenical spirit, Peters examines Christian symbols and faith in order to explain the proleptic expectation of the gospel, i.e, that Jesus Christ is the future made present.

Plöger, Otto. *Theocracy and Eschatology.* Translated by S. Rudman. Oxford: Basil Blackwell, 1968.
Plöger devotes part of his work to the book of Daniel's idea of a double resurrection—some to eternal life and others to eternal shame. He draws connections to Israel and the revival of the people of God.

Ramsey, A. M. *The Resurrection of Christ.* London: Collins Clear Type Press, 1961.
A study by the Archbishop of Canterbury on the place of the resurrection in Christian life and thought. This simple yet scholarly account includes historical evidence for the event in relation to modern critical studies.

Russell, Elizabeth and John Greenhalgh, ed. *'If Christ be not risen . . . ': Essays in Resurrection and* Sur*vival.* London: St. Mary's, 1986.
The concern of these essays is to emphasize the idea that eternal life is still as much a legitimate concern of Christian thought as it was in the original preaching of the faith and to redress the balance of our understanding of the gospel by a focus on death.

Schillebeeckx, Edward. *Jesus: An Experiment in Christology.* New York: Crossroad, 1981.
Schillebeeckx provides extensive exegetical study within a classic christological work.

Schep, J. A. *The Nature of the Resurrection Body.* Grand Rapids: Eerdmans, 1964.
His work investigates scriptural data concerning the resurrection body of Christ and of believers in both the Old Testament and the New Testament.

Schottroff, Luise. *Let the Oppressed Go Free: Feminist Perspectives on the New Testament.* Louisville: Westminster/John Knox Press, 1993.
Schottroff provides an exegetical examination of the women in the Easter narratives.

Simpson, W. J. Sparrow. *The Resurrection and Modern Thought.* London: Longmans, Green and Co., 1911.
Simpson provides a major treatment of the theology and history of the doctrine of the resurrection. He focuses on the theology of the resurrection as expounded by Paul and the physical resurrection of individuals as traced from the Apostolic age to modern days.

Smith, Robert H. *Easter Gospels: The Resurrection of Jesus According to the Four Evangelists.* Minneapolis: Augsburg, 1983.
This work focuses on how each of the canonical gospels uses the shared Christian tradition of the resurrection of Jesus. Smith gives a verse by verse commentary of each account, explores the situation of the evangelists, and summarizes their views of Easter.

Stendahl, Krister, ed. *Immortality and Resurrection.* New York: The Macmillan Company, 1965.
Four essays by other scholars investigating to what degree the New Testament affirms belief in immortality or in resurrection. Stendahl provides an introduction.

Stanley, David M. *Christ's Resurrection in Pauline Soteriology.* Rome: Pontificio Institute Biblico, 1961.
Stanley does for Roman Catholics what Gaffin does for evangelicals, namely, help them recover the soteriological function of resurrection.

Stewart, James S. *A Man in Christ.* London: Hodder & Stoughton Limited 1936.
Union with Christ rather than justification or eschatology is the real clue to understanding Paul's thought and experience. Stewart gives a fresh study of the New Testament to discover the central ideas of Christianity and to emphasize the resurrection as God's act and God's power.

Swain, Lionel. *The People of the Resurrection*. Wilmington: Michael Glazier, 1986.
Swain shows the resurrection is a metaphor for the destiny of Christ and the faithful.
__________*Reading the Easter Gospels*. Collegeville: Liturgical Press, 1993.
Approaching the gospels as stories, Swain uses reader response criticism to examine the texts to avoid misunderstanding regarding the paschal mystery of Christ. He writes with both the specialist and nonspecialist in mind.

Tenney, Merrill C. *The Reality of the Resurrection*. New York: Harper and Row, 1963.
A conservative New Testament scholar of the last generation who looked at the historical, experiential, and theological dimensions of the resurrection.

Torrance, Thomas F. *Space, Time and Resurrection*. Edinburgh: The Handsel Press, 1976.
Torrance gives a theological interpretation of the Easter message of the New Testament writers taken as a whole. While the book deals with some important scientific and philosophical questions in regard to resurrection and ascension, its core is concerned with the evangelical message of the resurrection.

Vos, Geerhardus. *The Pauline Eschatology*. Grand Rapids: Eerdmans, 1953.
Geerhardus deals with the subject of the resurrection change and how it affects believers along with the implications for humanity and the question of whether human resurrection is distinct from the process of the resurrection of Christ.

Wenham, John. *Easter Enigma*. Grand Rapids: Zondervan, 1984.
Wenham reconstructs and draws together pieces of New Testament information to show the possibility of harmonizing the resurrection accounts into a comprehensive historical sequence.

Westcott, Brooke Foss. *The Gospel of the Resurrection: Thoughts on its Relation to Reason and History*. London: Macmillan and Co., 1874.
Westcott shows the conception of Christianity as Christ's sovereignty and the resurrection as the power and motivation required for a life of sacrifice and hope.

Wilckens, Ulrich. *Resurrection*. Translated by A. M. Stewart. Atlanta: John Knox Press, 1977.
A New Testament investigation of biblical sources and texts behind belief in the resurrection. Wilckens treats the resurrection in the New Testament, the significance of the resurrection concept, and the proclamation of the resurrection in the New Testament.

## 1993 NORTH PARK SYMPOSIUM ON THE THEOLOGICAL INTERPRETATION OF SCRIPTURE

## THE RESURRECTION

### THE PRESENTERS

ELIZABETH ACHTEMEIER, Union Theological Seminary, Richmond

STANLEY HARAKIS, Holy Cross Greek Orthodox School of Theology

JOHN NEWPORT, Southwestern Baptist Theological Seminary

BEN OLLENBURGER, Associated Mennonite Biblical Seminaries

ROGER OLSON, Bethel College

CAROLYN OSIEK, Catholic Theological Union

CLARK PINNOCK, McMaster Divinity College

TED PETERS, Pacific Lutheran Theological Seminary

PETER STUHLMACHER, University of Tübingen

### RESPONDENTS

Steve Bouma-Prediger, North Park College

John Martz, Evangelical Covenant Church

Bruce Metzger, Princeton Theological Seminary

Walter Michel, Lutheran School of Theology at Chicago

Grant Osborne, Trinity Evangelical Divinity School

Thomas Parker, McCormick Theological Seminary

Jamie Phelps, Catholic Theological Union

# An Announcement

North Park Theological Seminary in Chicago, Illinois is pleased to announce that the ninth Symposium on Theological Interpretation of Scripture will take place October 14-16, 1992. The Symposium will start at 1:30 p.m. on October 14 in Nyvall Hall and will extend through noon on October 16.

The theme of the symposium will be The Church. The following persons have agreed to make presentations:

| | |
|---|---|
| Prof. Paula Barker | *History, Theology* |
| Prof. François Bovon. | *New Testament* |
| Dr. Carl Braaten | *Systematic Theology* |
| Prof. Richard Carlson | *Practical Theology* |
| Dr. James L. Garrett | *Systematic Theology* |
| Prof. Richard Hays | *New Testament* |
| Prof. C. G. Newsome | *Church History* |
| Dr. Stanley Walters | *Old Testament* |
| Dr. Don Wardlaw | |

Persons interested in attending the sessions should write before September 1, 1994 to:

Ms. Jackson Blanchard
North Park Theological Seminary
3225 W. Foster Avenue
Chicago, Illinois 60625

Meals may be taken at North Park, and assistance will be provided in finding nearby lodging.

# EX AUDITU

## VOLUMES AVAILABLE

*EX AUDITU* Vol. 1 (1985) consists of selected articles presenting the issues inherent in the theological interpretation of Scripture.

*EX AUDITU* Vol. 2 (1986) discusses the theme: "Church and State Relationship." In addition there are two lead articles, one by Peter Stuhlmacher on "EX AUDITU and the Theological Interpretation of Holy Scripture," and the second by Ben F. Meyer on "The Primacy of Consent and the Uses of Suspicion."

*EX AUDITU* Vol. 3 (1987). The theme is: "Creation."

*EX AUDITU* Vol. 4 (1988). The theme is: "The Church and Israel (Romans 9-11)."

*EX AUDITU* Vol. 5 (1989). The theme is: "What is Salvation?"

*EX AUDITU* Vol. 6 (1990). The theme is: "Prophetic and/or Apocalyptic Eschatology."

*EX AUDITU* Vol. 7 (1991). The theme is: "Christology and Incarnation."

*EX AUDITU* Vol. 8 (1992). The theme is: "Worship."

*EX AUDITU* Vol. 9 (1993). The theme is: "Resurrection."

Ten copies or more of one volume may be purchased for $10.00 per copy from Pickwick Publications.

To be published in April 1994:

*EX AUDITU* Vol. 10 (1994). The theme will be: "The Church."

Pickwick Publications, 4137 Timberlane Drive
Allison Park, PA 15101-2932

*CHRISTUS FABER*

*The Master Builder and the House of God*

**Ben F. Meyer**

Christus Faber presents the historical Jesus as the climactic keystone of the whole biblical tradition. Its final essay, "The Temple at the Navel of the Eart," is "a model of how to do what the Germans call gesamtbiblische Theologie."____ Sean McEvenue, Concordia University, Montreal.

ISBN 1-55635-014-7 $27.50

*CALVIN'S CONCEPT OF THE LAW*

**I. John Hesselink**

Insofar as I understand Calvin, the author has introduced us not only to the magnitude but also the problematic of Calvin's concept of the law. This merits our gratitude all the more, particularly because for the first time Calvin has been so incisively prese*A M B*nted from just this point of view chosen by the author . . . . I have studied this dissertation with great respect. It is an outstanding achievement.____Karl Barth (from his report to Basel University faculty)

There are very few thinkers in the history of the Church who have described the new Christian life with the care and clarity that Calvin did, and in John Hesselink, Calvin has a credible and worthy expositor. Must reading, for pastors as much as for students of Calvin.

*Calvin Theological Journal.*

ISBN 1-55635-007-4 $27.90

*AMBUSHED BY GRACE*

*The Virtues of a Useless Faith*

**Thomas W. Currie III**

An acculturated church will always find the gospel useful; indeed, that is how it seeks to render the gospel harmless. However, the "uselessness" of the gospel is precisely the key that helps the church discover the radical claim of Jesus Christ.

ISBN 1-55635-017-1 $10.00

*ON THIS ROCK*

*A Commentary On I Peter*

**Donald G. Miller**

This work contains an introductory section dealing with authorship, date, place of origin, original readers, theology, genre, and literary affinities; and an interpretation of the meaning of the text and its significance for today. The theology of the epistle is viewed in its relation to the Old Testament, to the Gospel report of the teachings of Jesus, and to the thought of other New Testament writings.

ISBN 1-55635-020-1 $30.00

*THE LITTLE CHURCH THAT REFUSED TO DIE*

*History of The Church in Little Gidding, England*

**William W. Moore**

The community in Little Gidding goes back to 1625 when it was established by Nicholas Ferrar. It became known through the fourth poem in T. S. Eliot's FOUR QUARTETS.

ISBN 1-55635-023-6 $16.00